AT THE
:TABLE:
OF THE
:G·R·A·I·L:

To the memory of:
Hannah Margaret Closs (1905–1953)
and
Nathan Comfort Starr (1896–1981)

AT THE TABLE OF THE G·R·A·I·L

MAGIC & THE USE OF IMAGINATION

EDITED BY
JOHN·MATTHEWS

Routledge & Kegan Paul
London, Boston, Melbourne and Henley

First published in 1984
Reprinted in 1985
by Routledge & Kegan Paul plc
14 Leicester Square, London WC2H 7PH
9 Park Street, Boston, Mass. 02108, USA
464 St Kilda Road, Melbourne,
Victoria 3004, Australia
Broadway House, Newtown Road,
Henley-on-Thames, Oxon RG9 1EN, England
Phototypeset in Palatino by Input Typesetting Ltd, London
and printed in Great Britain by
Billing & Sons Ltd, Worcester

Library of Congress Cataloging in Publication Data

At the table of the Grail.
Bibliography: p.
1. Grail—Legends—History and criticism—Addresses, essays, lectures.
I. Matthews, John, 1948—
PN686.G7A88   1984   398'.353   83—13794

British Library CIP data available

ISBN 0-7100-9938-X (pbk.)

:CONTENTS:

Contributors   vii
Introduction by John Matthews   1

Part I   Origins and patterns   9

1 The Grail of the Golden Age   11
   Geoffrey Ashe
2 The meeting of the waters   29
   Hannah Closs
3 Alchemical transmutation in history and symbol   49
   Adam McLean

Part II   Elements of the Grail tradition   67

4 Temples of the Grail   69
   John Matthews
5 The return of Dindrane   91
   Helen Luke
6 Sophia: companion on the quest   111
   Caitlin Matthews
7 The world's need   129
   Brian Cleeve
8 The desire of the heart: a meditation   145
   Lois Lang-Sims

v

Contents

Part III Magic and the use of Imagination   157

 9 Merlin and the Grail   159
   Gareth Knight
10 The Grail as bodily vessel   174
   Bob Stewart
11 The path to the Grail   197
   Dolores Ashcroft-Nowicki

Conclusion   217

12 Glatisant and Grail: an Arthurian fragment   219
   Peter Lamborn Wilson

Recommended reading   243

: CONTRIBUTORS :

DOLORES ASHCROFT-NOWICKI is Director of Studies for the Servants of the Light School of Occult Science, of which she was a founder member with the late W. E. Butler. She has travelled world-wide lecturing on aspects of the occult, and is the author of *First Steps in Ritual* (1982) and *The Shining Paths* (1983) both published by Aquarian Press.

GEOFFREY ASHE is best known for his wide-ranging studies of the Arthurian mythos, of which the most recent are *Kings and Queens of Early Britain* and *Avalonian Quest*, both published by Methuen in 1982. In 1966–70 he was secretary of the Camelot Research Committee, which excavated Cadbury Castle in Somerset in search of the real Camelot; and in 1981 he published radical new findings suggesting the identity of the historical Arthur. He is also author of *The Virgin* (Routledge & Kegan Paul, 1976) *The Ancient Wisdom* (Macmillan, 1977) and *Camelot and the Vision of Albion* (Heinemann, 1971).

BRIAN CLEEVE, born in England in 1921, served in the Merchant Navy during the war, and has been a broadcaster and novelist since then. He received a PhD from the National University of Ireland in 1956. He has written two books on mystical religion, *The House on the Rock* and *The Seven Mansions*, both published by Watkins in 1980, and some other works of a similar nature, not yet published.

HANNAH CLOSS was born in London in 1905 and died in Bristol in 1953. She was educated at the Slade School and the University of Vienna and her publications include a brilliant trilogy of novels about the Albigensian Crusade, *High are the Mountains, Deep are the Valleys* and *The Silent Tarn* (reprinted by Vanguard Press, New York, in 1978). Her highly original essays on the Grail and Catharism have so far remained neglected, the one included here being printed in 1948.

GARETH KNIGHT has been a dedicated student of magic for thirty years. He was trained initially in the occult school founded by Dion Fortune and is well known for a series of major books on the subject which combine academic erudition with practical experience. These include *A Practical Guide to Qabalistic Symbolism* (Helios, 1965) *Experience of the Inner Worlds* (1975) *A History of White Magic* (Mowbrays, 1978) and *The Secret Tradition in Arthurian Legend* (Aquarian Press, 1983). He has also written many journal articles and is in great demand as a lecturer. He was awarded an honorary doctorate for his work in this field and service to analytical psychology.

LOIS LANG-SIMS has spent much of her life in and around the precincts of Canterbury Cathedral, where she was for a time a guide, but she has also travelled far, to India and Egypt, which were spiritual as well as physical journeys. She has described them memorably in two volumes of autobiography, *A Time to be Born* (1971) and *Flower in a Teacup* (1973) both published by André Deutsch. She is also the author of a remarkable book of mystical theology in the tradition of Julian of Norwich and Charles Williams, *The Christian Mystery* (Allen & Unwin, 1980).

HELEN LUKE was born in England in 1904 and studied Italian Literature at Oxford University and the psychology of C. G. Jung in London and Zurich. In 1949 she moved to Los Angeles where she practised as a counsellor, and later founded the Apple Farm Community, where she now lives and teaches. She is the author of *Woman, Earth and Spirit* (Crossroads, 1981) *Dark Wood to White Rose: A Study of Meanings in Dante's Divine Comedy*

(Dove Publications, 1975) and *The Inner Story* (Crossroads, 1982). Further collections of her essays are planned for the future.

ADAM McLEAN is the founder of *The Hermetic Journal* which deals with alchemy and related subjects. He has also written numerous articles and is the author of *The Spiritual Science of Alchemy* (1978). As editor and publisher he is in the course of producing *The Magnum Opus Hermetic Sourcebooks* reprinting rare and valuable works at present available only in manuscript form.

CAITLIN MATTHEWS is a poet and musician who has spent many years studying the mysteries of the Divine Feminine, in particular as these relate to the figure of Sophia, Divine Wisdom and to the cult of the Black Virgin. She is the author of a long poem *The Search for Rhiannon* (Bran's Head, 1980) and is currently working on a book to be called *The Western Way* (Routledge & Kegan Paul, forthcoming).

JOHN MATTHEWS has spent the last twenty years studying the subject of the Grail and has lectured widely on this and related subjects. He was co-founder, with Grahaeme Barrasford Young, in 1978 of the arts magazine *Labrys*, and is the author of *The Grail, Quest for Eternal Life* (Thames & Hudson, 1981) and is at present working on a novel about Giordano Bruno and a full-length study of Prester John.

BOB STEWART is a Scottish composer, author and musician, living in the West of England. He has recorded four LPs including his own songs and instrumental works and wrote the theme music for Nicol Williamson's recording of *The Hobbit*. His published work includes *Where is Saint George?* (Moonraker Press, 1976) and *The Waters of the Gap* (Bath City Publications, 1981) a study of Celtic mythology and magic revealed by the evidence of excavations at temple of Sulis Minerva, Bath. He is at present working on a book about the British Underworld or Otherworld tradition.

PETER LAMBORN WILSON was born near Baltimore, Maryland in 1945. He studied at Columbia University and then travelled extensively in the Middle East, where he discovered a life-long attachment for Sufism. He was editor of *Sophia Perennis*, the journal of the Imperial Iranian Academy until the fall of the Shah, since when he has continued to travel widely. He has published several books of translation, worked in both radio and television and has written, among others the following: *Angels* (Thames & Hudson, 1980) *Divan* (Crescent Moon Press, 1978) and *The Winter Calligraphy* (Golgonooza Press, 1975).

:INTRODUCTION:

·

JOHN·MATTHEWS

·

At the end of the Grail text known as _Perlesvaus_, when the miraculous vessel has passed away to appear no more in that place, and the knight Perceval has departed for lands unknown, the Castle of the Grail was left untenanted and became ruinous. Many wondered what the castle had been, but the truth faded from memory and it become known as a haunted place. No one dared to go there except for two Welsh knights:

> they were fair knights indeed, very young and high spirited, and they swore that they would go, and full of excitement they entered the castle. They stayed there for a long while. And when they left they lived as hermits, wearing hair shirts and wandering through the forests, eating only roots; it was a hard life, but it pleased them greatly, and when people asked them why they were living thus, they would only reply: 'Go where we went, and you will know why.'[1]

To anyone who has not sat at the table of the Grail there must be a sense of bewilderment, even scorn for a group of people willing to perch inside such a dilapidated ruin as the Grail castle seems to be. For others there is the same sense of achievement, the same enthusiasm of discovery felt by the two Welsh knights. But like them, it is hard for us to tell you what the experience is like; we can only suggest that you 'go where we went, and you will know why'.

The Companions of the Grail did not all depart on a mystical

1

ship for the shores of Sarras, nor did the Grail itself suddenly become inaccessible for those who came afterwards. The Grail castle's ruins are not in some hidden location which can be discovered by means of a map reference: though there may well be signposts along the way. The Grail Company is here among us, in the world. Its members are just as likely to be ordinary individuals as intensely mystical personalities from some high-powered esoteric order. The Grail castle's boundaries have admittedly stretched to encompass towns and indeed countries far beyond Britain, and the Grail table is nowadays grown vast; but what of the Grail itself? There must be many for whom the prospect of finding the Cup of the Last Supper is uninviting because it is alien to their own religious tradition. And what of those who have no religious tradition at all? Are they excluded from the Table and the Quest? To them we would say that while the Grail has latterly been closely associated with the Christian tradition, it need not bear any single interpretation.

The elements of the Grail tradition are known to have come through many sources, to form a multi-religious hologram as diverse as those seated at the table itself. For those who were raised outside any tradition, or those who have rejected a formal discipline, it may be difficult to formulate any clear notion of what the Grail might mean. For them it may be helpful to consider that the framework of the stories, though loosely Christian, is part of the mellow ambience of the medieval world: one which was closer to ancient traditions of pagan under-standing and which responded more readily to a vigorously told tale than many of us can do today.

There are as many possible paths to the Grail as there are roads to Rome, and every one of them is valid. Arthur may well have been a Christian king, but he remained aware that his realm held other concepts which could only help strengthen the common purpose of the Round Table. When we sit at the Table of the Grail, in the castle of the Fisher King, who is Arthur's spiritual representative within Britain, we are similarly aware that around us are seated many who are not native to the land. From their experience they bring new ideas, promoting the spiritual health of all upon the Quest with their initiative and active participation. It begins to dawn upon us that there is a freemasonry among those on the Quest, just as there is among those who pursue the mystical path in all traditions. There is a common language, a mode of consciousness, almost a secret sign which can be read and recognized by all who are similarly engaged. Such realizations help fend off the feeling of isolation which can dog the steps of those who seek the Grail.

So we must not make the mistake of seeing the Grail as just a charming medieval legend. It is part of a much larger tradition: one in which we all share. The mystical tradition of any people is usually embodied within a set of written scriptures – holy writings – which tell of a hero and a quest. Although such scriptures are often considered to be the only valid source for mystical research, we must not forget those myths and sub-cultural stories which have preceded or grown up around them. In their own way these tell us a great deal about our spiritual quest, and are very much a part of our heritage. This does not, however, make them any easier to understand, for they are often made up of successive layers of meaning: the accretions of long ages of growth, change and rebirth. You will find many descriptions of the Grail in this book: as chalice or stone, dish or womb; as a cup 'from which each individual life receives its essential food and drink' (Ch. 5, p. 92), or as a witness to the Feminine Principle. For some it is only one of many such vessels; for others it has no real existence at all but serves rather as a luminous idea that shapes itself at will to the needs of the individual. To still others it is part of an ongoing process of transformation: an alchemical dream of the soul on its quest for human evolution or oneness with God.

Yet much as these views differ, they are at one in their belief in the Grail as guide, counsellor, helper, and as gateway to the interior life, the inner journey we must all travel to its end, beset by danger and doubt, fear and loss of faith. And, so long as our goal is a true one, and carries no taint of evil, the Grail remains always at hand like a light in the wilderness.

You may learn much from these pages, yet if you learn nothing more than to recognize the Grail within your own being you will have discovered a truth that will never desert you, that will shine forth on the path before you and show you the way to self-realization.

'Emotional experiences for their own sake and theoretical truths we have in plenty, but true feeling which leads to the perception of abiding values is still rare in our time' (Ch. 5, p. 103). No one who sets forth on the Grail Quest remains unchanged. The experience may seem slight, may almost pass unnoticed, yet images will keep recurring, forming themselves into chains of meaning, patterns in which we may see ourselves reflected in countless different ways.

No one who reads this book with open mind and heart will fail to see the patterns that form and dissolve again with each new definition, with each succeeding evaluation of the matter of the Grail. Again and again they will catch the echoes, perhaps distant at first, but growing clearer with each reading, until finally the Grail's message to each of us will resonate clearly through the chambers of the soul.

Several of the contributors to this book have chosen to give emphasis to the loss and, more importantly, the projected return, of the Feminine Principle. The importance of this seems clear. In an age marked more than ever by destructive urges, its masculine-oriented hunger for war, there is an ever-increasing need for the gentler, inner-centred approach of the feminine – an attribute present, though dormant, in men as well as women. In the imagery of the Grail we see this borne out in the episode of the Ship of Solomon, where Galahad, the Grail-winner, and his two companions take ship at last for Sarras, the Holy City. With them goes the body of the woman Dindrane, who gave her blood that another might live (see Ch. 5, p. 91). She is the lost Feminine Principle, who has withdrawn from the world and left behind a wound. The desire of every modern Grail seeker should be to bring back the vessel from Sarras, and with it the figure of Dindrane, dead to us no longer, alive to the needs of our time.

At the end of this book will be found a section consisting of a guided meditation and an original story. The first is designed specifically to set anyone who wishes upon their own Quest; though even those already on the path may find it rewarding. And in the story of Palamydes the Saracen, with which the

4

book ends, many will find the seeds of new lines of thought, ways to project their own vision into the common symbolism of the Grail. But read the other essays first; they are written by people dedicated to the Inner Journey, seen from many different points along the way. Maybe as you read you will begin to recognize ideas long since learned and forgotten. This may be your way into the landscape of the Grail. Once there, you can only return with new insights into your own state of being, truths that will make life seem larger and more light-filled than ever before; for on this journey, you are seeking absolutes.

We invite you then, like the two Welsh knights with whom we began, to enter the castle and sit down at the great Round Table of the Grail, which may at once fit within the walls of our own hearts, and stretch to encompass the stars. From there, the way is ours to follow, as and where we may.

The story of the Grail: a synopsis

There are almost as many stories of the Grail as there are traditions – and these are many. Most people today know of the Grail from Tennyson's indifferent version. In the fifteenth century it was Malory's *Le Morte D'Arthur* they turned to. But Malory's book was only a boiled-down version of earlier cycles of tales 'drawn out of the French'. Beyond this again lay Celtic myths which gave rise to the earliest form of Grail – the wonder-working vessel – though even here the concept was not so far removed from what we think of as the Grail today. To offset the problem posed by this vast complex of texts, a brief summary of what might be called the basic story is offered here. Much has, of course, had to be omitted, but it is hoped that this synopsis will help the reader new to the subject to find his or her way into the essays which follow.

Some traditions hold that the Grail originated as a jewel – an emerald – from the crown of the Light Bringer, Lucifer, the Angel of the Morning, which fell from heaven during the war between the angels. Others believe that Seth, the child of Adam and Eve, returned to the Garden of Eden, where he was given

5

the Grail as a sign to all men that God had not forgotten them. But whatever theory is adhered to, the first time the Grail makes an appearance in history is at the time of the Crucifixion of Christ. At this time Joseph of Arimathea came into possession of the Cup of the Last Supper, and used it to catch a few drops of blood and sweat from the body of the Messiah – from which point it became a hallowed object. Thence it was borne into the west by Joseph and his band of followers – the first Company of the Grail, who arrived at Glastonbury in Somerset, where they founded a church dedicated to the Mother of Christ and enshrining the holy cup. We next hear of the Grail in Arthur's time, when the first great Quest is recorded. It was then seen as inhabiting a castle, variously named as Muntsalvasche or Carbonek, which lay in a place not wholly of this world and where the Knights who swore to seek the Grail must journey, undergoing many perils and trials along the way. It is this quest or series of quests which forms the main source of information we possess about the Grail and its operations. At Camelot it appeared in a ray of brilliant light, and all the company were fed with the food and drink of their choice – a symbol of the spiritual food to be obtained from the Grail. In another text it is described as having five shapes or changes of shape which contain an inexplicable mystery. All seek it, some for good, others for evil purposes. It is only found by the good and the true. Three knights are named: Galahad, Perceval, and Bors. They alone of Arthur's men find their way to the castle and the mysterious Fisher King, wounded through the thighs and unable to be healed until a ritual question – usually 'Whom does the Grail serve?' or sometimes, 'Who is it that serves the Grail?' is asked and answered. At which both the King, and the land he rules, which is until then a desert, are restored. The three knights, along with the Grail, depart by ship for Sarras, the Holy City in the East, where the final celebration of the mysteries of the Grail take place, and Galahad, the purest of the three, expires in an odour of sanctity. Perceval returns to the Grail castle to become its new King, and Bors journeys to Camelot to tell of the miracles of the Quest.

Such is the story in its baldest outline; there are many other versions and countless adventures of the knights who seek it;

Grail

- Joseph of Arimathea (Glastonbury Abbey)

no Xian acceptance

but the essence remains the same. The message of the Grail does not change, either then or now, as we will hope to show in these pages.

Acknowledgments

Extracts from Charles Williams's poems, 'Taliessin in the Rose Garden' and 'The Last Voyage' in Ch. 5, are reproduced by kind permission of David Higham Associates. Materials from *The Grail Legend*, by Emma Jung, is reproduced in Ch. 8 by permission of Hodder and Stoughton Limited.

Note

1 *The High Book of the Holy Grail*, trans. N. Bryant, Brewer/Rowman & Littlefield, 1978, pp. 264–5.

· PART · I ·
·

: ORIGINS
· & ·
PATTERNS :

:1:

THE·GRAIL·OF·THE :GOLDEN·AGE:

.

GEOFFREY·ASHE

.

Perhaps the most powerful impulse underlying the attractiveness of the Grail stories is one of nostalgia. Whether for the dim and distant days of our own childhood, or the lost days of a time long vanished, the Grail seems to embody the need to rediscover this happy period. Thus the personal search, whatever form it happens to take, is at heart a desire for a seemingly unattainable thing, but which yet has its own reality. This precisely describes the Grail, and its imagery is reflected in nearly all the stories – from the pagan Spoils of Annwn to the Christian Queste del Saint Graal. Geoffrey Ashe sees this as the nostalgic memory of a time when paganism and Christianity were able to meet in something like harmony – as they perhaps were in the 'Arthurian' period. The pre-Christian Grail images of the Cauldrons of Rebirth and Inspiration helped to shape the later Christianized images in which the content of the vessel became of greater importance. But the past time, when the matrix was formed, remained buried in the subconscious of the race, like a distant golden gleam on far-off mountains. It reflected a need, which the search for the Grail fulfilled, as it still does, for something eternally present in which to believe – a need which sends people in quest of the Grail to this very day.

At various times, Christian doctrine and mythology have adopted a great deal that is pre-Christian. This is notably true of the Grail myth. Its special character does not lie in the adoption as such, but in its nature and results. What we have here

11

is a major instance of the process not 'taking'. It created a myth, without creating a fully and acceptedly Christian myth. The Grail mystery hovered in Christian imaginations, but never reached the point of being endorsed or defined by those who spoke for the Church.

Even at Glastonbury Abbey, where the Grail-bringer Joseph of Arimathea was part of the tradition, the Grail itself was not. The Abbey's fourteenth-century chronicler tells of Joseph's coming. He even adapts episodes from two of the Grail romances. But he replaces the wonder-working vessel with two 'cruets' containing drops of the blood and sweat of Christ – uncontroversial holy relics. (But see Ch. 10, pp. 174–96.) It certainly appears that the story had some early connection with Glastonbury; yet the plain statement that Joseph brought the Grail there is never made in the Middle Ages. It is never made, so far as I know, by anyone before Tennyson.

There were several reasons, besides the pagan factors themselves, for the Grail's failure to find a niche in the household of orthodoxy. For one thing it could not be identified with any recognized relic. It took different forms in different stories, and none of these had any clear link with Christian tradition outside the literature. The Church had little to say about the tableware of the Last Supper, and, such as it was, it had no points of contact with romances like Robert de Boron's *Joseph* or the *Queste del Saint Graal*.

Again, the spirit of the myth was foreign to medieval norms. This does not mean that it was heretical. The author of the *Queste* makes his story a vehicle for orthodox teaching – at tedious length indeed; and the crowning experience, attained by the chaste Galahad, seems to be a Christian vision of the nature of God and the Incarnation. But even in this pious text the quest is a personal adventure, aloof from the Church's collective life. While it leads to orthodoxy, it leads that way in an atmosphere of enchantment, secret knowledge, initiation. The orthodoxy is esoteric and therefore suspect. (See Ch. 6, pp. 111–28.)

Hence, the mainstream Christian rejection cannot be ascribed entirely to pagan motifs and clerical dislike of them. But the motifs were present, they were never fully domesticated, and the fact that they could not be is reflected in the rejection, even though they were not solely responsible for it.

What exactly they were has been a topic for much debate. The first extant version of the quest, and the only purely pagan one, is a cryptic Welsh poem called *The Spoils of Annwn*. Its author is supposedly the sixth-century bard Taliesin, but its present text is later by four hundred years. It describes (or rather, does not describe) a foray by men under Arthur's leadership into Annwn, a Celtic Otherworld or Underworld. They go by water, braving obscure perils, and only seven return. Their purpose seems to be to find a magical cauldron which is in the custody of nine maidens. (See Ch. 10, pp. 174–96.)

This poem has undoubted echoes of Celtic religion. Sacred cauldrons were well-known objects; a fine specimen was discovered at Gundestrup in Denmark. A Roman author, Pomponius Mela, mentions an actual sisterhood of nine virgin priestesses on the Ile de Sein, off the coast of what is now Brittany. They were healers and diviners, and could reputedly turn themselves into animals and control the weather. The group of nine Otherworld women reappears in the twelfth century, in Geoffrey of Monmouth's *Life of Merlin*. They live in the Apple-Island or Avalon. Their chief is the enchantress Morgan le Fay, who has similar powers to the women of the Ile de Sein, and, in her antecedents, is the Celtic goddess Matrona.

With the Grail romances themselves, from the 1180s onward, pagan imagery gradually gives way to Christian but never vanishes. As with the cauldron, women play a large role in the mysteries of the marvellous vessel, and continue to do so even when it is definitely Christianized. (See Ch. 5, pp. 91–110.) At first it seems to be associated with fertility-magic and the 'sources of life', as W. B. Yeats put it. Sometimes the Grail castle is in a Waste Land, and houses a wounded king. If the Grail-seeker asks a ritual question, the king will be healed and the Waste Land will revive: very much a *Golden Bough* idea.

Towards the end of the twelfth century, Robert de Boron is the first known author to say that the Grail was a vessel from the Last Supper, involved in Christ's sacramental ministry. Robert makes it a chalice or cup. Others make it a dish. In any case the 'life' of pre-Christian magic becomes Eternal Life, the transfiguration of the Waste Land of fallen nature. Yet even in the highly spiritualized *Queste del Saint Graal*, with the pure Galahad as hero, the vessel still produces literal nourishment. When it shows itself, veiled, to Arthur's assembled knights, they enjoy a supernatural banquet. In *Parzival* – where, incidentally, it becomes a stone – it regularly feeds its attendants. The author of *Perlesvaus* (best known in English as *The High Book of the Holy Grail*) hints at a mystery of transformation, speaking of the Grail as manifesting in five successive ways, finally changing into a chalice. What were its previous guises, how did they lead up to the last? He never says.

The same author tells us he used a document at Glastonbury Abbey. He is not the first to glance that way. Robert de Boron, in his Christian account of the Grail's origin, refers to its being brought to the vales of Avalon, i.e. central Somerset. Scholars have rejected the *Perlesvaus* author's claim on the ground that he describes Glastonbury in the story and gets it wrong, so that plainly he did not go there. In fact, however, he gets it right. The scholars never bothered to look properly, and missed the part of the Glastonbury hill-cluster he has in mind. His claim of a source-book at the Abbey may well have something in it. Certainly he knew the place and had a reason for his assertion.

In view of the Abbey's rejection of the Grail, the natural guess is that its contribution, if any, consisted of stories of early Christians and King Arthur – material for the context and characters rather than the central motif. But attention must be paid to a theory put forward by Geoffrey Russell, making out that the romancers' Christianization of a pagan quest derives from actual events, and Glastonbury supplies the key to them. According to this, the romances follow on confusedly from a much earlier phase when the paganism was fully understood, and Christians consciously recast it. Some such background was suggested before, by Jessie Weston, whose work impressed T. S. Eliot and underlies *The Waste Land*. She, however, did not bring in Glastonbury. Russell brought it in very precisely, with statements which can be partly checked.

He focused not on the Abbey but on the Tor, the highest hill in the cluster cradling the town. This is so outlandish-looking that visitors often ask whether it is artificial. It is not, but it

14

does show signs of having been artificially shaped. Worn and weathered terraces run all the way round it, on seven levels, with curious undulations and sudden plunges. At the summit is a ruined tower, the remnant of a church dedicated to the Archangel Michael. Attempts to explain the terraces by erosion or agricultural working have proved unsatisfactory. In 1966 Russell made a surprising suggestion. They were the remains of a huge prehistoric maze, following a complex backtracking course which is found in other contexts – in Greece, Crete, Italy, and elsewhere in the British Isles – and clearly had magical significance. Maze-threaders would have walked round and round the Tor and undergone some ceremony or initiation when they completed the last circuit. Russell argued that the first Christians at Glastonbury – the group headed, in legend, by Joseph of Arimathea – adapted the meaning of the maze for their converts, and substituted a Christian symbol, perhaps literally a cup, for some object used in the pre-Christian ritual. In the Grail stories we have a hazy tradition of this. The quest recalls the long, devious, complicated maze-threading.

In favour of Russell's theory is the fact that the Tor was regarded centuries ago as a point of entry to Annwn, the Otherworld or Underworld containing that cauldron which is the earliest known 'Grail'. The belief is attested by the legend of St Collen, who passed inside the hill and encountered the Celtic demigod Gwyn ap Nudd, Annwn's ruler. It has persisted to this day in local beliefs about the Tor having a hollow space inside it, which can be entered, but is full of danger. Mazes have Underworld associations in several mythologies, and it could be that Tor maze-threaders did actually finish by passing from the path on the hillside into an underground chamber.

These admittedly are flimsy connections, and Annwn is too vague a concept to prove anything. Russell's notion of an adaptation of pagan ritual to Christian ends seems tenuous. Nevertheless, on the main issue, he was right. Field-work in 1979 showed good reason for believing that the Tor maze is real, and that Glastonbury was a sacred site in Celtic paganism and earlier. It opens windows on a pre-Christian world which can be seen percolating through into Christian mythology and even

15

Christian practice, and has its relevance for the Grail, though this may not be as precise and direct as Russell thought.

For instance, the same spiral maze-pattern that appears on the Tor was employed in Crete to represent the Labyrinth. In the oldest mythical stratum this had a presiding goddess-figure, the Mistress of the Labyrinth, who may survive in the classical version as Theseus's guide, Ariadne. There are grounds for thinking that the Tor maze had a similar presiding goddess, that Chalice Well just below was her sacred spring, and that she was the Mother whom the Celts called Matrona. This is the same deity who reappears in the guise of the enchantress Morgan le Fay, lady of Avalon, head of the sisterhood of nine.

Credibly her cult helped to inspire something else – the dedication of Glastonbury's first church to Mary, Mother of Christ. This happened so early as to be completely out of line. No such dedication is on record anywhere else in the British Isles till centuries later. Glastonbury clearly had some special motive for it. The significant point is that here alone in north-west Europe, the dedication is early enough to fit into the first phase of the Virgin's cult, when, in Italy and the Christian East, she was taking the place of goddess-figures not yet forgotten – Artemis, Athene, Aphrodite, Isis, Cybele. At Glastonbury she may have done the same with Matrona, whose memory had been preserved for a while by the terracing of the Tor and the perpetual flow from the spring at its foot. *Perlesvaus*, the Grail romance claiming a Glastonbury connection, is also the one in which Mary's role is most evident.

To range farther afield, Russell correctly pointed out that the seven-levelled Tor might have been intended to correspond mystically (like many sacred hills) to a 'cosmic mountain' which figures in several mythologies. (See Ch. 2, p. 34.) It is supposed to unite the earth and the heavens, and to be surmounted by a paradise of the gods. The authors of the Grail stories show no awareness of the myth. But a greater one, Dante, discovered the mountain in Islamic literature. He Christianized it poetically as the seven-tiered Mount of Purgatory with the Earthly Paradise at the top, and a way upwards through the heavens to the climactic vision of the *Divine Comedy* . . . which, as Charles Williams observed, is probably in substance the same vision Galahad beholds in the Grail. Any search for direct influence – speculation about secret doctrines of the Templars, for instance – is doomed to be inconclusive. We can only say that certain things happened in medieval imaginations, tended in the same direction, expressed the same logic of the spirit. But we can say that.

Dante, of course, was a genius who could have done almost anything with almost anything. No comparable figure stands behind the Grail mythos. In this too something entered Christian imagination from an older world, whether at Glastonbury or elsewhere. However, it was complex and ill-defined. In the absence of the single creative genius, its infiltration depended, far back, on a special atmosphere – the atmosphere of Celtic Christianity in the British Isles.

The 'difference' of the Celtic Church has often been misconstrued and exaggerated. Protestants have tried to make out that it was separate from the main Catholic body, divergent in doctrine and without allegiance to Rome. This is an error. The Celtic Christianity of the early centuries was neither schismatic nor unorthodox. But barbarian inroads and other factors threw it on its own resources for many years. It developed practices of its own. These caused bitter argument when Rome could at last move in to restore conformity. But even bishops such as Colman at the Synod of Whitby, who opposed papal rulings and refused to comply with them, never challenged papal headship in principle, or the appeal to a divine commission on which it was based.

These disputes do not reveal some abortive Reformation. However, they are eloquent of things unsaid. They went deeper than they appeared to go. The points at issue, such as the fixing of the date of Easter, were rallying-cries in a clash of attitudes. The Celts were Catholics in a different spirit, less clear-cut and authoritative. And an important part of the difference, whether or not the advocates of Rome fully grasped it, was a difference of attitude to the old gods and the pagan, magical world prior to Christianity. This is the remoter background to the growth of the Grail mythos.

The Celts of Britain and Ireland did not regard everything

pre-Christian as anti-Christian and therefore to be suppressed, replaced, or edited out of recognition. For them, the old mythology could survive as part of the new scheme of things, without entirely losing its character. Elsewhere, saints might take over from gods in local folklore, Mary might take over from goddesses; but it was emphatically a takeover, with the new figures annexing the pleasanter aspects of the old ones and consigning them to oblivion or poetry. Among the Celts, similar changes were apt to be more subtle and less dismissive. Many beings enjoyed a respected continuity when Christians of other lands would have damned them.

Some have supposed that this happened because there actually was a kind of affinity. An eighteenth-century notion that the Druids were proto-Christians, even that Christianity is (in effect) a form of Druidism, has lingered to this day. But no such fancies are needed. The clearest reason lies in an accident of history. Everywhere else in the former Roman world, the Church had been persecuted by pagan authorities. The old gods were therefore seen as hostile. They were malignant demons in disguise, who had deceived humanity and inspired the persecutions. In Britain it was otherwise. Persecution was on a small scale, and brief. It never spread to Ireland at all, because Ireland was outside the Empire, and in any case there were no Christians there, or very few, when it occurred.

The result was that for the Christians of these islands, the native gods and demigods had fairly clean hands. Clerics might denounce them, but they were not felt to be enemies. The mythology that went with them was not diabolic. A certain live-and-let-live was possible. They could not remain divine, but they could pass nobly into legend as kings and queens, heroes and magicians. Gods were humanized into monarchs such as Lud and Lear. Also, pagan motifs could attach themselves to the new religion even where it could not assimilate them. St Brigit, for instance, acquired attributes of an Irish goddess of the same name. Her feast was observed on 1 February, the date of the goddess's fire-festival, and a sacred fire was kept burning in her convent at Kildare. Irish poets spoke of her as 'mother of the Great King's Son', even 'mother of Jesus', apparently implying that she was Mary reincarnate; and she was referred to as a priest or bishop, though the Church never ordained women. Both these aspects of her suggest a recollection of Druidism, which did ordain women, and may have taught a form of reincarnation. As we have seen, the goddess Matrona probably survived in both ways. The Virgin assumed some of her attributes at Glastonbury, while in legend she became Morgan le Fay, not indeed a goddess, but a benign, super-human enchantress.

One way in which Celtic Christians accommodated beings whom other Christians could not admit was by allowing the existence of neutral angels. The normal view was that all angels had either remained loyal to God or fallen with Lucifer, so that they were either good and in heaven, or bad and in hell. Hence spiritual beings had to be either celestial or demonic. Dante mentions angels who took neither side, but he confines them to a dismal life in hell's antechamber. In effect they are lost as the devils are. Some Celts, however, gave them an intermediate status. St Brendan, on his famous Atlantic voyage, was said to have encountered hundreds of them in bird form flying over a flowery island.

Neutral angels, ambiguous spirits, make an appearance in the Grail cycle. Their presence is a symptom of the whole under-lying process – a process rooted in Celtic Christianity, able to acclimatize magic cauldrons, fertility-rituals and much else. Likewise with several of the human characters. Bron, a leading companion of Joseph, and in some versions identified with the 'Fisher King', is the British god Bran – Bran the Blessed as he is called in the *Mabinogion*. The greater Merlin, who of course extends through the whole Arthurian Legend, sums up the special atmosphere in his own person. He is the son of a human mother and an evil spirit whose evil has been neutralized. As C. S. Lewis remarked, he is a kind of Druid, yet he is also a Christian. He has occult gifts, yet he is responsible for the Round Table, which has its ancestry in the table of the Last Supper.

The romancers who created these stories and characters evoked what was probably, in some degree, the reality of the fifth and sixth centuries in Britain. It need not be supposed that anyone literally went Grail-seeking. But the spiritual ambiguity, the mingling of pagan and Christian elements, could well have been a fact. A Merlin could really have had it both ways.

However, the Britain of the authors' own time was quite different, and France, the home of most of them, had never known Celtic Christianity at first hand – the closest contact was via the Bretons, who, centuries earlier, had brought their religion and mythology from Britain, but had since diverged considerably. Grail romance took shape in a Christendom where the Celtic attitude existed no longer. Anything rooted in that attitude was discrepant, out of keeping. Many have tried to connect the Grail with actual heresy, usually Catharism. An outright heretical link or content is unlikely. Though orthodoxy never had any place for the Grail, there is no sign of active hostility, or attempts to suppress the literature. But partly because heresy was flourishing, orthodoxy was hardening. Anything that seemed to go outside official Catholicism was suspect, probably sinister. Magic was becoming taboo, and on the way to becoming simply evil, a forbidden art. We can trace the change here and there in the Arthurian literature itself. Thus Morgan, on her first appearance in Geoffrey of Monmouth, is 'good'. She is a wise healer. Presently, however, the idea of a 'good' Celtic enchantress with a foot in both worlds is felt to be inadmissible. Morgan turns into a witch and trouble-maker. Under pressure, even the Grail stories lose some of their early strangeness, and become more ·like innocuous Christian allegories.

That came later. The heyday of the Grail theme was a time when the hardening process had begun but was not yet ascendant. What can be detected in these romances is not a covert leaning towards heresy or paganism, but a half-conscious, still-possible nostalgia for an earlier world of Christi-anity-*and*-paganism. The authors were Christians. However, they could dream of a Christianity with a 'Something Else' quality, a questing religion in a world of mystery and magic – a world with potentialities which the Church tended more and more to blot out. The ultimate inspiration was Celtic, and it let in the Grail, itself of Celtic ancestry, as the focal image.

A less important but noteworthy parallel is the medieval vogue of the romance of St Brendan, the same who met angels disguised as birds. The Irish had tales called *immrama* of voyages over the western ocean, full of pre-Christian marvels – strange islands, sea-monsters, countries of eternal youth. Brendan was a sixth-century Irish saint famous for his travels by boat. His legendary 'Life' credited him with a long series of adventures in the Atlantic, in search of the Earthly Paradise. The relation between St Brendan's Voyage and the surviving *immram* yarns is a difficult problem. Borrowing occurred in both directions. But the literary result, though Christian, drew on many themes which were not. During the Middle Ages, versions of the Voyage were composed in most European languages. Not only was the theme popular as the Grail theme was, it overlapped it. Both went back to Celtic Otherworld-quests by water. Both drew pagan ideas and imagery into a Christian story. *Perlesvaus* even has an episode which is a sort of *immram*.

Grail romancers sought to re-evoke a 'having-it-both-ways' milieu which they associated, more or less rightly, with a vanished regional form of Christianity. They knew that it belonged several centuries before their own time, in the days of the Celtic Britain of which Arthur had supposedly been the principal king, though perhaps, in historical fact, a little before the Celtic Church took its characteristic shape. Their accounts of the Grail's origin make it a Christian object but a very mystifying Christian object, by no means a conventional relic. The setting of its later appearances is pictured appropriately. Normally the romances portray Arthur's world as Christian, but weird things happen in it, and the norm itself is not invariable: in *Perlesvaus* the old religion is still powerful, with alarming aspects, and some of the knights are crusaders against the heathen.

This ambiguous world, in which the Grail is a typifying and focusing image, is not 'good' in a Utopian way. It is a world of high ideals but also much evil. The quest, in fact, exposes its failings and weakens the chivalry of the Round Table. The romancers do not portray a Golden Age in any absolute sense. They do portray a world with a richer spiritual atmosphere, and a hidden glory lurking in it, giving glimpses of something utterly above the everyday Waste Land, for those who enter its presence with the right dispositions. The Grail is a point of direct contact with a spiritual and supernatural realm. (See Ch.

4, p. 78.) In its fully Christian form it becomes the token of a special divine friendship, a special closeness to God. Sometimes it appears as the vehicle of a special sacrament unfolding the mystery of the Incarnation, God become Man to bring the gift of Eternal Life. The Grail-seer encounters the things of eternity through the senses, with an assurance denied to normal existence.

That last motif is itself closer to paganism and the mystery-cults than to Christianity. The Church enjoined, as it still enjoins, faith in things unseen. Yet the desire to see was a real human yearning. Outside the romances, there are medieval legends of the consecrated host at the altar visibly turning into a likeness of Christ, confirming the doctrine of the Real Presence. Visionary happenings of much the same kind occur in the romances. But in Arthur's world, the authors imply, it was not a question of rare miracles but of a contact with divinity which the Grail supplied all the time. When the Grail departed, the secret glory departed with it. The realm of Arthur declined, deprived of its transcendent treasure. In this conception we have something like the widespread belief in a lost Golden Age, even though the Arthurian age is not presented as golden for humankind generally.

The sense of loss, and the attempt at a literary reinstatement, are related to the passing away of Celtic spirituality. Can they be related to anything else?

Perhaps they can. One twelfth-century phenomenon was a complex shift in the status of women, and in male attitudes to them. The strongest material factor was the repeated absence of nobles on crusade. Their wives took over some of their functions at home, with a consequent rise in social importance. In one field, literary patronage, a queen was the chief figure. Eleanor of Aquitaine promoted Arthurian romance and the troubadour love-cult, with its fantasization of the adored lady, which helped to shape such themes as the Lancelot-Guinevere affair. (See Ch. 3, pp. 49–65.)

These matters concerned only a minority. But a change which pervaded all society was a religious one – the growth of devotion to the Blessed Virgin, with an immense investment of money and labour in church-building for her, and a popular mythology of her unique role and her miracles. It is hard to say what the relations were between this and the actual status of women, or between either and courtly love. What is clearer is that the heightened glorification of Mary reflected a sense of something lacking in a masculine Church; and that this had more than a touch of nostalgia, tending towards a re-enthronement of female divinity as worshipped in past ages, so far as theology allowed it. (See also Chs 6, 9 and 10.)

Much the same impulse can be seen at work in some of the Grail literature. The 'different' religious past, which it drew back confusedly to the surface, had palpable female aspects. There were female Druids as well as male ones. The ancestral cauldron was in female custody. The Grail itself was originally a female symbol if it had any sexual connotation at all. The Glastonbury connection was a link with an ancient Marian shrine, perhaps the only one this side of the Alps marking a direct or near-direct transition from Goddess-worship, the worship of Matrona-Morgan, the lady of Avalon.

In harmony with all this, several of the romances depict the Grail as borne by women . . . a total defiance of medieval Church practice. *Perlesvaus* has its Glastonbury associations, frequent devout allusions to Mary, a vision suggesting that she played a part in the revelation, and a plain statement that she personally visited the Grail chapel during the ritual. The *Queste* has Galahad achieving the final goal in a ceremony called 'the Mass of the Glorious Mother of God'. Outside the romances Mary is spoken of, in her Litany and elsewhere, with imagery that relates to the Grail. Poets actually call her 'the Grail' and, in one remarkable Welsh text, 'the cauldron'. Dante's vision at the close of the *Divine Comedy*, which seems to be much the same as Galahad's, is granted through her intercession. Again it is not clear what the relationships are. But the impression of an unexplored background is strong.

The image of the Waste Land – the tract which has become sterile, but can be revivified through the Grail – points to a larger significance of the theme as a whole. Loss-and-recovery is central. The Grail itself, at first, is known and accessible to many – to Joseph, to his companions, to his British converts.

23

Then it passes into a phase of withdrawal when it is known only to its keepers, and Britain suffers. Then the questing knights rediscover it, and attain a glimpse of what was so long withheld.

What happens after that? The accounts disagree. The Grail is taken up to heaven, or away out of Britain, to an island or a retreat in Asia. In some sense, however, the experience of it may still be possible. Romancers who tell the tale of its origin assert that its secrets are preserved in a book. To some extent they themselves are restoring it to the world. Anyone today who seeks to renew the quest through a meditation or spiritual exercise is not out of harmony with the myth. It is one version, in fact, of a Golden-Age archetype which is perennial. (See also Ch. 11.)

Human minds do not seem to work normally or naturally in terms of progress. Far more compelling is the concept of a glory or promise which once existed, then faded, but is not truly lost; a glory or promise which can be recovered and reinstated for a fresh start, with intervening corruption swept away. The Grail, possessed-and-lost-and-found-again, is the focus and symbol of a desired mode of spiritual life associated with Celtic Christianity. This, for the romancers, flourished once but has succumbed . . . but can still perhaps be revived, at least in imagination.

Now the same mode of thinking appears in the real history of Christianity, on a far vaster scale. The reformers in the time of Erasmus, Luther and Calvin knew nothing of the Grail quest. Yet their minds, however diverse from one another, followed in the same kind of track as the minds of the romancers. The Church had once had its Golden Age, in the apostolic purity of the first centuries; corruption had overspread it; but Scripture, and the continuing witness of a few who had kept faith, made it feasible to restore the pristine rightness and begin afresh.

Nor is the syndrome confined to Christianity. Its Protean energy is amazing. In modern Judaism, for instance, the reformist and liberal movements never acquired the dynamic force of Zionism (in its ideological, pre-chauvinist period). Zionism insisted on Israel's recovery of its long-lost Land, where once David reigned as the Lord's anointed, and the Temple stood on its holy mount. In the nineteenth century Israel's state was dead, the Temple destroyed, the people scattered among the nations. So it had been for a long, long time, and almost all 'enlightened' and 'rational' Jews accepted the fact and sought to assimilate. Yet it was the seemingly mad dream of a restoration – of Jews reoccupying the Promised Land and refusing any other proposed home – that took hold and gained ground, decade after decade, proving more potent than all the rationality arrayed against it. Likewise in Imperial India, the early, British-schooled nationalists who talked of parliaments and industrialization made no headway. The only leader able to rouse India's millions was Gandhi, who condemned westernized progress as a perversion. Instead he proposed to bring back an idealized pre-conquest India of saints and scholars and village communes and handicrafts. Independent India did not eventually go his way, but the mass pressure for independence came, in the first place, from the recovered-Golden-Age mode of thinking and not the progressive mode.

Examples can be piled on examples. French revolutionaries appealed to Rousseau, with his doctrine of a virtuous natural society in the distant past, wrecked by bad institutions, and capable of being restored by good ones. Russian revolutionaries appealed (and this is interesting) not strictly to the Marxism of the Communist Manifesto, but to an enlarged version taught by Engels and Lenin, making society begin in an idyll of 'primitive communism', which the Revolution could reinstate on a higher level by ending the succession of class tyrannies that had taken its place.

The poetic exponent of this theme is William Blake. He expresses it in his myth of the Primal Being, Albion, whose sleep has been the disintegration and cutting-down of divine humanity, and whose awakening will be its rebirth. Blake pointed out acutely that 'the stories of Arthur are the acts of Albion'. The king's legendary career is an image of basic truths about the human condition. Which brings us back to the Grail. As a lesser but perceptive author (A. E. Waite) once observed, not only is the Grail given an Arthurian setting, there is a real parallelism of idea. The finding of the Grail has a counterpart in the prophesied return of Arthur. The main legend of Arthur, indeed, is a fuller embodiment of the Golden-Age mystique

25

itself. The setting given to the Grail is appropriate for another reason than the association of Celtic Christianity with a stretch of history in which Arthur figured.

The Golden-Age element in Arthur's legendary reign is a constant. Its nature varies. In the stories that involve the Grail, the glory is spiritual and withdrawn from secular life. In the rest, which of course are the majority, it takes different forms in different literary phases. The early Welsh tradition, rooted in far-off victories over Saxon invaders, makes Arthur the arch-hero of a British heroic age, chief prince of the Island of the Mighty, a realm of larger-than-life warriors and wild fairy-tale exploits. Geoffrey of Monmouth, the first author to present him as a quasi-historical monarch, keeps and even expands the warfare but civilizes the Golden Age. In Arthur's time, he says, 'Britain had reached such a standard of sophistication that it excelled all other kingdoms in its general affluence, the richness of its decorations, and the courteous behaviour of its inhabitants.' Later, with the advent of French courtly romance, the Golden Age becomes more purely elite. The glory is centred on the Round Table and chivalric ideals applying to the nobility only. Arthur is a model of aristocratic courage and courtesy. Little is said to show how good he is as a ruler, and whether his subjects in general are well off.

Understandably, there tends to be a failure of fusion. When the Grail enters and even Lancelot proves unworthy, it calls the glory of chivalry in question. The Golden Age is not fully articulated till Malory. He, however, in his great English version, holds everything together by what C. S. Lewis calls a three-tiered scale of values. Evil is simply evil. But good is of two kinds: first the earthly good of knighthood, valid on its own level; and secondly the heavenly good of the Grail, which can draw a Galahad away from the first, but need not invalidate it.

Thus Malory can suggest that throughout most of Arthur's reign, a noble way of life did flourish in Britain. In the end, human shortcomings doomed it and the end was tragedy. The knighthood destroyed itself in internal conflict and Arthur passed away. But – Malory tells us – his death remains uncertain. 'Some men say in many parts of England that King Arthur is not dead, but had by the will of Our Lord Jesu into another place; and men say that he shall come again.' He is *rex quondam, rexque futurus*, king that was, king that shall be.

Here also then, the lost glory is not truly lost. Arthur preserves it in his mysterious immortality, and will return in the hour of need to renew it. The immortality takes two principal forms. He may be alive in an enchanted island, healed of his wounds by Morgan le Fay. Or he may be sleeping in a cave. The latter is the folklore version. His cave is located in quite a number of places, from Somerset through Wales to the north of England and even Scotland. Both stories owe a debt to a Celtic myth about a god lying asleep in a cave on a western island. As with the Grail, paganism breaks through.

In view of all the instances of this pattern of thinking – and there are many more, ancient and modern – we might well ask where it comes from. Applied to historical realities, it does not tally very convincingly with knowledge and experience. Golden Ages have seldom been really golden (perhaps never, except in restricted fields such as art), and would-be restorations are apt to turn sour, as with Rousseau's disciple Robespierre, whose technique for bringing back natural virtue was to chop off heads. Yet the pattern persists, in myth and legend, and in religious and political action. It surely corresponds to something profound.

Traditional Christianity might say that its substratum is a fact about the human condition, deeply imprinted on the psyche: that which is called the Fall. Humanity once dwelt in an earthly paradise. A breach of the law of the paradisal state resulted in exile, and 'brought death into the world and all our woe' – Paradise Lost. Yet there can be a way back, a way of redemption – Paradise Regained. (See Ch. 4.)

If this can be admitted as true, in whatever sense, the rest follows. Human beings create myths in the same shape: glory, eclipse, recovery. These have the power to haunt and motivate even when they are baseless. The Grail is lost but found again. Arthur departs but will return. Pure primitive Christianity, in the eyes of Luther, lay crushed under a corrupt Church, but the spirit of the apostles would be reborn and overthrow priestcraft.

Mother India, in the eyes of Gandhi, had been shut away in a British jail, but her children would set her free, to come forth with her youth renewed. Even Russia's avowed atheists adopted a programme based, in effect, on Paradise-Lost-and-Regained, with an ancient classless society rising to rebirth out of millennia of bondage. If such things are images of Fall and Redemption, we have a key to them. But they lead back to a single question behind them all. What meaning should we give to Fall and Redemption?

:2:

:THE·MEETING OF·THE·WATERS:

·

HANNAH·CLOSS

·

Theories about the origin of the Grail tradition exist in such numbers as to cause bewilderment rather than illumination: one of the most frequent bones of contention being the derivation of Grail lore from either Eastern or Western sources, one or other being championed by individual writers. What has seldom been attempted is an approach which seeks to reconcile the two, pointing to a dual origin, or even a unified urge which sprang into being in various parts of the world at the same time. Yet from this unified point of origin comes the harmonizing influence of the Grail itself, reminding us that out of the reconciliation of opposites comes rest, and the recognition of the true self. The simple power of the Grail images demonstrates how this may be achieved. To meditate on the symbols of the Grail is to activate them. Once activated, they become signposts in our own quest, pointing towards a personal point of harmony and reconciliation.

I

Few though the images of the Grail may be, their richness conjures up an infinite world – whether it be the green valleys of Usk or the dim forests of Broceliande – a world in which we may expect to encounter, at any turn of the path, the magic fountain of Owain's adventure, or catch between the trees a glimpse of Guigemer pursuing the fateful hart. Endless is the quest through the perilous wood. Dare we hope that, faint and doubting, we may reach at last, where the thicket lightens, the cell of Trevrizent, though the clouds still shroud the horizon that promised sight of the Grail?

The quest is still unfulfilled – even for scholars. Amongst those who have contributed most to the elucidation of problems relating to the Grail was the late Jessie Weston, to whom T. S. Eliot acknowledges a profound debt in the notes to his *Waste Land*. In the book he particularly quotes, *From Ritual to Romance*,[1] as in other of her works, she set herself the task of proving the actual existence of a definite Grail Mystery. It was her belief that an ancient fertility cult still discernible in folk ceremonies the world over, but having an esoteric spiritual meaning traceable in Hellenistic-Oriental mystery religions ultimately sublimated to a Christian gnosis, was transported by the foreign legionaries to the furthest bounds of the Roman Empire. Finding a congenial soil in the realm of Drudical lore, it was adopted by the Britons, though sooner or later its practice, on account of the violation of one of the 'Grail' maidens, was relegated to the secrecy of the mountain fastnesses.

As in the East, this search for the ultimate Secrets of Life involved initiation and a test on different planes of existence. The text which Jessie Weston considers to reflect the earliest existing version of the Grail story[2] gives the description of such an actual test. The hero or rather the would-be initiate (he fails on the higher plane) is Gawain. Gradually, however, what was originally the account of an actual happening was converted through the influence of Christian relics (Glastonbury and Fescamp) into a romance of which Perceval, whom she considers as a folk-tale character, originally unconnected with the Grail, becomes the hero. With Chrétien de Troyes and Wolfram von Eschenbach, the ritual myth, according to her, becomes purely literary.

In tilting against the adherents of the purely Celtic school, Jessie Weston rightly warns us that visits to the Otherworld are not always derivations from Celtic fairy lore. (See also Ch. 10.) Nevertheless, obsessed with the fertility aspect suggested by the dead king on the bier, the waste land, the sexual symbolism of lance and spear, she has hardly done justice to the divergence of certain versions from her accepted scheme. Their dismissal to a realm of literary fantasy and confusion remains unsatisfying. Is there really not a fundamental connection, for instance, between the seemingly conflicting versions which see the Grail now as a vessel, now as a precious stone, and a deeper reason for the 'introduction' of Perceval? Jessie Weston refused, as she herself admits, to be sidetracked down a bypath that can but lead into mists of a Celtic twilight. It is possible that we shall have to venture into a realm of far deeper shadows to achieve the quest and explain the perpetual re-occurrence of images that seem to combine two distinct patterns, which, in spite of local and periodic divergencies ultimately reveal an underlying affinity. Then we shall learn too that the repetition of such symbols may not depend only on conscious borrowings and factual transmission but on a repeated upwelling from the unconscious of a forgotten heritage, whether in the individual or in the group.

What follow are but a few suggestions in that direction. For the purpose of our own inquiry it will be necessary to consult not only literature but the products of fine and applied art. Ideally, of course, such a study would have to embrace also the province of music.

One of the chief recurrent images of Celtic myth and legend appears to be that of a visit to or from the Otherworld. It is significant that the landscape thus conjured up so often bears the same or similar features which, though they appear in different combinations and not always all together, enjoy one basic peculiarity – that of a realm somehow detached from this present world. It may be described as at most times, or to all but a chosen few, invisible. It may be visibly cut off by ocean, river and lake, by mountain rock or by mist, or hidden within the mountain itself. Sometimes it can only be entered by the overcoming of a test or through the sustaining of a mortal wound. But always it is cut off by some barrier from the world of daily existence. Thus Tristan and Guigemer, wounded beyond hope of healing are borne in a rudderless or fairy boat across unknown seas; thus in the lay of Ivonek, the lady following in the track of her elfin lover's blood has to venture into the very bowels of the mountain to reach the fairy world on the other side. Owain has to perform the magic rite at the

well and overcome its consequences. The castle of the Grail
itself lies in a mountain fastness, beyond the ocean, on the bank
of an impassable river, or by a mysterious lake. It is impossible
in this short space to enter into all the variations, even of the
Grail landscape. Enough to point out that from concepts as
widely divergent as the barbaric raid to secure the magic cauldron in the *Harrowing of Annwn* in which the magic land is
conceived now as an island fortress, now as a dim subterranean
land, lighted by lamps, now as hell, to the Christianized mysticism of the *Perlesvaus*, the image is retained. It occurs most
clearly in a reference in the *Book of Taliesin*:[3]

> Perfect is my seat in Kaer Siddi
> Nor plague nor age harms him who dwells therein.
> Manawyd and Pryderi know it.
> Three utterances around the fire will he sing before it.
> And around its corners are oceans currents
> And the fruitful [wonder-working] spring is above it
> Sweeter than wine the drink in it.

The resemblance to *Perlesvaus* is striking:

> La nef a tant coru e par jor e par nuit, issue com a Deu
> plot, que il virent un chastel en une isle de mer. . . . Il
> esgarde desouz un molt bel arbre . . . e voit la plus bele
> fontaine . . .

> [The youth had hardly journeyed a day and a night, coming
> as God had planned, when he saw a castle set upon an
> island in the sea. . . . He drew rein beneath a most beautiful
> tree . . . and saw a most lovely fountain . . .]

We must consider now whether this land of youth, this magic
realm of plenty or spiritual bliss is after all so essentially Celtic.

If we turn to the field of art, we shall discover in Asiatic art
countless examples, often in symbolic or conventionalized form,
of mountainous peaks embraced by heaving waters. To this
theme we shall return presently. For the moment let us limit
ourselves to the representation, on so-called Byzantine reliefs,
of a spring or a fountain entwined with foliage amongst whose
fruits and tendrils perch birds, or from whose waters beast and

bird may drink. Or again we have, as on a Sassanian metal dish, the tree itself flanked by two antelopes. At their feet is water that in many cases gushes from the tree's roots.

We are obviously confronted with the tree or fountain of Life. It is due to the research of the late Joseph Strzygowski and Heinrich Glück[4] that we have been able to get a clear picture of the perpetuation of the Iranian Paradise, the Otherworld landscape which early Christendom borrowed (and adapted to its own purpose) from Mazdaism – that ancient religion in which nature expressed itself in symbols. It may long before have travelled with Celtic migrations to the West. Its roots lie buried deep in the Indo-European tradition. Is it surprising that the imagery is continually reborn in medieval legend both in West and East?

Franz Kampers,[5] in tracing the story of the Grail to Oriental myth and Arab legends surrounding the fabled figure of Solomon, points to numerous references and elaborate descriptions of the tree of life in the Garden of Paradise so frequently associated with stories of the Eastern Kingdom of Prester John. The tree which appears now heavy with luscious fruits, now sparkling with jewels, is even described as illuminated. As such it has strayed into the legend of the Grail itself, for instance, into a curious anecdote in Gautier de Doulens's *Continuation of the Grail*, where we hear how Perceval comes to a tree in which he sees a child who gives him no answer to his question concerning the Fisher King. Later he sees a tree illumined with candles which changes to a chapel. Kampers goes on to say:

> Both trees are probably identical. The given explanation, that the child climbed up and down the tree because it wanted to show Perceval how vast is the world, was scarcely needed to prove that we have here lit on the sun tree . . . whose boughs spread over the whole world.

The identification is proved by a passage in Robert de Boron's version in which Perceval again meets with a similar tree with two children at the crossing of the ways – or from which issue forth the four streams of Paradise. But the imagery seems to lead us further back. I could not but be struck by the strange resemblance that the incident bears to a legend from the *Bhāga-*

vata Purāna[6] in which the hermit Markandeya beheld on a peak of the earth a young fig-tree bright with fruit and leaves.

> On a branch thereof that looked to the North-East he saw a babe lying in the hollow of a leaf, consuming the gloom with his own radiance. . . . Then the child drew a breath and Markandeya like a gnat passed into his body. And he beheld lying therein the universe in its fullness. . . . As he gazed upon the universe, the child's breath cast him out . . . and he fell into the ocean of the dissolving world.

That the Paradise in which the Tree stands is often thought to be situated on the cosmic 'Mountain of the World' is proved by legend and art alike. Indian myth may have seemed remote enough and by many it may be considered a still farther cry to Buddhist Japan. Yet it is precisely here that we find several striking visual expressions of the Mountain, which, curiously enough, may throw some light on the Grail. For the moment we will consider only the Tamamushi shrine in the Horijushi monastery at Nara, on one side of which is depicted a most fantastic representation of the mystic mountain Meru. Encircled by coiling dragons which revolve it at its base, and rising in four tiers like a branching conifer, the mountain shoots into the heavens where, between two discs evidently representing sun and moon, fly winged creatures and genii mounted on the backs of birds. Beneath the lowest of the tiers or rocky continents, from each of which sprout shrubs and pavilions, appears a small temple in which the Buddha sits enthroned between two attendants or Bodhisatthvas.

On either side of this subterranean temple stands a bird with sweeping plumage – perhaps a phoenix – surrounded by a flickering line. Surely the ancient Aryan image of the revolving universe has here been translated into the language of Buddhism. But if we recall the prototype-Vishnu's own mountain Meru around which sun and moon revolve, may we not also be reminded of Celtic lore – of Malduin's revolving island and the fortress of the solar hero Curoi; above all of the turning castles in *diu Krone*[7] and *Perlesvaus*, whilst in the Grail Temple described with such fantastic elaboration by Albrecht von Scharffenberg in the *Jüngere Titurel*, the dome was covered with blue sapphire and strewn with gleaming carbuncles, amidst which appeared the sun and moon, moved on their course by a hidden mechanism. (See Ch. 4, p. 75.) But we are reminded no less of the magic column in Orgeluse's enchanted castle in Wolfram's *Parzival* which he himself maintains was brought by Klingsor from India – Feirefiz's land.

It is significant that the legend of Prester John once more provides a similar image. The turning palace and chapel which in the latter crown the terrace structure like the firmament are hence not absolutely dependent on Babylonian astrological monuments. As in the case of Arthur's Round Table, which, according to F. Kampers,[8] also revolved, Arab and Babylonian cosmogony and Semitic legend centring on the fabled treasure of Solomon may well have played a part in the development of the Grail romance, but the more we become conversant with the evolution of northern and Iranian art, the clearer will become the hidden Indo-European root, and possibly *roots even deeper* from which that imagery has sprung. It was perhaps no mere stroke of artistic ingenuity that made Scharffenberg conceive his Grail Temple as a circular and radiating building.[9]

The influence of Templar architecture may have played its part, but even so we are led back to the centralized form of the Armenian churches and thence to the Iranian Fire Temple. How this latter was conceived standing in the midst of the holy garden or Paradise may very likely be seen in the ornamentation of Sassanian dishes.[10] It is possible that the very concept of encircling the ritualistic procession around the venerated symbol ultimately derives from a primal stage in man's religious consciousness, whilst it has been suggested that this rotating movement in Aryan ritual, added to references in the Veda to the thirty days dawn, points to the arctic origin of the northern peoples in the interglacial period.[11] (But it should be made clear that the term northern is here used without political perversion and not merely in regard to Indo-European tribes. Actually it embraces also the 'Amer-Asiatic' and 'Atlantic' races who may have migrated southward before them. Hence certain 'northern' tendencies, for instance, in the art and culture of Egypt.)

In the far north where the sun does not rise high in the heavens but actually wanders *round* the earth[12] and is, moreover, for six months wrapped in darkness, dawn is not a daily phenomenon, but denotes the advent of a whole season. There the sun's rising may well be a source of physical and spiritual rebirth. Perhaps some such unconscious memory is really reflected in the *Veda* where we read:

> She, the daughter of the sky, has appeared after, the young maiden in white robes. . . . She follows the course of the Dawns that have passed away, the first of the endless dawns to come. . . . rise up. Living life has come to us. The dark has passed away. The light comes. She has abandoned the path for the sun to go. We have come where men prolong their life.[13]

Incidentally, it may be noted that the old English goddess of Spring, Eostre, has been identified by some with the Aryan goddess of the dawn.

Be that as it may, it is certain that long after any migration southward and the change to a diurnal phenomenon, the image of the rising sun persisted with such intensity that it was taken over from Iran by Christianity itself. 'At the flaming of the dawn, when the gates of heaven are thrown wide . . . the Saviour rises out of the far East, the fount and habitation of Light.'

The sun, therefore, the Light, the Radiance, may well have been conceived as the fount of Life itself.

At first such ideas may have been visualized only in abstract symbolism. In the course of time, however, the process of anthropomorphization takes place. The sun becomes a deity, Surya, Mitra, Vishnu. But the primal concepts linger on. The light, the sun, is now a tangible object of a raid, a heroic feat, whether it be Indra's theft of the food-providing broth-pot or the expedition of Arthur and his warriors to Annwn, to the land of youth, to secure the pearl-rimmed cauldron which also possesses amongst other properties the reputation of being a vessel of plenty. Thus in the Veda we read how Indra trans-pierced the Gandharva in the limitless skies to provide nurture for his worshippers. 'Out of the mountains he shot, held fast the ready-cooked broth. Indra let loose the unfailing shaft.'

The springs of the Celtic land of youth abound, as we saw

at the beginning of this essay, in wine and mead. In the Vedic Sun-realm we likewise find not only milk and broth but mead. The last, however, is often identified with the Soma – the draught of the immortals. 'On the highest step of Vishnu lies the fount of mead. May I attain to this dear place, where men, devoted to the Gods, regale [inebriate] themselves; they the boon-companions of the wide-stepper.'

This 'third stride' of Vishnu – so often reiterated in the Veda – has given rise to much speculation. It is more than likely that the three strides refer rather to cosmic regions than to the time of day. The following Vedic hymn may offer suggestions. (Indu, incidentally, is a frequent epithet for Soma.)

> Where light is perpetual, in that realm where the sun is placed, to that immortal world bring me, Pavamana; flow, Indu for Indra.
>
> Where Vivasvat's son is king, where the inner chamber of the sun [is] where the eternal waters [are], there make me immortal; flow, Indu for Indra.
>
> Where in the third heaven, the third sphere, the sun wanders at will, where the regions are filled with light, there make me immortal; flow, Indu for Indra.
>
> Where yearning and desire [are satisfied] there where the region of the sun [is], where delight and sustenance are found, there make me immortal; flow, Indu for Indra.
>
> Where joy and pleasure dwell, and mirth and happiness, where the wishes of the wisher are fulfilled, there make me immortal; flow, Indu for Indra.

We are certainly in the 'land of youth' but we may also call to mind Wolfram von Eschenbach's description of the Grail as *'der Wunsch von Paradis, . . . Erden Wunsches uberval'* ('the wish for Paradise . . . which excels all earthly excellence').

The Soma has often been related to the Moon (apart from which there seems no Moon-worship in the Veda). But we have already read of the Soma in Vishnu the Sun God's highest step and the imagery here clearly points to the *sun's inner realm*. Thus Vishnu's highest step seems best to apply to the immortal realm of light – is in fact a land of the immortal dead.[14] This is borne out by the fact that the Soma is guarded by the Gandharvas, those strange creatures who can adopt bird or animal form, and who have at the same time been identified with the host of the spirits of the dead.

II

Step by step, the affinities between ancient Indo-European concepts and the Grail spring into sharper focus. The land of immortality where every wish finds fulfilment, where the Gandharvas (one recalls the 'bird' father of Ivonek and note particularly in this case Lohengrin) are in charge of the holy vessel – the sun, but perhaps also the moon (even as two vessels often appear in the Grail legend itself).

But the lance too finds its place, for Indra, who loots both sun and Soma, is described as wielding not only the thunderbolt and the arrow but also the spear. He is accompanied by the Maruts, a swift-footed host of youths in gleaming armour who are often interpreted as the storm winds, but also like the Gandharvas[15] as the spirits of the dead.

It is natural that Jessie Weston refers to them with gusto as helpers of Indra who, freeing the waters, brought fertility on the land. In their traditional dance (represented in ritual mime by the priests) she sees indeed a germ of the folklore sword-dance and even prototypes of the Knighthood of the Grail. Certainly the rain-making capacity of Indra must have been of primary importance to the dwellers of the plains and it may be justifiable to build up, step by step, a theory of the Grail romance which centres on the Waste Land, though that aspect does not seem to exhaust the problem. As she herself admitted, in some versions of the Grail legend the theme of the Waste Land has lost its point, or, as in Wolfram von Eschenbach's *Parzival*, plays practically no part at all. But in the latter case, there appears, it is true, what may be the remnant of an original substitute. First, as she herself states, the very nature of Amfortas's wound, whose sexual symbolism Wolfram in no way euphemizes, suggests a fertility motif which supports her theory. At the same time another point in Wolfram's description, and one that has caused great perplexity to scholars, namely, the treatment of the wound, may perhaps cast a yet clearer light on the subject.

The agony of Amfortas's wound was rendered most unendurable through frost. Now it appears that no less an authority than Hillebrandt held that at the time when the Vedic peoples inhabited a colder region, Indra must have been a Sun-God who *melted the frost* on the approach of Spring. Hence the strange idea of laying the spear (Indra's weapon) on Amfortas's wound to alleviate the agony attains some sort of sense, as the residue of ancient beliefs mingled with medieval alchemy and folk customs, a fact borne out by the allegations of Suhtschek (to whose theories we shall be referring later) to the effect that a similar ritual is practised by the natives of Sistan today in treating the plague.

Another image that has given rise to much speculation is that of the Fisher King. Admitting the possible influence of Babylonian, Semitic, Christian and Hellenistic legend, it seems that striking affinities may nevertheless be drawn between the Grail Fisher and Indo-Aryan and Buddhist imagery. The golden fish is, for instance, a symbol of the first avatar (incarnation) of Vishnu. Transferred to the Mahayana Buddhism of Tibet, the fish, being golden, is regarded as symbolizing the preciousness of Samsaric beings who are to be freed from ignorance; immersed in the ocean of Samsara they are drawn by the Fisherman to the Light of Liberation. It was, however, once again through one of the treasures of Buddhist Japan[16] that a deeper significance was revealed to me. Here, drifting on the ocean which, like some vast lake girt by rocky tree-clad continents, surrounds the central boss figuring the mountain Meru, we find the actual figure of the Fisherman himself. As in the imagery of the Grail, the Otherworld landscape and the Fisherman appear united.

We have, then, an ever recurrent group of images surrounding the central idea of the *life-giving Light*; the sun-vessel (cauldron or pot), and the weapon used in its recovery; the secret landscape with cosmic mountain and tree where the light withdraws and where is likewise the fount of immortality. Desire and yearning for a happier or higher state of existence necessitate a quest for that secret realm easily associated with the immortal dead. (See also Ch. 1.) The imagery lingers on in Nonno's description of the Argonauts in which a bowl (the heavens or heavens with the sun) hovers over the illuminated tree on the cosmic mountain. Sometimes the sun-vessel is actually a boat.

Doubtless the fertility, the sex aspect, forms an integral part but may one not also perhaps divine from the first a latent hankering for the transcendental which is borne out by the tendency of 'northern' art (from the Celtic West to the Asiatic East) towards abstraction, infinity and a symbolic conception of landscape? Already in a silver bowl from Maikop, Kurgan, South Russia[17] dating from between the third and second millenniums B.C. we have an instance of beasts moving in the ritualistic circumambulatory manner we have noted, in a symbolic landscape of mountain, tree and water. Perhaps such conceptions are really likely to be rooted in the nature of peoples who spent half their year in darkness, though not in the extreme cold that characterizes the Polar regions since the second Ice Age. When climatic conditions and other factors urged them in repeated migrations to drift southward, such ideas may gradually have found expression in vegetable and animal form (though still abstract or symbolic) the process of personification becoming ever stronger as they intermingled with races who, unlike themselves, held anthropomorphic ideals in religion and art. But behind the consequent evolution of systematized religions and the practice of varying fertility cults, the yearning for the light remains – the imagery persists – now, as in Indo-Aryan or Celtic myth, in the rape of the sun-vessel and the quest for a paradisal 'land of youth'; now, after an assimilation of Syro-Phoenician mysteries and identification with sexual symbolism and the dying God, in an ultimately embraced Christianity. Thus expressed as a Mystery of the Holy Grail it could even invoke Christian relics through identification of Cup and Spear with the instruments of the Passion.

It cannot, however, be denied that Wolfram's Grail differs from the latter imagery. His Grail is a precious stone – a radiant jewel. But is the jewel not also a solar emblem? We meet with it on the tree of Life – the illuminated Sun-tree. We find it in the three jewels of Vishnu's helmet and above all in the

Buddhist *padma mani* – the jewel in the heart of the lotus which is itself of solar origin. It too leads to a gnosis and to liberation. It appears to be the Indo-Iranian concept. But it suggests perhaps, too, that the essence of the Grail is to be found in more than original fertility aspect; that the latter, though an integral part of the mystery, is subordinate to the concept of the radiance, the Light. But how was it that a German knight at the commencement of the thirteenth century should have chosen the Iranian in place of the usual Western form?

Friedrich von Suhtschek[18] challenged the whole academic tradition of Western literary history when he maintained the Arthurian cycle to be of Iranian origin and Wolfram's *Parzival* and Gawain's romance a free translation from the Persian. His view is extreme. Is it not more likely (as it has indeed been the purpose of this essay to prove) that there may well be various developments of a Grail concept deriving, part consciously part unconsciously, from a long forgotten source? The poet responds to every vital influence from outside, apprehends an analogy, grasps without knowing it the archetypal image. In Wolfram's case, however, there may be reason to suppose a greater degree of contact with the Eastern stream. Connections with the East, through the Crusades, the Arabs and even long before them were far stronger than most of us suspect.

There may not have been, as Suhtschek would insist, an actual 'Parzivalnama'. Enough perhaps that there certainly existed not only the curiously similar Manichaean tale of the 'Pearl' – the story of a quest and an initiation on the part of a fatherless and poorly clad youth – but that there were sufficient tales of Iranian chivalry to fire the imagination of a European knight. None the less the affinities are so remarkable that it almost seems as though Wolfram were describing the setting of such a Manichaean citadel as Kuh (Mount)-i-Sal-Chwadeha (his Muntsalvasche seems a perfect echo of the name) on the lake of Hamun in Sistan, whilst Gawain's adventure in Klingsor's magic castle gives the most astounding accurate picture of the Buddhist monasteries of Kabulistan and above all the palace in Kapisa, with its fantastic throne on wheels (the rolling bed), gigantic stupa and all. Particularly important for us is that this very corner of the globe, the borders of Persia and Afghanistan, was the melting-pot not only of various religions but also of influences in art, and that it is in Iran that we find, as already noted, the perpetuation of Mazdian concepts of that Holy or Secret Landscape which afforded a starting-point for our inquiry. In Iran, indeed, that Paradise, through the grace of God's spirits – the radiance of the Chwarna – is made manifest on earth. Thus in the Awesta it is written of the Chwarna:

> It appears now as bird, now as a creature swimming or diving, as a ram or in the form of some other beast or it passes over into the milk of a cow. Chwarna causes the streams to gush from the springs, plants to sprout from the earth, winds to blow the clouds, men to be born; it guides the moon and stars on their path.[19]

Nature becomes a symbol, continually reborn through the spiritual fount of all life – 'for ever spending, never spent'. But the crux of the whole matter in regard to Wolfram's Grail is that, like the Manichaean Jewel, it possesses the qualities of the Chwarna itself. Moreover, upon that Manichaean stone alights a dove, to set upon it the Hanma Seed, just as Wolfram's dove brings a sacramental wafer to the Grail. It is on Good Friday (significantly on the advent of Spring – the northern sun's rebirth) that the power of the Grail or the Manichaean stone is thus renewed. Wolfram's Grail likewise possesses the qualities of the Buddhist *cintamani* – the wish jewel – Wolfram's *'Wunsch von Paradis'* ('Wish for paradise'). There are Buddhist paintings of the divine maiden bearing the joy-spending jewel. She might well be an Asiatic sister to Wolfram's Repanse del Schoye. It is significant that the latter married, in the end, the paragon of Eastern chivalry – Feirefiz.

Above all the Manichaean jewel or Pearl is the symbol of compassion. In Wolfram's version, does not the very significance of Parzival's initial failure lie in the fact that he does not ask 'King, what ails thee?' It takes him years to redeem that youthful lack of understanding, and significantly – though he is able to regain eligibility to the Grail kingship only through bitter experience, through inner growth and self-realization – understanding must ultimately come through the guru – the hermit Trevrizent. How important a part is assigned to the hermit's teaching in Wolfram's version! I would here quote an analogy with a passage I discovered quite independently of any Grail research in a book on Tibetan Yoga. 'This accepted conviction or truth hath not been arrived at merely by the processes of deduction and induction, but essentially because of the Guru's teachings which have made one to see the Priceless Gem lying unnoticed within one's reach.'[20] What is it that the Guru teaches Parzival? The need of *'demut'*, i.e., humility, and self-recognition – *'Datta'* (give), *'Dayadhvam'* (sympathize), *'Damyata'* (control) – the doctrine of Eliot's *Waste Land*.

It is precisely that quality which the great emperor in the Alexander romance lacked, and which there too was symbolized in a stone sent from Paradise – the landscape with which we are by now so familiar: 'Go and say to Alexander that it is in vain he seeks Paradise; his efforts will be perfectly fruitless for the way of Paradise is the way of humility, a way of which he knows nothing.'

Influences from the East were doubtless transmitted through the Arabs and the Crusades, but the direct key to Wolfram's Grail probably lies in the riddle surrounding the much-disputed Kyot, whom Wolfram claims as his source. The very existence of this mysterious personage has been denied by many who would see in him only a mask for Wolfram's originality and, according to medieval standards, unforgivable adulteration of the source. But is not the true test of creative imagination the vitality and poetic power with which he has obviously rendered both story and symbolism so that even if its source be Eastern it has become with him a fervent expression of the ideals of Western chivalry?[21] Who was Kyot? An Armenian, as Suhtschek suggests? Or, as Wolfram himself maintains, a Provençal – a terrain that can certainly embrace Languedoc? Surely it is more than likely that there, in the land of the Albigenses, a territory imbued with Manichaean beliefs and Arab-Sufi influences from across the Pyrenees, legends would find not only access but the most fruitful soil in which to develop, not only as literature but possibly even as a cult. If Jessie Weston is right in believing that an Attis-Mithras Grail cult flourished in Roman Britain, then a Manichaean mystery, originally deriving as we have seen

43

from similar sources, may still more easily have found a home in the citadels and vast fortified grottos of the Ariège.

The Cathar citadel Montségur has been regarded by Otto Rahn[22] as the Castle of the Grail. However, any cult centring on the castle of Montségur must have been subsequent rather than antecedent to Kyot's story, for we know that it was only in the years immediately preceding the threatened Albigensian Crusade that the ancient ruin was refortified as a Cathar citadel. If it was conceived as a Grail Castle it was most likely as the expression of a wish-fantasy in which grim necessity and fashionable aesthetic snobbery mingled with the craving of a hyper-civilized people for spiritual rebirth. But the intermingling of ambition, of human frailty and passion does not cancel the power of the spirit's yearning. The quest remains. Still the Grail-bearer of Montségur haunts the imagination of the Pyrenean peasants – in the shape of Esclarmonde, a synthesis perhaps of the two Esclarmondes, one of whom – the great Cathar abbess – dedicated Montségur to the Cathar faith whilst the other died as a martyr at the stake.

Is it mere chance that the legendary Esclarmonde did not die, but was actually transported to the mountains of Asia? She makes one think, moreover, of one of those reincarnations of Repanse del Schoye's spirit as conceived by a modern German poet, Albrecht von Schaeffer in his own poem on the Grail.[23]

> Die is Titurels, des Alten, Tochter;
> Tragerin des Grales, lebt in ewiger
> Jugend durch den Duft in dem Gemache
> bis die Tochter eines neuen Konigs
> ihr die Burde abnimmt und die Wurde
> stirbt am Ende schmerzlos; wird geboren
> augenblicks an audrer Erdenstelle;
> heisst Beate oder auch Renate[24]
> lebt mit Menschenlos; zu lieben leiden
> ohne Wissen eingedenk der Heimat
> und des Einhorns und des reinen Dienstes
> kensch wie keine; endlich stirbt sie
> ganzlich.

It is old Titurel's daughter,
Carrier of the Grail, who lives in eternal youth
By the fragrance of the apartment,
Until the daughter of a new king
Takes on the burden and the dignity.
She dies in the end, painlessly, is reborn
Instantly in another part of the earth,
And is called Beate or Renate,
Living by the lot of mortals: to love, to suffer
Without knowledge, yet mindful of her home
And the unicorn, and pure service
Chaste as none: In the end she is totally extinguished.

There are, nevertheless, numerous points of analogy between Montségur Manichaeanism[25] and Wolfram's Grail, amongst them the discovery in the Pyrenean citadel of earthenware doves. The dove as we have seen was closely connected with both Wolfram's Grail and the Manichaean pearl. It was, moreover, the badge of Wolfram's Templiesen – the name he gave to his knighthood of the Grail. This warrior caste, by the way, which stands in seeming opposition to Cathar pacificism, almost recalls the ideas on militarism expressed in the *Bhagavat-gita*. There is, moreover, the question of the Manisola – the secret feast of the Cathars – which still awaits further elucidation. Was it perhaps a mystic meal such as Jessie Weston associated with her Attis-Mithras cults? In any case it would involve an inquiry into the festivals of the dim past – the Aryan feasts of the dead. So once again the circle would close, leading back to the Land of Light, the realm of youth, of departed spirits.

We should also have to inquire into the report that the skeletons of the Cathars have been found arranged in a radiating circle, which suggests analogies not only with the circumambulatory and radiating formal arrangements in art referred to so often above, but also with the Tantric designs in which Jung has discovered the magic power of the archetype. Indeed, it is perhaps ultimately only through the study of the ever-recurring Grail images that we shall understand the extraordinary creative power of a symbolism that has continued to have a hold over us for thousands of years, and which, if rightly comprehended, might lead us to a recognition of the hidden unity between East and West.[26]

For the way of the Grail is the way of self-recognition, of acceptance of the Shadow. In the dualism of the world of appearances, the darkness apprehended perhaps by primitive northern man in the nightly, or half-yearly, disappearance of the sun, cannot be denied, but it can be transcended. The path, whether it lead through the death-simulating gloom of a Celtic-Hellenistic mystery ritual; through occult alchemical searchings for the divine essence sleeping in the heart of matter (an aspect presented by Flegetanis in Wolfram's poem) or along the purifying paths of a Manichaean gnosis, has ultimately the same goal – the liberation from darkness into a realm of light, of higher consciousness, where the radiance of the spirit is no longer obscured but burns more eternally even than the never-dying sun of the cosmic heavens or the mystic jewel crowning the mountain of the world; where man breaking the bounds of all otherness enters at last into the holy landscape to recognize his true self in the likeness of God.

A deeper elucidation of the story of the Grail might indeed help in bringing about an understanding of that unity between East and West which Wolfram von Eschenbach and many of his contemporaries apprehended and which he embodied so fervently in a figure from India's *Westereiche* – Parzival's half-brother, Feirefiz. Had their spirit not been obscured in the centuries that followed, the world might never have been led to its present pass.

Notes

1 Doubleday Anchor Books, New York, 1957.
2 Wauchier in his continuation of *Perceval*, she maintains is here drawing from a version anterior to Chretien's.
3 R. S. Loomis 'The Spoils of Annwn', in *Proceedings of the Modern Language Society of America*, December 1941.
4 Joseph Strzygowski, *Spuren indogermanischen Glaubens in der bildenden Kunst*. Heinrich Glück, *Die Christliche Kunst des Ostens*, Cassirer, Berlin, 1923. Both books contain numerous examples of the 'Paradise' symbols.

5 Franz Kampers, *Das Lichtland der Seelen und der Heilige Gral*, Cologne, 1916.

6 Strzygowski *op. cit.*, plate 127. Quoted by L. D. Barnett in *The Heart of India*, Murray, London, 1924, pp. 65f.

7 A curious compilation of Arthurian and Grail romances by the thirteenth-century German poet Heinrich von dem Turlin of which Gawain is the hero.

8 Kampers *op. cit.*

9 Strzygowski *op. cit.*, plates 205–7 reproduce S. Boisseree's architectural reconstructions.

10 *Ibid.*, plate 19.

11 B. G. Tilak, *The Arctic Home of the Vedas*, Poona, 1903; Biedenkamp, *Der Nordpol als Volkerheimat*, Jena, 1906.

12 Strzygowski believes that the ambulatory and semi-radiating form of the fully developed Gothic apse may be attributed to the unconscious persistence of those original concepts.

13 E. Thomas, *Translations from Vedic Hymns*, Murray, London, 1923.

14 It may be noted here that in Heinrich von dem Turlin's *diu Krone* the Castle of the Grail is described as the realm of the dead.

15 Leopold von Schroeder, *Die Wurzeln der Sage vom heiligen Gral*, Vienna, 1910.

16 A bronze mirror from the treasure of Shosoui in the Todajdshi monastery at Nara illustrated in J. Strzygowski, *Dürer und der nordische Schicksalshain*, Heidelberg, 1937, plate 47.

17 *Spuren indogermanischen Glaubens in der bildenden Kunst*, plates 11 and 123.

18 Wolfram von Eschenbach's *Reimbearbeitung des Parzivalnama*, *Klio* no. 25; and his *Parzivalnamanbersetzung, Forschung und Fortschritte*, 10.

19 *Asien's Miniaturenmalerei*. Strzygowski in collaboration with Heinrich Glück, Stella Kramrisch and Emmy Wellerz, Klagenfurt, 1933.

20 W. Y. Evans, *Tibetan Yoga*, Wentz, London, Oxford University Press, 1927.

21 A heartfelt appreciation of Wolfram as a poet is to be found in Margaret Richey's *The Story of Parzival and the Grail*, Oxford, Blackwell, 1935.

22 Otto Rahn, *Kreuzzug gagen den Gral*, Freiburg, 1933.

23 Albrecht Schaeffer, *Parzival*, Leipzig, 1922.

24 The heroine in A. Schaeffer's novel *Helianth*, Insel Verlag, Leipzig, 1922, who is brought into relationship with Akhenaten, the heretic pharaoh of Egypt.

25 Samuel Singer has pointed to Manichaean heretical influence in regard to Wolfram's 'neutral angels' in *Wolfram und der Gral: Neue Parzival Studien*, Herbert Lang, Berlin, 1939. Whilst Rolf Schroder in *Die Parzivalfrage*, Munich, 1928, considers the Manichaean problem at length.

26 Celtic concepts related to an ideal Byzantium are reflected in the poems of Charles Williams, *Taliessin Through Logres* and *The Region of the Summer Stars*, Cambridge, D. S. Brewer, 1982.

:3:

:ALCHEMICAL·TRANSMUTATION IN·HISTORY·AND·SYMBOL:

·

ADAM·McLEAN

·

Again and again throughout this book we shall meet the imagery of transformation: as in the Grail itself, changing mysteriously through five shapes ('that ought not to be spoken of') into the final one of the cup. This imagery, which conceals the most potent mystery of the Grail, its ability to shape things to itself, has long been recognized as closely aligned with the mysteries of spiritual alchemy. As the inner changes are manifest in the secret realm of the Grail lords, so are they made apparent in the outer world, affecting deeply the historical process whereby no single aspect of creation is allowed to remain static.

Closely aligned with this alchemical process, are the effects of the esoteric feminine principle within the exoteric shape of Christianity – a matter to which we shall be returning during the course of this book. For there are parallels, some of them indicated here, which point the way towards a new trans-sexual polarity being brought about through the agency of the Grail. It is to this cosmic alchemy that individual seekers must devote themselves, and a recognition of this is of the utmost importance for the understanding of the contemporary signifi-cance of the Grail.

The mystery of the Grail is intimately bound up with the unfol-ding of Christianity. It existed as an esoteric stream nourishing those who penetrated through the outer rituals and dogmas of the church, and, indeed, even today the Grail mystery remains a source of inspiration to inner mystical Christianity, while the outer face of the Christian impulse, the church, maintains a polarized dogmatism. This Grail mystery tinges all who encounter it with an inner questing, as it still possesses strange powers of transmutation.

The outer Christianity of the church has carved out definite roles for clergy and laity, static guidelines for channelling the spirit. These outer formulae, hallowed by long tradition, are now only shackles and rigid moulds into which living souls must be pressed. The outer rituals and spiritual exercises of the organized church, the prayers, hymns and moral sermons, seem to be dead and empty to the searching soul. Yet a strange sparkle remains within Christianity, a mystery that still enchants and draws the soul. Within the outer husk, the hardened shell, a spiritual light seems to glow, and a mystery dimly perceived can still attract our souls – the mystery of the Grail.

This mystery, this inner stream, is not something new, but has been bound up with Christianity from the earliest times. It still remains eternally present even though the church polarizes and distorts the essence of the spirit. We will come to recognize it as an inner feminine element living within the stream of patriarchal churchly religion. To encounter this inner stream, the feminine component of the Christian mystery, is to be tinged, transmuted, alchemically transformed. (See Chs 1, 6 and 9.)

Thus the Grail, on one level, is a source of transformation, and I intend in this essay to illustrate how this transmutation has operated in two realms. Firstly, I will sketch through a historical perspective some ways in which the Grail mystery transmuted the outer forms of Christianity – the transmutation in history. Then I would like to show further, some ways in which the Grail mystery expresses itself in the realm of symbols, and illustrate the subtle transformation of pagan archetypes into certain alchemical symbols – the transmutation in symbol.

Transmutation in history

If we try to penetrate to the heart of the events of Christianity we meet great problems, as the events surrounding the historical personality of Jesus Christ, and the unfolding of Christianity during its first century, are so incompletely documented as to allow theologians an enormous field for their speculations and disputes. However impossible it might be to see these events clearly, one point I think is certain, that Christianity arose as a reaction against the prevailing rigidly codified Jewish religion of that time that killed the spirit. Jesus Christ seems to have felt himself to have a mission to transform the polarized, distorted patriarchal religion of his fathers and bring about a new means for humanity to relate to the spirit. Thus we note the soft, forgiving side of Christianity as an antithesis of the hard, unyielding masculine codes of the Patriarchs. Christianity attempted at its inception a balancing of the feminine and the masculine components of the soul. Initially, the impulse was towards the integration of these two polarities, and not to their separation, nor the further stage of denying or repressing the feminine component.

Christianity would in all probability have remained a religion devoted to the balancing of these opposites, had not the Pauline impulse worked to change its direction. This led eventually to Christianity becoming a largely state religion, and ultimately it had to sacrifice its inner spiritual balance as it became the agent of social control in a patriarchal society. When Christianity united with Roman imperialism, it became more and more given up outwardly to a patriarchal domination. The inner spiritual balance was distorted, while the outer forms of the religion adapted themselves to becoming instruments of patriarchal social control. Ultimately the inner feminine side of Christianity was forced to become esoteric, hidden even from the outer dignitaries of the church.

This is well pictured in the Grail legends. For example, Robert de Boron expressed this by having Jesus after his crucifixion give esoteric instruction to the imprisoned Joseph of Arimathea, who subsequently establishes the Grail mysteries under the guardianship of hereditary Keepers of the Grail.

This mystery stream of an esoteric Christianity guarding a hidden wisdom of the feminine facet of the spiritual quest, was preserved intact for a millennium, only occasionally surfacing and tingeing outer history. Thus we can see its influence upon the Gnostic stream of the third to the sixth centuries, where there is an attempt to found a religion or at least a theology in which the feminine and masculine elements of the human soul are both represented in mythic structures. The Gnostics were profoundly working to incarnate mythologies where syzygys of spiritual beings, emanations of the Divine, are seen as balancing the masculine and feminine archetypes.

This inner stream in Christianity also perhaps is seen in the Pelagian heresy in Britain. During the fourth century a form of Christianity arose in Britain that challenged the central codified religion of Rome. It recognized an inner freedom for humanity to be inspired by the Holy Spirit, which disturbed the patriarchs of Christianity who wished to lay down decrees and codes, and not to recognize any individual mystical insight. The Pelagian heresy was put down by force. At about the same time in Ireland and Scotland, an independent form of Christianity was arising which one can see as possessing a more feminine side. Ireland was sufficiently remote from the centralized Roman church to have a large measure of independence, and also, since Ireland had never been brought under the yoke of Roman military and civil power, the old pagan religions had continued. This pagan religion still worked in the Celtic peoples and tinged their version of Christianity. So at this time we find the interweaving of the pagan religions of the Celtic peoples, which recognized and articulated the feminine in its mythic structure, with the independence of Irish Christianity. This Celtic church sent missionaries all over Europe during the sixth, seventh and eighth centuries, and many of these Celtic monks had a profound influence on the development of European Christianity. We can see that this independence was coloured with elements of the Grail mysteries, particularly in its recognition of the feminine principle in the divinity. This connection is brought out in the Grail legends in the cycle of de Boron or Chrétien through such figures as Merlin, an archetype of Celtic paganism, and we see there how it is Merlin who sets the Quest of the Grail as a goal for the Arthurian court.

We see that the Grail mysteries, holding an esoteric initiation into the feminine side of the Christian mystery, continued in secret for over a millennium, only occasionally producing a ripple on the outer surface of history. Where the centres of these Grail mystery schools were held remains uncertain. Many writers have identified various different sites as being the centres, the 'Montsalvach', of Grail mystery schools. Rather than trying to argue about which of these centres was the 'true' Grail Castle, I believe it is more constructive to realize that this esoteric Grail tradition was quite widespread and indeed had many such mystery centres throughout Europe and the Middle East.

The twelfth century was a time that brought great historic change to western religious tradition. Contact with the Arabs in Spain brought new learning into Europe. The Arabs in their conquest of Greek Alexandria had gathered together a vast store of ancient wisdom, and at this time, many centuries after the initial heat and religious fervour of the foundation of Islam, a period of tolerance, particularly to be found in Spain, allowed Arabic scholars the luxury of working on old texts of Greek philosophers, Aristotle, the Neoplatonists and Gnostics. Some of this material they were prepared to share with such European scholars as Robert of Chester, who brought back from Spain at the end of the eleventh century translations of works on alchemy, algebra, astrology and mathematics.

The crusades to the Holy Land also brought back new impulses into western Christianity from the encounter with Jerusalem. During the earlier Crusades, there were founded certain Christian chivalric orders which were dedicated to retrieving the lost wisdom and relics to be found at the ancient centre of historical Christianity. We especially note the formation of the Knights Templar with their impulse to protect and recover the ancient wisdom and sacred geometrical principles of the Solomonic Temple in Jerusalem. The Great Schism in 1054 of the Eastern and Western churches over the question of the role of the Son-Christ in the realm of the Spirit, gave a new freedom to the Western church to explore new ways of working. The Eastern Church was becoming increasingly patriarchal, identifying with the Father aspect of the divine, and seeing the Son and the Holy Spirit as proceeding from the Father. The Western Church wished to preserve a theology in which the Father element was balanced with the Son. From this point on there was no possibility of the feminine aspect of the Christian mystery being outwardly expressed in Eastern Orthodox theology, whereas the Western church retained an openness in its theology to a less polarized expression.

The Albigensian heresy began to make an impact upon the western church during the twelfth century. At the centre of this heresy lay a profound dualism, a view that the outer world was evil and that humanities and individual salvation could only be had by the renunciation of the worldly. The simplicity of this dualism began to attract large numbers of converts and the church felt itself threatened by the rise of this Cathar heresy.

All these influences impacted upon the Western church in the early twelfth century and established Christianity stood at a crisis point needing to absorb these streams into its domain without being overwhelmed by them.

It seems that at this crisis point, the esoteric schools guarding the inner secrets of Christianity, the guardians of the Grail mystery, perceived that the time was right for revealing some of this mystery knowledge which they had preserved hitherto in secret.

With this historical sketch of these times, we can now look at the ways in which this Grail wisdom began to tinge and transform outer Christianity.

The body of mystery knowledge, the rituals and practices of the esoteric schools of Christianity we see as working with the Grail element, the feminine side of Christianity, was not revealed directly but was rather woven into an elaborate series of legends. These legends, which presented through a series of dramatic pictures the esoteric lore of the Mystery schools, were not revealed through the church but were put into the hands of poets and troubadours. We can well imagine such great tales capturing the imagination of the people, contrasting with the dryness of scholastic theology and the intoning of prayers and orations. These tales brought to the common people a living picture of Christianity working in the world and they could identify themselves with the archetypal characters in the stories. The people could even recognize in the stories thinly veiled allusions to pagan elements. These legends began like a ferment to tinge and transform people's consciousness, and through working with them, they became dimly aware of the inner feminine element which was not found in the external Christianity of the established church. This inner power of the spiritual quest began to make its impact on outer culture. The legends were first written down towards the end of the twelfth century from about 1180, firstly by Chrétien de Troyes (French stream), Robert de Boron (British stream) and Wolfram von Eschenbach (German stream). These three seem to have been assigned the task of giving archetypal expression to the legends for the French, British and German peoples respectively. Within a few decades a profusion of Grail legends appear, showing how widespread and influential the stories must have been.

The guardians of the Grail put into the hands of the people an esoteric lore woven into the archetypal pictures of a story, which if allowed to work in the soul could produce an inner openness to a more feminine aspect of Christianity.

As an antithesis to this, other mystery schools dedicated to a more patriarchal view, were moved by this crisis point in the church, to transform its outer facet in their own fashion. Orders of Masons and Temple builders were orchestrated during the late twelfth century to build the great Gothic cathedrals. Esoteric principles of sacred architecture were put at the disposal of the church, probably through the Templar Order, which had researched these principles in its concern for the structure of the Temple in Jerusalem – Solomon's Temple, the esoteric architecture of the Jewish patriarchal tradition.

The early history of building the Gothic cathedrals is shrouded in mystery, little explanation being given by orthodox history as to where the impulse for this new style of sacred architecture arose, of how the activities of the builders could be co-ordinated, or indeed how economically this impulse could have been sustained (over a hundred vast cathedrals and many smaller abbeys and churches were being built simultaneously during the twelfth and thirteenth centuries). There seems little doubt that this vast project was orchestrated by a tight knit esoteric order (probably related to the Knights Templar) who put their energies and abilities at the disposal of the church.

The impulse behind the cathedral building was to provide

the established church with imposing edifices which would consolidate and demonstrate the outer worldly masculine power of organized Christian religion. These masculine cathedrals were often built upon the sites of pagan sanctuaries with a feminine dedication. The best known example of this being Chartres with its 'black virgin', which had been for many centuries before the Gothic cathedral was built, one of the most famous shrines to the feminine principle in all of France.

As a result of these two impulses – the making exoteric of the Grail mystery which concerned the inner quest of the feminine principle in Christianity – and the cathedral building consolidating the outer worldly masculine power of the organized church – an inner change occurred in the Christian religion.

On the one hand, the church was being pressed into a masculine stance, fighting crusades in the Holy land, putting down with great severity the Cathar and other heretics; and on the other hand, it did not wish to go entirely along the road of the Grail Christianity. It needed to incorporate the feminine in a form which was within the control of the masculine principle. The solution to this problem was achieved by the champion of orthodoxy, St Bernard of Clairvaux. He encouraged Christians to identify with one facet of the triple goddess, the spiritual virgin aspect, identified as Mary. St Bernard instituted the adoration of the Virgin Mary, and established a simple ritual for ordinary people to enable them to relate to her. This is, of course, the exercise of the Rosary, the circle of beads each corresponding to a petition alternatively addressed to the Virgin and the Son, balancing the male and the female principles in a religious exercise. The Virgin Mary facet of the Triple Goddess was a remote figure, and being cut off from the other aspects of the Goddess, lacked the primal power and earthly energies of the unified Goddess which we recognize in paganism. Thus the church incorporated the feminine in a way which left the masculine polarity dominant.

We should see behind this historical process in the outer church the transforming power of the Grail mystery – the feminine mystery had to be woven into the fabric of the church. The Grail mystery impulse failed at this time, however, entirely to transform the church religion and retired to its role as an inner esoteric school.

At the centre of the Grail mystery is a ritual of the Eucharist. It seems that during Initiation, the candidate experienced a ritual ceremony of the Mass in a form very different, more profound and spiritually elevating than the Mass in the outer church. The sacred power of this ritual is described in the Grail legends in many ways – in the procession of the Grail before Perceval-Parzival in Chrétien and Wolfram, for example, and in later versions such as the *Queste del Saint Graal* ascribed to Walter Map, where at the close we find Galahad performing a very spiritual ritual mass. The legends often emphasize that the Grail was the actual physical vessel which Christ had used at the celebration of the Last Supper, and rather than seeing that the mystery lay in this sacred object, perhaps what the legends intended to convey was that there was a continuity in the Grail mystery through the celebration of this ritual – that it was performed in the same manner as Christ performed it.

Just at the time the Grail legend became outwardly revealed at the end of the twelfth century, a profound change occurs in the celebration of the Mass in established Christianity. This concerned the position of the officiant-priest in regard to the altar. Before this time, the Mass was celebrated with the priest behind the altar facing the congregation. His ritual actions were entirely revealed and exposed to the gaze of the congregation. With the new cathedrals and their rigid structure, different from earlier round churches, the altar is placed at the far end of the choir. The position of the priest performing Mass was changed. Now he stood in front of the altar, facing in the same direction as the congregation. But now his ritual actions were not visible to the people. The ritual of the Mass was hidden in a priestly mystery. Later, even rood screens were built across the choir so that the congregation would see even less of the ritual proceedings. Thus we note here, the church at its crisis point, further wishing to consolidate the spiritual power of the priesthood, makes the mass into a secret mystery. This is in a sense a reaction to the revelation of the Grail quest, which puts the onus on the individual to go on the search for spiritual illumination. In the legends it is not churchmen who achieve the Grail but the naive figure of Perceval-Parzival, the son of the widow. He does not need the mediation of a priest to participate in the ritual enactment of the mystery.

The earlier form of the Mass, where the priest stood behind the altar facing out to the congregation, corresponds to the position of the Christ at the Table of the Last Supper, and to the form of the Table of the Grail under the protection of Joseph of Arimathea as recounted in Robert de Boron (Figure 1).

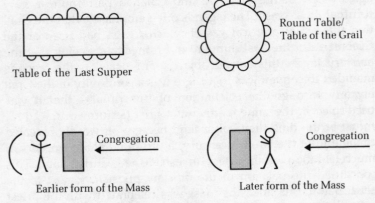

Table of the Last Supper

Round Table/ Table of the Grail

Congregation

Congregation

Earlier form of the Mass

Later form of the Mass

Figure 1

Interestingly, in recent times, after the Second Vatican Council reformed the structure of the Catholic Mass in the 1960s, the priest adopts the former position as regards the altar.

I have pictured something of how the Grail mystery, centred upon an inner feminine element in Christianity and an esoteric ritual initiation of which the Eucharist was a pale reflection, tinged and transformed outer history. The spiritual energies of this esoteric tradition were never allowed to flow out openly in the world, but only to affect the current of events indirectly. We can recognize the influence of this mystery stream behind certain movements and impulses in Christianity during the first millennium. The Grail guardians tried in the twelfth century, while the organized church stood at an important crisis point, to effect change within the spiritual direction of Christianity and allowed their secrets to be woven into allegorical romances, the Grail stories or legends. The church responded to the challenge that it incorporate the feminine mystery into its structure, by on the one hand consolidating its masculine power and influence in outer society through the building of the imposing edifices of the Gothic cathedrals and at the same time allowing an aspect of the Goddess that would not challenge the masculine domination, the Virgin Mary facet, to be a focus of spiritual worship.

The Grail mystery returned underground, wrapped itself again in its esotericism and waited for another time to unfold its inner revelation. Such a point was reached after the Reformation, when this inner Grail mystery of the feminine side of Christianity, surfaced again in the Rosicrucian movement of the early seventeenth century. At this time another attempt was made by the guardians of the mystery stream to allow their esoteric wisdom to influence outer events. The Rosicrucians tried to incarnate an esoteric Christianity within the Protestant movement, which was in orthodox Lutheranism and Calvinism unyieldingly patriarchal and unbalanced, in order to provide a much needed resolution of the polarities of Protestantism. Thus we should see the Rosicrucian movement as being inwardly related to the Grail mystery. The spiritual alchemy that was the esoteric foundation of Rosicrucianism can be seen as a development of the Grail impulse.

The inner living spiritual energy of the Mystery of the Grail has tinged and transformed outer historical events in subtle though important ways. It has always pointed humanity towards recognizing the necessity of balance: a polarized working with the masculine facet in religion. At its centre has lain the essential feminine symbol of the cup or chalice. For the second section of this chapter I would like to illustrate some ways in which this great symbol of the Grail transformed the symbols of the Celtic pagan world, and produced a Christian esotericism in Rosicrucian alchemical symbolism.

The transmutation in symbols

Corresponding to the outer transformation of the Christian tradition through the preservation and bringing of the feminine mystery into outer expression, the Grail mystery stream also worked inwardly, transforming certain constellations of symbols. We can see this revealed in many different facets but here will focus on the ways in which the Grail subtly tinged pagan celtic symbols and later found expression in alchemical symbolism.

We shall here pursue only the transmutation illustrated in Figure 2.

CAULDRONS	→	THE GRAILS	→	THE ALCHEMICAL VESSELS
of the Celtic tradition (first millennium)		as recounted in the legends (12th century)		particularly in Rosicrucian esotericism (12th-18th century)

Figure 2

These cauldrons, Grails and alchemical vessels are all feminine mystery symbols. Interestingly, there are in each of these traditions, three expressions of each symbol. This tripling of the symbols is by no means artificial but corresponds to the three facets of the Triple Goddess: the Old Woman – Virgin – Mother aspects.

In the Celtic tradition we find three cauldrons. The Cauldron of Annwn was the cauldron of rebirth, ancient primal symbol found in the earliest celtic legends. It appears in the important poem, *The Spoils of Annwn*, from the Taliesin tradition. There it is the goal of a quest undertaken by the celtic Arthur, who sails in his ship *Prydwen* through seven caers or castles with his company of knights, seeking the spoils of Annwn, the 'underworld'. The cauldron is described there as being gently warmed by the breath of nine maidens (the muses or attendants of the triple Goddess) and with a rim of pearls around its edge. The inner experience of the cauldron of rebirth can only be achieved by the journey through the seven caers, the inner castles of the quest. (See also Ch. 1, p. 15.) This cauldron can thus be associated with the Old Woman facet of the Goddess, the protector of such dark mysteries. She is the Calleach, or Hecate, the Dark Goddess.

The Cauldron of Ceridwen, also mentioned in the Taliesin literature, is quite different. It is a cauldron of inspiration, of initiation, the source of the beginnings of wisdom. Ceridwen prepared for initiates in her mysteries, a potion which contains the essence of all wisdom. In the famous story of Taliesin, it is he with his former name Gwion, who is set to stir and tend this vessel. However, three drops of the potion fall on his fingers, and attempting to ease the burn he places this in his mouth and absorbs the boiled down essence of Ceridwen's wisdom, becoming an initiate, the Taliesin, 'radiant browed'. This cauldron of inspiration corresponds to the Virgin–Young Woman facet of the Goddess, the protectress of initiates, those entering the mysteries.

The third cauldron is found in many examples from Celtic legend, but this aspect is perhaps best known as the Cauldron of the Dagda. The cauldron here is a source of plenty. It is the cauldron seen as a food vessel. Its spiritual nourishment is endless and bottomless. Here we have an example of the Mother–provider facet of the female archetype. Under this aspect of the Goddess we have eternal plenty and fecundity, both physically and spiritually.

These three cauldrons in the Celtic myths are the vessels of the Goddess. They are vast primal elements in Celtic mythology. The three Grails which correspond to these are not such vast archetypal vessels, but rather appear as more simple items potentized with spiritual energies.

The first Grail which we meet particularly in Robert de Boron's recension of the legend, is the Chalice, the Cup of the Last Supper, in which Joseph of Arimathea caught the blood that flowed from the wounds of the Christ on the cross. This vessel is thus charged with spiritual force. While Joseph is imprisoned this vessel is brought to him by the Christ being and he is instructed in the esoteric lore of the Grail. This Chalice is thus a vessel of redemption, giving a new beginning to all those initiated in its mystery, through contact with the blood of Christ. This blood aspect is one of the central mysteries of

Christianity (see Ch. 10). It is the essence of the Christ's being that entered and united forever with the Earth. It is that part of Christ left behind to the Earth after his body ascended. It enters and penetrates the body of the Earth and a part is held back in the vessel of the Grail Cup, which therefore must come under the Old Woman facet of the Goddess, the dark body of the Earth planet.

The second Grail, found in Wolfram von Eschenbach, is the Grail as Stone. In his Parzival, it is quite unequivocally described as a 'Stone of light', a stone that gives all who behold it spiritual enlightenment. In Wolfram it appears during an elaborate cere- monial Procession of the Grail, an intricate ritual event which passes before Parzival as he sits as guest at the Table of the Fisher King, Amfortas. This procession primarily involves the ladies of the court, and the Grail itself is borne by the Queen Repanse del Schoye. Parzival initially fails to recognize the importance of this ritual object and is not able to read the strange letters on the surface of the stone, which in fact spelled out his own name. He also fails to ask the question of the Fisher King as to what ails him, a question which once asked would redeem Amfortas and end his suffering. Thus in his initial meeting with the Grail, Parzival fails both to recognize his own role as Grail guardian and to see that he has a role in redeeming the suffering of the Fisher King. This Stone of the Grail, brought before him by a procession of women, is the stone of initiation into the Grail mysteries:

> If he gazed at the Stone for two hundred years,
> His beard would not turn grey
> Such force gives the stone to man
> That his flesh and bones
> Promptly become young again
> And the stone is called the Grail.

This initiation mystery is associated with the young woman – Virgin facet of the Goddess.

The third Grail we meet in Chrétien de Troyes's version of the story. Here the Grail is a dish or platter that provides the company at the Castle of the Grail with spiritual nourishment. In Chrétien's version of Perceval's first visit to the Grail Castle, he there participates in an elaborate ceremonial meal at which the dish of the Grail was present and passes round the company. The old King or guardian of the Grail, receives only the Host from the Grail for his nourishment. So this Grail is connected with the nourishing aspect of the triple Goddess – the Mother facet.

In the alchemical tradition we also find certain vessels corresponding to our cauldrons and Grails. In early alchemy these are straightforwardly seen merely as articles of chemical apparatus, however, the spiritualization of the alchemical mystery through its contact with such esoteric traditions as that of the Grail, tinged and transformed these simple pieces of apparatus into spiritual archetypes, inner faculties of the soul.

The first we consider is the Crucible. This open vessel was made to be fiercely heated in the fire, and was used to calcine or burn to ashes any substance placed within it. This calcination is a form of purification of substance and can be experienced as a kind of rebirth – the passing of the outer imperfection into an ashy residue wherein lies its essence. In particular, Gold was purified by being melted in a special form of crucible in the cupellation process. Here any other metal contaminating the Gold was burnt off in the form of an ash or slag. This purification or rebirth process can thus be seen as coming under the domain of the Old Woman facet of the Goddess.

The next item of alchemical apparatus we have to look at is the Retort or Flask. Substances were placed within this vessel in order to undergo an inner transformation. Often the alchemist sealed up his substances in such a retort and left it for many months or years, allowing an inner digestion to take place. This is the process of interiorization, corresponding to the initiation experience of the Ceridwen Cauldron. It can be placed under the facet of the Young Woman.

The last alchemical vessel we consider under this heading is the Alembic, the Still. The alchemist places into the alembic the substances he wishes to purify by distillation. Then by applying heat, the essence is driven off, purified and condensed in the still-head of the alembic and passed into a receiving vessel. The inner process corresponding to this outer experimental procedure of purification through distillation, connects with the

Mother facet, in that a new purified substance is separated off from the 'Mother Liquor' placed in the alembic.

We can see that these three alchemical procedures, taking place in vessels or feminine interior spaces, were interpreted spiritually by being tinged with the Grail esotericism, this becoming especially marked in the late sixteenth and early seventeenth century during the Rosicrucian period of alchemy.

We can summarize these associations in Table 1.

TABLE 1

CAULDRONS	Annwn	Rebirth	Old Woman
	Ceridwen	Inspiration	Maiden
	Dagda	Plenty	Mother
GRAILS	Chalice	Vessel of Blood	Old Woman
	Stone	Spiritual enlightenment	Maiden
	Platter	Nourishment	Mother
ALCHEMICAL	Crucible	Calcination	Old Woman
VESSELS	Retort	Interiorization	Maiden
	Alembic	Distillation	Mother

I have tried to sketch some ways in which the Mystery wisdom of the Grail has subtly worked behind outer history and indicated how the formative energies of its esotericism transformed pagan Celtic symbols into the familiar hallowed objects of the Grail legends, and centuries later found its expression again in the esoteric Christianity behind the Rosicrucian movement.

This Grail mystery is not bound in the past but is eternally present, and will be found working esoterically behind the outer Christian religion as long as its theology remains polarized and denies the feminine mystery that is an essential part of the fabric of Creation. Indeed, I believe we have witnessed during the last decade the beginning of a new cycle in which Grail wisdom will pour out into our civilization. During this period we have seen a growing interest in the ancient Stone Circles and related ritual centres, together with an awareness of the 'earth forces' that work at such sites, and their special connection with the feminine, the Goddess. These sites can be seen as the new vessels of the Grail.

I believe that as we look towards the end of this century, this Grail mystery will become more important in public awareness, becoming identified with the living esoteric body of the Earth planet herself. The Grail wisdom seeks now to reach out to our civilization and asks us to go on the quest to discover and relate our beings, and through this our civilization, to the living energies of the Earth.

We must not pursue the mystery of the Grail as a dead branch of scholarship, as something bound to the past, but seek it as a living source of inspiration eternally with us. Its mystery stream still seeks new vessels and symbols for incarnating its esoteric impulses, and I can only hope that we will all recognize the ways in which it strives to unfold itself to our times.

·PART·11·

·ELEMENTS·

OF·THE

GRAIL

TRADITION

:4:

:TEMPLES OF·THE·GRAIL:

JOHN·MATTHEWS

The way to the Grail lies within: this much is made clear by the nature of the Quest, in its imagery of the divine search for what is best in humanity. So the body, which has always been recognized mystically as an impediment to the realization of spiritual freedom, becomes a testing ground, in which the good and bad elements of the individual do battle, the one seeking to know God, the other running from Him. The Temple, of which the body is an image, performs a similar function, in the Grail story more especially so, where it reflects the duality at the heart of all matter, and the desire of humanity to conquer its divided self by stretching up to meet the descending love of creation. It is this which, as we saw in Geoffrey Ashe's essay, prompts the nostalgia of earlier times, when harmony existed everywhere and division remained unknown.

I

When Sir Lancelot, in Thomas Malory's *Le Morte D'Arthur*, comes at last, after many adventures, to the Chapel of the Grail, an unearthly voice warns him not to enter. Hesitating outside the door, he none the less looks within, and sees:

> a table of silver, and the Holy Vessel, covered with red samite, and many angels about it . . . and before the Holy Vessel . . . a good man clothed as a priest. And it seemed he was at the sacring of the mass . . .[1]

69

Watching the events that follow, Lancelot sees the celebrant holding aloft the image of a man, as though he would make an offering at the altar. And, when it seems as though he would fall from the effort, Lancelot enters the chamber out of a pure desire to help. But he is struck down by fiery breath, and blinded by the light which flows from the Grail. For Lancelot is a fallen man, and besides he does not know the way into the presence of the Grail.

That way is a hard one, for it consists of entering the Castle and Temple of the Grail, which is so designed that it serves as an initiation test for all who wish to share in the mysteries. Lancelot's experience is echoed by many who set out unprepared, and who end by being blinded by what they cannot understand. Properly followed, however, the way towards and through the home of the Grail can offer a means of knowing, of understanding the light. Many temples have fallen in ruins, but it is said that the true Temple is never destroyed, any more than is the path to God. We would do well to keep this in mind as we examine some of the images assumed by that imperishable temple throughout its long history, hoping that we may thus learn something of our own part in the continuing mysteries of the Grail.

II

The earliest traditions relating to temple-building depict them as dwelling places for God; where the Creator, invited to enter his house, may choose to communicate with his creation. The earth upon which the temple stands is thereby sacred earth – either through its being placed at that spot, or by a hallowing touch of the divine which calls forth the building as a marker for those in search of the sacred experience. Thus it becomes a *temenos*, a place set apart, where an invisible line shows that here is sacred space, to enter which means to enter the sphere of the divine, the reflection of the heavenly on earth.

For this reason the forms most often incorporated into the design of the temple are those of the circle and the square, symbolic representations of heaven and earth, so that many consist of squared stones set up in circles (the Megalithic temples), or rectangular buildings supported by rounded pillars (Hellenic and Egyptian temples). These can be seen as archetypal images of the masculine and feminine, so that the circle of the heavens and the square of earth unite in a single image.

This may be expressed graphically by the *vesica piscis*, two overlapping circles (Figure 3) which illustrate the link between God and his creation which takes place in the temple, whether directly or through the agency of priests and seers. Plotinus understood this perfectly when he wrote (using a slightly different analogy), '. . . he belongs to Him, like two concentric circles: they are only one when they coincide and only two when they are separated.'[2]

Figure 3

It is the state of *spiritual* separateness, expressed most easily by the imagery of the Fall, that causes the failure of Lancelot and those who came after; and it is for this reason that the Grail temple exists, to show the way back to a state of unity with the divine impulse of creation.

It is for this reason also that we first read of the Grail in an aftermath to the story of the Fall. For it is said that the Grail was entrusted to Adam at the beginning of time, but that after the Fall it remained behind, since it was too holy an object to be taken into the world. But there is a tradition which says that Seth, a child of Adam and Eve whom the Gnostics revered as a hidden Master, made the journey back to the gate of Eden, in search of the Sacred Vessel. There, he was permitted to enter, and remained for forty days, at the end of which the Grail was given into his keeping, to serve both as a reminder of what had been lost, and as a sign of hope and redemption to come – though this remained unrecognized until the time of Christ, when the symbol of the Grail as Chalice became established in Christian belief.

What is most especially important here is, 'that those who possessed the Grail after [Seth] . . . were by this very fact, able to establish a Spiritual centre destined to replace the lost Paradise, and to serve as an image of it'.[3] It is this image that is served by the temple of the Grail, and it is also, as we have seen, a place where God and his creation can meet and converse as once they had in Paradise.

In this way the temple can be seen to represent a cosmic evolutionary diagram. It is as though the temple builders, by inviting God to descend into the *temenos*, were asking not only to be guided along the path towards the unity of perfection, but also anticipating (however heretically) that God would further evolve through contact with them. God is spirit and humanity matter and the two cannot evolve separately – they are indeed like two interlocking circles, which are only complete when superimposed precisely one upon the other – at which they become one. Thus all temples and churches were intended as physical glyphs to be read by both mankind and their gods, as a mirror reflecting back images of the temporal and divine upon each other.

This imagery is carried on in the iconography of the Virgin Mary, who becomes a human temple and a vessel for the divine, and whose reply to the Angel of the Annunciation is iconographically represented in reversed, mirror writing. This is done so that her words may be read by the angelic power above her, and Mary herself is sometimes referred to as 'a mirror of the greatness of God'.

Thus the earliest temples we know – the stones which gave Megalithic man his name – were erected in circles: set up on power points in the ground, so that they served as living extentions of the earth Herself – the Mother holding out her arms towards the Moon, the Sun and the Stars. These huge astrological observatories were built as much for the gods as for mankind – not just to honour them but to invite them to participate in the ritual living out of life in and around them. Or to quote Plotinus again:

> those ancient sages who sought to secure the presence of divine beings by the erection of shrines . . . showed insight

into the nature of the All [perceiving that] though the Soul is everywhere its presence will be secured all the more readily when an appropriate receptacle is elaborated . . . serving like a mirror to catch an image of it.[4]

In its most complete and complex form this cosmic mirror for the reflection of God becomes also an initiator into the divine mystery of creation, the most perfect object of the Quest. As such it may be expressed by the eternally fixed but changing pattern of the maze, and it is no accident that the architects of the Gothic cathedrals such as Chartres, in an endeavour to encode the mystery of the temple into the design of the great medieval churches of Europe, chose to include this form so often on both floors and walls.[5]

The temple of the Grail was a logical outcome of this, and it is not surprising to find how closely it conforms, throughout its many representations, to the traditional archetype.

III

The imagery of the Grail Temple is consistent. It is usually at the top of a mountain, which is in turn surrounded either by impenetrable forest or deep water. Access, if any, is by way of a perilously narrow, sharply edged bridge, which became known as the Sword Bridge. To make entrance even harder, the whole temple, or the castle which contained it, would often revolve rapidly, making it almost impossible to gain entry by normal means. Once within, more perils awaited, and for those few who succeeded in reaching the centre, where lay the Chapel of the Grail, the experience could, as in Lancelot's case, be both chastening and parlous. Nor was the castle without its human guardians; at an early stage in the mythos a family of Kings, supported by a specially chosen body of knights, appeared to serve and protect the sacred vessel.

The most completely developed description of the medieval Grail Temple is to be found in the Middle High German poem *Der Jüngere Titurel* (c. 1270) attributed to Albrecht von Scharffenberg. Here the lineage of the Grail Kings is traced back to

Solomon – a detail which, as we shall see, is of some importance – but the setting is firmly medieval in its details. According to Albrecht, Titurel, the grandfather of the famous Grail knight Parsifal, was fifty when an angel appeared to him and announced that the rest of his life was to be dedicated to the service of the sacred vessel. Accordingly he was lead into a wild forest from which arose the Mountain of Salvation *Muntsalvasche*,[6] where he found workers gathered from all over the world, who were to help him to build a castle and temple for the Grail – which at that time floated houseless in the air above the site, supported by heavenly hands.

So Titurel set to work and levelled the top of the mountain, which he found to be of onyx and which, when polished, 'shone like the moon'. Soon after he found the ground plan of the building mysteriously engraved on this fabulous surface.

The completion of the temple took some thirty years, during which time the Grail provided not only the substance from which it was built, but also food to sustain the workmen. Already the Grail is seen as a provider – a function which it continues to perform. But more rarely, and importantly for our argument, it is here seen as contributing *directly* in the construction of its own temple, making one a part of the other, the design non-human in origin.

At this point in the poem Albrecht devotes one hundred and twelve lines to a description of the temple so specific in detail as to leave one in little doubt that he is describing a real building.[7]

The temple is high and circular, surmounted by a great cupola. Around this are twenty-two chapels arranged in the form of an octagon; and over every pair of these is an octagonal bell-tower surmounted by a cross of white crystal and an eagle of gold. These towers encircle the main dome, which is fashioned from red gold and enamelled in blue.

Three entrances lead inside: one in the North, one in the West, a third in the South from which flow three rivers (thus indicating a debt to the image of Paradise with its rivers and gates whereby they flow out). The interior is rich beyond compare, decorated with intricate carvings of trees and birds; while beneath a crystal floor artificial fish swim, propelled by hidden pipes of air fuelled by bellows and windmills. Within each of the chapels is a altar of sapphire, curtained with green samite,[8] and all the windows are of beryl and crystal, decorated with other precious stones.

In the Dome itself a clockwork sun and moon move across a blue enamelled sky in which stars are picked out in carbuncles. Beneath it, at the very centre of the temple, is a model of the whole structure in miniature, set with the rarest jewels, and within this is kept the Grail, a microcosmic image itself of the whole universe of creation.

It is clear that what is being described in Albrecht's poem is a type of the Earthly Paradise. Details such as the three rivers, as well as the overall layout of the building, frozen and perfect in its jewelled splendour of artificial birds and fishes, all support this conclusion. The first home of the Grail is being rebuilt in medieval terms, but it remains a copy, a simulacrum of the true temple whose reality it merely mirrors.

But the image is not limited purely to mythical, or indeed literary, manifestations. It is possible to trace the origin of Albrecht's temple to an actual site, though this did not come to light until the 1930s, when the Orientalist Arthur Upham Pope lead an expedition to the site of the ancient Sassanian (Persian) temple known as the Takht-i-Taqdis, or Throne of Arches, in what is now Iran. Attention had already been drawn by earlier scholars[9] to the literary evidence suggesting a link between the semi-legendary Takht and the Grail Temple, but it was not until Pope published his findings that it became known that the reality of the Takht so closely approximated the description of the thirteenth-century poet.

The site contained evidence of a great central dome surrounded by twenty-two side chapels (or arches) as well as other architectural details similar to those described in the *Jüngere Titurel*. Even Albrecht's mountain of onyx was accounted for by the presence of mineral deposits around the base of the site. These when dried out by the sun, closely resembled onyx.

Pope's excavations also confirmed that the Takht had once contained a complete observatory, with golden astronomical tables which could be changed with the seasons. A star map was contained within the great dome; and to facilitate matters even further the entire structure was set on rollers above a hidden pit, where horses worked day and night to turn it through the four quarters, so that at every season it would be in correct alignment with the heavens. Literary evidence from Persian writings such as the *Shah-Nama* further supported the details of the site, and made clear the nature of the rites which had been celebrated there. These were of a seasonal and vegetational kind, and, when performed by the priestly rulers of ancient Persia, ensured the fertility of the land and the very continuation of its people's life. Pope commented that the beauty and splendour of the Takht 'would focus, it was felt, the sympathetic attention and participation of the heavenly powers',[10] so that once again we have an expression of the desire for direct intervention of God into a man-made temple – a temple which furthermore revolved as did both the Grail Temple and, in certain versions, the walls of the Earthly Paradise – and without which it cannot be said to be complete.

IV

Many of the attributes discussed so far bring to mind an even more famous temple – that of Solomon at Jerusalem, the story of which is indissolubly linked with that of the Ark of the Covenant, itself an image that shares many of its attributes with those of the Grail. It is also the story of a chosen race and their communications with their God.

Built to house the Presence of God (Shekinah) the Solomonic temple was the concretization of an idea which began with the revelation of Moses, who created the first Tabernacle to contain the Ark. From within this holy house God spoke 'from above the mercy seat, from between the two cherubim that are upon the Ark of the Covenant'.[11] But the Tabernacle was never intended as a permanent home, and it was left to Solomon to complete the fashioning of a final resting place for the Ark at Jerusalem.

But even this remained merely a pattern for the Heavenly Temple, the Throne of God, the Temple Not Built By Human Hands: it possessed also a secondary, spiritual life, made from stones crystallized from the river Jobel which flowed out of Eden. So there is a sense of an image behind an image; while the link between the heavenly and earthly dimensions of the temple is part of the Edenic mystery, and therefore of the Grail – which in turn performs the same function as the Ark as a place for the meeting and mingling of God's essence with that of his Creation.

This can be taken a step further by reference to the Qabbalistic tradition, where the earthly temple is said to possess 'two overlapping aspects: one heavenly and one divine'.[12] Moses, who received the plan of the temple in much the same way as Titurel in Albrecht's poem, is enabled to witness the mystery performed in the divine dimension, where the high priest is the Archangel Michael. Beyond this is a still higher and more secret sanctuary, where the 'high priest' is the 'divine light' itself.[13]

So the mysteries of the Grail, which undergo a tripartite division into mind, heart, and spirit, echo the formation of the Solomonic sanctuary into the Temples of Earth and Heaven and the Temple of Light. Worshippers entering the outer court were said to have reached Eden; beyond this, in the Holy of Holies, the dwelling place of the Ark or the Chapel of the Grail, are the mysteries of the heavenly world, where the concerns of mind and body are left behind and those of the sanctified heart begin. Of those who went in search of the Grail, few except Galahad went beyond this point, and those who did were assumed into Heaven. It is as though, looking out of a window, the eye was lead beyond a glimpse of the immediate world, to gaze up into the heavens, and on looking there was suddenly enabled to see beyond, through all the dark gulfs of space to the Throne of God itself, there to be lost in light.

Lancelot was struck down and half blinded by that light, for which he was unprepared. Only his son Galahad was allowed to look directly into the heart of the Grail, and then only at the direct invitation of God – an answer and a reversal of the continuing invitation of mankind to God to enter the temple built in his honour.

Of the several non-biblical accounts of the Solomonic temple which exist, that of the Islamic historian Ibn Khaldun is one of the most interesting, for in it he states that the vaults below the temple, which are still generally believed to have been the stables for Solomon's horses, were nothing of the kind; they were built to form a vacuum between the earth and the building itself, so that malign influences might not enter it from below.[14]

There is here a suggestion of dualism in the opposing of the dark forces of the earth against those of the sky, and this is born out by what we know of the construction of Greek and Roman temples, where the *adytum* stretching *below* the earth was of equal or perhaps greater importance to the building above ground, and which served as a meeting place for the subterranean gods and their worshippers.

By medieval times, when the original site of the Solomonic temple had become a Muslim shrine, the chamber mentioned by Ibn Khaldun had become known as a place of entrance and exit for the spirits of the dead, while of the original structure nothing now remained above ground. The Crusaders however, continued to refer to it as the *Templum Dominum*, and it became sacred to the three major religions of the time. For the Jews it was the site of Solomon's Altar of the Holocausts, while to the Muslims, as the place from which the Prophet had ascended to heaven, it came for a time to rival Makkah (Mecca), and was attributed with the property of 'hovering'. Thus the geographer Idrisi referred to it in 1154 as 'the stone which rose and fell' (*lapis lapsus exilians*), which interestingly recalls Wolfram von Eschenbach's description, in *Parzival*, of the Grail as *lapis exilis*, sometimes interpreted as 'the stone which fell from heaven'. And it seems that here we have a paradigm for the whole history of the Grail and of the temple built to house it. The Grail, originating in Paradise, can also be said to have 'fallen' by being brought into this world by Seth. Through its use by Christ to perform the first Eucharist, it is hallowed, and the world, like the lost Eden, redeemed, so that it too 'rises'. Equally, both the stones used in the building of the temple, and the design for its construction, can be seen to have 'fallen from heaven'.

The Solomonic temple was to give rise to several imitations in the history of the Western world, one of which at least concerns us in our examination of the temple of the Grail. During the Crusades it became common practice among the knights to chip off fragments of the rock upon which the Temple had once stood. These they would take home as talismans of their visit to the Holy Land. One such man, a French knight named Arnoul the Elder, brought back one such piece to his home at Ardres in 1177, along with a fragment of the Spear of Antioch and some of the Manna of Heaven (though how he obtained the latter is not related). According to the Latin *Chronicle* of Lamber d'Ardres, Arnoul then proceeded to have built a castle to house these holy relics.

It was of curious design, containing rooms within rooms, winding staircases which lead nowhere, and 'loggias' or cloisters (a feature of Chrétien's Grail castle) and 'an oratory or chapel made like a Solomonic Temple'.[15] According to Lambert it was here that Arnoul laid to rest the objects he had brought with him, and it is interesting to note that these objects coincide precisely with the 'Hallows' of the Grail. The spear had long been identified with that which had pierced the side of Christ as He hung on the Cross, and as such had become one of the features of the Grail temple. Manna, the Holy Food of Heaven, is the substance which the Grail provides, either physically or in spiritual form. The stone from Jerusalem was part of the 'stone which rose and fell' and thus recalled the Grail stone of Wolfram. So that we have, assembled in a temple or castle constructed to resemble the Solomonic temple, all the elements of the Grail story originating from the Holy Land.

Nor do the links with Solomon and his Temple to the greater glory of God end here. Two important facts remain to be considered. The first concerns the Ark of the Covenant, which may be seen as the Grail of its age, and concerning which a well-founded tradition of the Ethiopian church maintains that it was removed from Jerusalem before the destruction of the Temple, by Menelik, a child of Solomon and Sheba. It is still kept hidden in the cathedral at Aksum in modern day Ethiopia, and has remained a central part of sacred practice. Known as the *Tabot* (from the Arabic *tabut 'al 'ahdi*, Ark of the Covenant) it is carried in procession at the festival of Epiphany, to the accompaniment of singing, dancing and feasting, which recalls the time when 'David and all the house of Israel brought up the Ark of the Lord with shouting and with the sound of the trumpet.'[16] Replicas of the *Tabot* are kept in every church in Ethiopia, and where these are large enough to possess a Holy of Holies, this representation of the Ark is kept within, as it was of old in the Temple of Solomon at Jerusalem.

Is it possible that we have here one of the contributing factors of the Grail story? It has been pointed out[17] that stories concerning a quest for a sacred object, undertaken by the fatherless son of a queen, may well have reached the West, and there become the basis for another story of a fatherless child (Parzival) who goes upon such a quest. Add to this the nature of the Ark itself, plus the fact that apart from the *Kebra Nagast*, in which this story is found in full, the only other known source is Arabic, suggests that the semi-mythical Flegetanis, Wolfram von Eschenbach's supposed informant who was also of Arabic origin, may have been the disseminator of this narrative. Just as Flegetanis/Wolfram speaks of the Grail as being brought to earth by a troop of angels where 'a Christian progeny bred to a pure life had the duty of keeping it',[18] so, similarly, does the *Kebra Nagast* speak of Menelik, the child of Solomon and Sheba, bringing the Ark out of Israel to reside in a specially protected *temenos* in Ethiopia.

Two further thoughts may be added. We have heard how Lancelot fared when he entered the chapel of the Grail to help the 'man dressed like a priest' who was serving at the Mass. Even though his intention is good, he is not permitted to touch or to look upon the mystery. So, too, in the story of the Ark's journey from Gebaa, described in the *Book of Kings*, when it had reached the threshing floor of Nachon, the oxen pulling the cart on which the Ark rode, began to kick and struggle and 'tilted the Ark to one side; whereupon Oza put out his hand and caught hold of it. Rash deed of his, that provoked the divine anger; the Lord smote him, and he died there beside the Ark.'[19]

Again the mystery is too great to be looked upon, or touched by one who is unprepared. Whereas in the Grail poem of Robert de Boron, we find the story of Sarracynte, wife of Evelake of Sarras, whose mother had for a time shared the guardianship of the Grail, in the shape of a host, and kept it in a box, which is specifically described as an ark.[20] She at least was allowed to touch it without harm, but such cases are rare in the mythos.

A visit to the Temple of the Grail must come first, and its perils must be overcome.

V

We have already noted that the most frequently occurring forms in temple design are those of the circle and the square. The significance of these forms becomes clearer when examined in the light of the construction of Roman cities and compared with the adventures of Gawain at the Grail Castle.

The plan upon which all Roman cities were based, like that of Titurel's Grail Temple, was supposed to have been divinely inspired, revealed to Romulus in a dream. It really consists of two separate designs, which together make up the total image of the city. These two designs incorporate the circle and the square; like the four square walls of the Earthly paradise, Rome is built on the principle of the rectangle.

The *urbs quadrata* is divided across and across by the *cardo* and the *decumanus*. The *cardo* corresponds to the axile tree of the universe, around which the heavens revolve, and is therefore a type of the same artificial, astrologically inspired plan as that of the Takht and the Grail Temple. The *decumanus* (from *decem* 'ten') forms the shape of an equal armed cross when it intersects the *cardo*. Within this complex were situated the temples dedicated to the sky gods, the masculine pantheon inherited from the Greeks; while adjacent to the *urbs* stood the citadel of the Palatine Hill, a circular form known as the *mundus*. This was the home of the dark gods of the underworld, and of the older, feminine worship of the Earth Mother, the Dark Goddess who held the secret of birth and death in her hands. In token of this, the centre of the *mundus* contained a hole in the earth, covered by a stone called the *lapis manalis*, which was only raised three times a year for the entrance and egress of dead souls, following the pattern established by the Greek temples and followed later by the Solomonic builders.

Here we have an example of the hidden darkness at the centre of things, the ancient Mother worship existing alongside the masculine deities, and illustrated by the forms of circle and square.

In the aspect of the Grail Temple known as the Castle of Wonders, we find taking place the adventure of Gawain and the magic chessboard. Gawain, the sun-hero whose strength grows greater towards midday and subsides towards evening, enters the feminine realm of the circular castle, where he finds a chessboard set out with pieces which move of their own accord at the will of either opponent. Gawain proceeds to play a game against an unseen adversary – and looses. Angrily he tries to throw the board and the pieces out of the window of the castle into the moat, and it is at this moment that a woman rises from the water to prevent him. She is identified by her raiment, which is either red or black, spangled with stars, as an aspect of the Goddess, and after at first rebuking Gawain for his anger and thoughtlessness, she becomes his ally and tutor, reappearing later in a different guise as his guide on the Grail quest.

It does not take much stretching of the imagination to see that here we have a restatement of the masculine and feminine elements associated with the temple. Gawain enters a circular (feminine) *temenos* and finds within it a square (masculine) chessboard, which is none the less chequered in black and white, a reconciliation of the previously opposing figures. When he tries to dispense with the board, he is prevented from so doing by an agent of the Goddess who, in subsequently helping him, teaches the necessity of establishing a balance between the masculine and feminine sides of his nature.

The image is born out by a further story from the Grail mythos, which brings us back to the themes of both the Solomonic temple and the Ark of the Covenant.

In Malory and elsewhere there are numerous references to the Ship of Solomon, the mysterious vessel which carries the Questing knights or even the Grail itself, to and from the everyday world into the timeless, dimensionless place of the sacred vessel. In fact, however, it does more than this, being in some ways not unlike a kind of mystical time machine, programmed to bear the message of the Grail through the ages, from the time of Solomon to the time of Arthur.

It was built, not by Solomon himself, but by his wife, who is called Sybyll in the medieval *Golden Legend*, but is identified with Bilquis, the Queen of Sheba. She, according to another Grail tradition, gave a vessel of gold to Solomon as a wedding gift – a cup which later became enshrined in the cathedral of Valencia as a type of the Grail.[21]

According to the story related in the *Queste del Saint Graal*, certain objects were placed within the ship, which was then set adrift, unmanned, to sail through time as well as space to the era of the Grail quest. These objects were: Solomon's Crown, the Sword of King David, a great bed supposingly made from the Rood Tree, and three branches from the Edenic Tree of Knowledge, one of red, one of white, and one of green, which were arranged to form a triangle above the bed from which a canopy could be suspended.

We should not be surprised to find images of paradise contained in the Solomonic ship – for the vessel is clearly an image of the Temple, this time afloat on the sea of time: its destination the country of the Grail. But perhaps the most important detail is that it contains wood from the tree which supposedly grew from a branch, taken from Eden by Adam and Eve, and planted in the earth. From this tree, it was widely believed in the Middle Ages, the cross of the crucifixion was constructed, and part of it used to make the Ark of the Covenant. The presence of this wood within the floating temple of Solomon's ship makes for some fascinating speculation. The ship, as has been said, was built at the behest of Solomon's wife. It thus becomes doubly an expression of the feminine archetype, often regarded as a vessel, and sometimes shown iconographically as an actual ship.[22] It is thus the prototype of all the traditional imagery of the human vessel, the womb of the earth and the womb of woman; Mary as the living Grail who carries the Light of the World within her, and the blood which will at length be spilled into the Cup which will in turn become the Grail. Within this female temple are placed the images of kingship: sword and crown; together with the three branches from the Tree of Knowledge, coloured in red, white and green, the colours of the alchemical process. Read in this way the myth becomes clear: it can be seen as an expression of the masculine contained within the feminine – of the square within the circle, images of the Grail Temple in all its aspects.

In the *Quest* the Grail knights voyage for a brief time together in the mysterious vessel. When the healing of the Wounded King is achieved, the final act of Galahad and his companions is to carry the sacred vessel to Sarras, the Holy City which is itself an image of paradise on earth. They do so in the floating Temple of Solomon, and in token of his Christ-like role Galahad lies down on the great bed which had been made from the wood of the Rood Tree. Symbolically, he is undergoing a species of crucifixion, and in doing so brings about the completion of the Grail work for that age.

After Galahad's death, however, we may believe that the ship returned to these shores, bearing the Grail hither again, to await the coming of the next Quester, and of the time when it would be redeemed again, and help thereby to redeem the time in which this far-off event occurred – our own time perhaps.

But the image of the temple as vessel, and of the Grail as a human vessel, brings us to the most fundamental aspect of the Grail Temple – or indeed of the temple everywhere – the Temple in man. This notion has been a common one since earliest times. In the *Chandogya Upanishad* it is held that:

> In the centre of the Castle of Brahma, our own body, there is a small shrine, in the form of a lotus flower, and within can be found a small space. We should find who dwells there and want to know him . . . for the whole universe is in him and he dwells within our heart.[23]

Or, as one might say: In the centre of the Castle of the Grail, our own body, there is a shrine, and within it is to be found the Grail of the heart. We should indeed seek to know and understand that inhabitant. It is the fragment of the divine contained within each one of us – like the sparks of unfallen creation which the Gnostics saw entrapped within the flesh of the human envelope. This light shines within each one, and the true quest of the Grail consists in bringing that light to the surface, nourishing and feeding it until its radiance suffuses the world.

'Chaque homme porte à jamais l'age du son temple', 'each

man is the same age as his own temple', wrote Henri Corbin, adding that the completion of the temple on *Muntsalvasche* was a kind of second birth for Titurel who, after this, we next see four hundred years old but perfectly preserved. The Temple of the Grail is really a divine clearing house for the souls of those who go in search of it – a kind of judgmental paradise, whose glass walls (like the floor of Solomon's Temple) reflect the true nature of the seeker and demand that he *recognize himself.*

The image of man *is* the image of the Temple, as writers as disparate as Corbin, Schwaller de Lubicz, F. Bligh Bond and Keith Crichlow have all noted. Man must make himself into a temple in order to be inhabited by God. *This* is the object of all the tests, the Sword Bridge and the turning door, the Perilous Bed and the blinding light of the Grail. The concept begins with the Egypt of the pharaohs, if not earlier, in the caves of mankind's first dwelling; and it continues through Platonic and Neoplatonic schools of thought. To them the temple was microcosmically an expression of the beauty and unity of creation, seen as a sphere. Expressed thus, it was reflected in the soul, and became indeed, 'a bridge for the remembrance or contemplation of the wholeness of creation',[24] words which could be as well applied to the Grail or the divine enclave of which it is a part.

This is the origin of the temple of light (the *haykat al-nur*), the macrocosmic temple which lies at the heart of Islamic mysticism, of which the Sufi mystic Ibn al-Arabi says: 'O ancient temple, there hath risen for you a light that gleams in our hearts,'[25] for which the commentary runs: 'the gnostic's heart, which contains the reality of the truth', is the temple.

Here we are back again in the world of the Solomonic Grail temple, the image of which, transformed and altered, together with that of the Earthly Paradise, were enclosed in the world of the Arthurian Grail mythos. And that world becomes transformed in turn, back into the Edenic world of primal innocence, the original home of the sacred vessel, possession of which 'represents the preservation of the primordial tradition in a particular, spiritual centre'.[26] The centre which is of the heart.

Ibn al-Arabi wrote[27] that the last true man would be born of the line of Seth. Do we not have in this statement a clue to the destiny of the Grail bearer who will come among us at the time of the next 'sacring' of the divine vessel? All the Grail knights were followers of Seth – who was the first to go in quest of it – and their adventures are transparent glyphs of the human endeavour to experience the divine. Most of us, if we found our way into the temple unprepared, would probably suffer the fate of Lancelot. But the Grail Temple exists to show us that the way is worth attempting, that the centre can be reached, if we are only attentive enough to the message it holds for us.

But what happens when we do finally reach the centre? If we look at what we have learned so far about the image of the temple on earth and in the heavens, we may begin to arrive at an answer.

All the temples are incomplete. They can only be made whole by the direct participation of God, who must stretch down to meet and accept the rising prayers of his creation. So with the Grail, it too must be hallowed, made complete, by the touch which makes blood of wine and flesh from bread. The Grail is made whole only when it is full, and it is not for nothing that the shape most often assumed by it is that of the chalice. If we see this as two triangles, one above the other, meeting at the apex point to form a nexus, we can see that it is an image of this divine meeting of upper and lower, temporal and divine. The same event occurs in the sanctuary of the temple, and is best expressed, as we saw earlier, by the figure of the *vesica piscis*, the two overlapping, interlocked circles which can represent God and mankind, and in the centre of which, outside time or space, the opposites are joined; the male and female, dark and light imagery we have been examining and which are represented, in the Grail story, by the chessboard castle.

We can see also that, in the human temple, this is expressed by the need of each individual to reach upwards and to be met halfway. We are all Grails to some degree, lesser or greater; but we are empty vessels until we offer ourselves to be filled by the light.

It is perhaps time that we looked again at some of the symbols which have built up throughout this study. Indeed, there comes a point at which unsupported words can no longer make sense of the complex of ideas presented. In the simple image with which we began, that of the *vesica piscis*, we have most of the story. The centre of the design with the outer edges of the two circles taken away (Fig. 4) makes the shape of the Grail. Turned upon its side, it is still the same, except that now it represents the image of the Grail as Temple, the building above, the adytum below, or as they may be seen: God and Goddess with, between them, at the meeting point of time and place, the figure of mankind. And, in the *temenos* between, the reconciliation of opposites, the perfection of the sacred space, sained by the touch of the divine which interpenetrates the temporal at the point of human experience. So that this experience can be shown as an exchange, to which we can contribute equally with God – as was suggested earlier, the image of the temple is at once a glyph of creation and of the evolution of the gods.

Figure 4

The images of the ship and the chessboard castle, the *urbs quadrata* and *mundus* of the Roman world, are also harmonized within this single point of interaction. The object of Gawain's visit to the Castle of the Grail was to be humbled and made to recognize the chequered pattern of all life, which is black and white, male and female equally and in proportion. The importance of the containing vessel cannot be overemphasized. The lower part of the Grail is of this world, penetrating time and space at once, its upper part is already in the paradisial state of beyond-time and beyond-space. At the centre is the Temple, the sacred space at the heart of the circle, the adytum which stretches below the earth but is open to the sky. Thus the ancient temples were the simplest and most direct means of contact with the divine, as today the most simple and direct method is the building and establishment of the inner temple, that of the heart. Dealing with the response in mankind to the voice of God, the Word, the Gnostic *Authoritative Teaching* says: 'the senseless man hears the call, but he is ignorant of the place to which he has been called. And he did not ask . . . "where is the temple into which I should go and worship my hope".'[28] This could hardly be clearer. In the quest of the Grail, the failure to ask an important question is the cause of the failure of many knights who arrive at the castle. It is Lancelot's failure, and it is the failure of all who do not listen to the Voice of the Light.

Qabbalistic teaching has it that 'the temple has been destroyed, but not the path of purification, illumination, and union that lay concealed in it'.[29] For when the perfected soul of mankind 'rises like incense from the golden altar of the heart and passes through the most inward curtains of his being to the holy of holies within'[30] then the two cherubim who stand guard over the Ark of the Covenant (of the heart) 'are united in the presence of the One, in Whom the soul recognizes its eternal life and its own union with Him. Henceforward the soul is called the eternally "living" [*hayah*], the "one and only" [*yehidah*]',[31] the perfect. The Light has come like veritable tongues of fire upon all who reach the centre of the temple and find there the seat of God in the heart of His Creation.

This was the aim of the Grail knights, of the *Templiesen* of Wolfram von Eschenbach, of the priest-kings who built the Takht-i-Taqdis or the Capitoline temples of Rome. Before them it was the desire of the people who erected their stone circles to echo the dance of the cosmos – awaiting that moment when God would reach down and hallow their seeking with a touch. And so we wait now, who are modern Grail questers, for that touch that awakens the light within: as must all who seek to enter the Temple of the Mysteries.

Notes

1 Sir Thomas Malory, *Le Morte D'Arthur*, New York, University Books, 1961, bk 17, ch. 15.
2 Plotinus, *Enneads*, quoted in K. Crichlow, *Soul as Sphere and Androgine*, Ipswich, Golgonooza Press, 1980, p. 23.
3 René Guenon, 'The Symbolism of the Graal', in *Tomorrow*, Winter 1965, vol. 13, no. 2.

4 Crichlow, *op. cit.*, p. 23.

5 Louis Charpentier, *The Mysteries of Chartres Cathedral*, Research into Lost Knowledge Organization, London, R.I.L.K.O., 1972.

6 This later became confused with an actual site: Montségur, a stronghold of the Cathars in Southern France. From this grew a tradition that they were guardians of the Grail, a supposition which has yet to be firmly proved, though there is some evidence to support it. See John Matthews, *The Grail: Quest for Eternal Life*, London, Thames & Hudson, 1981.

7 Albrecht von Scharffenberg: *Der Jüngere Titurel*, Augsberg, 1477 (?).

8 Green is a colour much associated with the Grail. In some versions the vessel originates as an emerald from the crown of Lucifer, the angel of light; while in Islamic tradition, the Black Stone of the Ka'aba, recognizably an image of the Grail, is carried on a cloth of green *archmadi*.

9 In particular Lars Ivar Ringbom; *Graltemple und Paradies*, Stockholm, 1951. For Pope's account, see 'Persia and the Holy Graal', *The Literary Review* (New Jersey), I, 1957, pp. 51–71.

10 *supra*.

11 Exodus 25:22.

12 *Zohar: Terumah 159a*, quoted by Lee Schayer, 'The Meaning of the Temple', in *Sword of Gnosis*, New York, Penguin Books, 1974.

13 *supra*, p. 363.

14 Ibn Khaldun, *The Muqaddimah*, London, Routledge & Kegan Paul, 1958.

15 see 'The Arthurian Tradition in Lambert D'Ardres', by Urban. T. Holmes in *Speculum*, XXV, 1965, pp. 100–2.

16 2 Samuel 6:15.

17 Helen Adolf, 'Oriental Sources for Grail Romances', *Publications of the Modern Language Association*, LXII, 1947, pp. 306–23.

18 Wolfram von Eschenbach, *Parzival*, trans A. T. Hatto, Harmondsworth, Penguin Books, 1980, p. 232.

19 2 Kings 6; 6–8.

20 Robert de Boron, *Joseph D'Arimathea*, trans. H. Lovelich, Early English Text Society, London, 1874.

21 Estha Quinn, 'The Quest of Seth, Solomon's Ship and the Grail', *Traditio*, XXI, 1965, pp. 185–222. I am indebted to this article, which contains a full treatment of the Ship of Solomon.

22 See the picture of the Virgin as Vessel in Matthews, *op. cit.*, p. 86.

23 *The Unpanishads*, trans. Juan Mascaro, Harmondsworth, Penguin Books, 1965, 8:1.

24 Crichlow, *op. cit.*

25 Ibn al-Arabi, *The Tarjuman Al-Ashwaq*, Acra, Theosophical Publishing House, 1978.

26 Guenon, *op. cit.*

27 Ibn al-Arabi, *The Bezels of Wisdom*, trans. R. W. J. Austin, London, SPCK, 1980.
28 *The Nag Hammadi Library* ed. and trans. James M. Robinson, Leiden, E. J. Brill, 1977, p. 282.
29 Quoted by Schayer, *op. cit.*, pp. 364–5.
30 *Ibid*.
31 *Ibid*.

:5:

:THE·RETURN·OF DINDRANE:

·

HELEN·LUKE

·

It seems to have passed largely unnoticed that it is always the knight,
the masculine representative of the Quest, who goes in search of the
divine vessel – perhaps because it is a feminine symbol to begin with,
but also because women do not need the quest, are already vessels of
the Holy Blood, their archetype the Virgin, and are therefore Grail
bearers rather than seekers. Each may give birth, therefore, to the new
Grail Lord. It is to these 'whole women', the Grail priestesses, that we
should turn for enlightenment, and in so doing discover that we have
always known the Grail secret, merely failing to recognize it, as men
fail to recognize the feminine element within themselves and women
their symbolic masculinity. Out of this realization, as we have said
before in this book, comes a new syzygy, an intermingling on all levels
which presents us with a healing face of creation we have never seen
before, but which is the true nature of the Grail.

C. G. Jung, writing of archetypes dormant in the unconscious,
says that they are activated when one-sided attitudes prevalent
at a particular time and place are in urgent need of a compensa-
tory image. By the end of the first millennium of the Christian
era the rejection of the body, of the feminine, of matter itself,
had reached a peak. There were some who actually believed
that the material world was a creation of the devil, and earlier
there had even been an unsuccessful movement within Christianity denying that women had souls. In a letter written in 1953

91

Jung said that the twelfth and early thirteenth centuries saw '. . . the beginning of Latin alchemy and of the natural sciences and also of a feminine religious symbol, the Holy Grail.'[1]

The Grail itself is indeed a supreme symbol of the lost values; for without the vessel of the feminine all the 'ten thousand things' must exist in a state of unrelatedness to each other – a chaos without meaning. The Grail is the cup from which each individual life receives its essential food and drink: it is the chalice containing the mystery of blood and spirit: it is a maternal womb, the body of Mary herself. Without a vessel no transformation on any level can take place – no cooking of ingredients in a kitchen, no chemical experiments or alchemical search for 'gold', no *metanoia* in a human soul, no incaranation of the Word to dwell among us.

Almost another millennium has passed since the Grail legends rose from the unconscious, and their vitality has never faded. Again and again poets and story-tellers have breathed new life into them – have, indeed, re-created them. The need for the affirmation of the feminine has not lessened since the twelfth century and has become particularly insistent in our own technological age.

The many legends surrounding the Grail image are for the most part concerned with the adventures of the knights, of the men who seek to find its meaning in their own souls. But the liberation of woman and the fight to establish her equality with men in hitherto masculine fields of work and thought has meant that she too has great need of a much more conscious awareness of the symbols of her own deepest feminine roots. Many women today are even contemptuous of the nature of the feminine being – of that which contains and nurtures and is still, which responds to people and things without any will to use or manipulate them, which guards in silence the mystery of life. If women do not themselves take up the quest of the Grail within, it is certain that their new-found equality in the masculine sphere will lose its meaning and become another 'wasteland'. A great hope for the future lies in the fact that so many individual women are now entering upon that quest.

Charles Williams, who died in 1945, was in my view one of the great re-creators of the Grail myth in our century. His Arthurian poems are not easy to read – often so obscure that even C. S. Lewis, his friend, who wrote a commentary[2] on them, had occasionally to admit defeat, but the more often one returns to them the more vividly they speak to the imagination, particularly through the poet's profound insight into the fundamental nature of woman; and we are left with shining and unforgettable images.

I shall discuss two of these poems, 'Taliessin in the Rose Garden' (*The Region of the Summer Stars*, Oxford University Press, 1950) and 'The Last Voyage' (*Taliessin Through Logres*, Oxford University Press, 1938). First, however, it is necessary to say something of the people from the legends who appear in these poems. Dindraine is Sir Percival's sister who appears briefly in the *Morte d'Arthur* of Sir Thomas Malory, though Malory does not name her. Williams called her sometimes Dindrane (from Welsh sources) and sometimes Blanchefleur (from the French poems). Taliessin does not appear in Malory. He was the great Welsh legendary bard and seer – the twice-born child who tasted of the cauldron of wisdom of the mother goddess, Ceridwen. Williams made him the central figure of many of his poems (as the king's poet at Arthur's court). Taliessin in Williams's story loves and is loved by Dindrane; it is a total commitment on all levels, but it is not consummated in the flesh since both have freely and consciously chosen celibate vocations.

Guinevere in the Rose Garden poem is, of course, Arthur's queen, through whose love for the king's friend, Lancelot, the fellowship of the Round Table was finally split and Arthur brought to his death. In the other poem, almost the last of the cycle, we meet Sir Galahad, Sir Perceval and Sir Bors. These are the three knights who, in Malory, achieved the Grail, and who took ship with it on its voyage to Sarras, the eternal place, where it was withdrawn from the war-torn kingdom of Logres. 'Logres' is the temporal kingdom of Britain; the forest of Broceliande is, in our language, the unconscious; Caucasia, for Williams, stands for the flesh and Carbonek for the spirit; Camelot is the temporal city.

There is one phrase that recurs in the poems whereby Williams defines the wholeness of such a woman as Dindrane.

'Flesh knows what spirit knows but spirit knows it knows.' It expresses the truth that the material and instinctual world remains innocent, at one with itself – every stone, plant, insect and animal fulfilling unconsciously its nature as it was created to be. But since consciousness dawned in man (as in the myth of the Fall) he has been split between the opposites, between light and dark, male and female, conscious and unconscious, good and evil – all in opposition to each other. The feminine was identified with flesh, the masculine with spirit, but the woman who is one-in-herself in full consciousness is the woman who 'knows she knows'. She has integrated the life of the spirit with the instinctive life of her flesh through the living in this world on all levels of the love which is the way of conscious return to the unity of all the opposites. The same integration, of course, applies to man, but he more usually must approach it from the opposite end of the spectrum.

As the poem 'Taliessin in the Rose Garden' opens, the king's poet is walking among the roses making poetry and he sees three women at the entry to the long garden path: Queen Guinevere talking to Dindrane and a maid doing garden work beyond. The sparkling red of the queen's great ruby ring and the glowing red of the roses unite in Taliessin's imagination with the red of falling blood and there follows a long meditation on the nature of woman.

Guinevere was a queen; on her was laid the great responsibility of carrying for her country the symbol of the feminine side of the holy marriage between Heaven and Earth, the symbol of humanity united to God, of the flesh infused by the spirit – giving birth in due time to the new king.

> Glorious over Logres, let the headship of the queen
> be seen, as Caucasia to Carbonek, as Logres to Sarras

But Guinevere had betrayed her vocation

> under her brow she looked for the King's friend
> Lancelot

Here at the outset Taliessin foresees that the Queen's betrayal of her feminine wholeness, her refusal to accept her great responsibility for the symbolic image which she carries as queen (the 'consummate earth of Logres' he calls her) will mean that the 'falling blood' which could have been the redemptive blood of sacrifice, will become the blood of war, bringing destruction of the kingdom when finally the king is forced into awareness by his own misbegotten son Mordred and makes war on his friend Lancelot to his own undoing. Thus any civilization is doomed when the 'queen' (the leading feminine principle, the dominant attitude in women) loses integrity of heart and succumbs to what someone has called 'love as a release of tension' in place of commitment to the relatedness of the true *eros*.

We may here ask why it is that through the ages adultery in a woman has been regarded as so much more terrible a thing than in a man. For centuries and in many places a woman was put to death if discovered in adultery. It is not enough to answer that the domination of men over women has been the sole cause of this attitude. There is also a profound psychological reason.

Nature is equally promiscuous, whether it be male or female, but since woman is so much closer to the unconscious than man she is far more likely to be swallowed by the instinctive life and so lose her humanity if she separates her body from her feeling values. Because the flesh is symbolically feminine man has projected on to woman his deep fear of the chaos and lack of order with which the growth of human consciousness is always threatened. This projection is mercifully waning and the extreme cruelties visited upon a promiscuous woman are a thing of the past. But an individual modern woman ignores at her peril the fact that very real damage may be done to her psyche if she gives her body indiscriminately without a commitment to relationship of heart and mind. Whether this commitment is lived through a life-long marriage or for one night only is not the point. Depth of feeling, not frequency is the vital thing. It is not a matter of conventional taboos or moral condemnation; it is a question of the fundamental difference between the masculine and feminine psyches.

I am not, of course, implying that a man is absolved from a similar feeling of commitment; far from it. No person of either sex can come to wholeness without full consciousness of the values of *eros* and willingness to accept the ties and the sacrifices which all true relatedness demands. Because, however, these values are the dominant principle for a woman, she is in much greater danger of disintegration if she betrays them than is a man, and the effects of her betrayal on the environment are deadly. It was Guinevere, not Lancelot, who bore the greater responsibility for the final disaster.

In the story of Lancelot and Elayne and of his begetting of the Grail hero upon her we can feel at once these distinctions. Lancelot was tricked into spending a night with Elayne, thinking that he was lying with Guinevere. It was therefore an inevitable fate and Lancelot remains morally innocent. It is inconceivable that Galahad, the High Prince, the whole man who 'achieved' the Grail, could have been born from a union of Guinevere and some great knight with whom she might have lain, unconscious of his identity. Symbolically that would be so false that we revolt at the very thought. Elayne, Galahad's mother, loved Lancelot that night and ever after with all her heart and soul as well as her body, even though she could never be with him again, and she accepted the pain of this knowledge. Our reason replies that so also did Guinevere love Lancelot – both he and she were equally guilty of betraying the king, her husband and his friend. Both of them were equally faithful on another level to their love for each other. Why then if Lancelot could father the Grail Prince could not Guinevere have been his mother? First, of course, because Guinevere, while accepting Lancelot, was at the same time pretending to be faithful to her husband – she had her cake and ate it. Her devotion was never whole, and she betrayed her symbolic feminine vocation as queen, as well as her personal husband. But still more important, it is an ultimate necessity for a woman that in the instinctual area she be *conscious of what she is doing* as was Elayne, if she is to give birth to the divine hero within – conscious, not in the rational analysing sense, but in the sense of awareness of her own feelings, and a responsible commitment of her body and heart together. If she were to be tricked in this area she would be less than woman – merely female (or possibly in these days an imitation man).

There is a trinity of women at the beginning of 'Taliessin in the Rose Garden', the three being a queen, a virgin soon to be a contemplative nun, and an ordinary working woman. In all women this trinity exists, lived or unlived, either positively or negatively. We may know and live the 'queen' through our sense of responsibility, not only for those around us but for all mankind. 'Through words and deeds the superior man moves heaven and earth – even if he abides in his room,' says Confucius. This is the royal quality – awareness of the symbolic power of everything we are. Or, for we are free to choose, we may identify with the queen and demand to be first all the time, to be served and protected and personally admired. The working woman is equally essential: to live in the present and do each task as it comes, tending the growing things, both of the earth and in the psyche. Without this we are no longer human; but, again, if the work we do, whether with hands or mind, absorbs our whole personalities, it becomes one of the most seemingly virtuous ways to evade reality. These two persons of the trinity are easily understood.

But what of the virgin? In our time it has become almost a shameful word. I was told the other day of a boy aged twelve who said to his mother, talking of a girl his own age, 'She's nothing but a virgin.' Asked what he meant by this, he replied, 'Oh, a virgin means a complete dud, boring and dull.'

A young woman who is still a virgin at twenty often has a miserable sense of inferiority on this account. A 'virgin' in common speech means a woman who has never had intercourse with a man, but in its more ancient and deeper meaning a virgin is a woman who, whether she has had intercourse or not, has no *need* to unite physically with a man in order to become whole, one-in-herself, for she has known intercourse with the god within. This has always been the symbolic meaning of the life of the nun. As the bride of Christ, she seeks the inner marriage of the human and the divine. It is easy, however, to see how the affirmation of a vocation to prayer and contemplation can sink into the negative repression of the sexual desires themselves. Chastity, which means purity of heart, has come all too frequently to mean a denial of the purity of instinct itself. No one can become 'virgin' in the true sense without going through the fire of instinctual emotion. This experience, however, does not necessarily include fruition on the physical level and the time has surely come not only for a resurrection of the true meaning of the word 'virgin' but for a return of respect for those whose inner truth may demand virginity in the ordinary physical sense.

Robert Grinnell, in his book *Alchemy in a Modern Woman*,[3] writing of a woman patient who suffered from frigidity, says that this problem in a woman may come from her high ideals in the realm of *eros*, together with a mistaken interpretation of them through a typical masculine over-valuation of physical sex. Grinnell adds that *eros* in a woman may be called a 'sort of feminine conscience' which takes her beyond the demands of the ego and lifts her out of her momentary desires. Thus the natural woman is transformed into the woman who 'knows she knows'.

Virginity and the quest for the holy marriage within are emerging from behind the walls of the cloisters, which through so many centuries have guarded that great symbol, and in our time, only individual women can give it new life. To one the god may come through her sexual fruition, to another through suffering its absence – and both are 'virgin' in the deep sense.

To return to the poem, Taliessin, musing on these things – the glowing ruby, the red rose, the falling blood – and on their meaning in woman, sees a great vision of the Zodiac. Each of the twelve houses, he says, is a door to the whole, 'All coalesced in each.' But Cain, by killing Abel, split the Zodiac at a blow and through the incoherence of the houses at war with themselves the blood flowed and the way of return 'climbed beside the timed and falling blood'. The shedding of blood can only be redeemed by the offering of blood. Then, as Taliessin looked on the stricken world, he heard

> The women everywhere throughout it sob with the curse
> and the altars of Christ everywhere offer the grails.
> Well are women warned from serving the altar
> who, by the nature of their creature, from Caucasia to
>   Carbonek,
> share with the Sacrifice the victimization of blood.

The woman's monthly shedding of blood is the outer sign

and an inner symbol of her female capacity to give birth. Williams means, I believe, that the menstrual blood of woman is a continual reminder of the truth that after the Fall, after the split in creation, there can be no 'return', no healing of the split, without sacrifice, without the giving of blood. If the woman or the feminine in man does not 'bleed' there is no creation in this world. Therefore, he says that women 'share with the Sacrifice the victimization of blood'. The piercing of Christ's side was the wound in the heart of his feeling nature. (The liver was thought by the ancients to be the seat of the emotions and is on the right side.)

I do not know any other writer, theologian or psychologist who has given this very profound, yet very simple and, once seen, obvious explanation of the intuitive revulsion which many feel at the thought of a woman priest celebrating the Mass. If a truly mature woman, fully aware of her 'animus' (the masculine aspect of her unconscious) were to read services and preach sermons it would not offend. The Mass, however, is a *symbolic* rite, and no matter how developed her spirit may be a woman remains biologically female. Since her shedding of blood, says Williams, is in her flesh an equivalent of the blood of the victim, therefore, if *in her flesh* she offers the blood of Christ she usurps on the wrong level the function of the spirit. 'Flesh knows what spirit knows,' Williams goes on, 'but spirit knows it knows.' In this, of course, he is emphatically *not* saying that individual women cannot know they know; indeed he goes on to show this with great clarity. He is speaking only of her symbolic feminine role in a ritual, not of her individual being. A symbol is, of course, that which makes one the two levels of reality – spirit and matter, inner and outer truth.

There is usually a symbolic meaning hidden behind an old wives' tale. During the Second World War I lived in a small village in Berkshire where a local woman cooked for our family. I remember that she told me she never tried to make jams during the days of her menstrual period since it was well known to be useless; the jam or jelly simply would not set! In other words, no *transformation* could take place at these times – the separate ingredients, the fruit and sugar, could be mixed but could never transform into the third thing – that which is both and neither. The relevance to the transformation of the bread and wine on that other level of the Mass is plain. Projected on to such things as the making of jam it is nonsensical in the light of our scientific knowledge, but the ancient symbolic truths which express the mysteries of being have always been preserved both in folklore and in the rituals of the great religions.

Though in the ancient world there were everywhere priestesses they were never, I believe, charged with killing the sacrificial animal or offering its blood. The tearing to pieces of victims by the women in the Dionysian rites was not a priestly act but a ritually contained release of instinctual frenzy. The priestesses served as links to the unconscious through their mediumistic power – the sibyls, for instance – they tended the sacred fire, as did the vestal virgins, fulfilling the great religious functions of woman; but they did not wield the knife of sacrifice or offer the blood. Rather it is their task to draw up the waters under the earth from the well of the unconscious that all may drink of the *aqua permanens*, as the alchemists called the water of life. It is the measure of the masculine one-sidedness of our culture that there have never been priestesses of this kind in institutional Christianity.

It would be useless for the church at this stage to attempt to introduce new rituals for priestesses. A true rite is born, not made, and if consciously contrived is merely sentimental. Nor does the answer lie in the current urge to admit women to the priest's role. Nevertheless, we cannot put the clock back in a mood of nostalgia. In most Protestant sects the communion service is not a symbolic transformation rite but a commemorative meal, so that there should be no objection whatever to women ministers. Only to the Catholic, Orthodox and Anglican rites do the words of Charles Williams apply. But the demand for women in the priesthood is perhaps one of the indicators that for growing numbers of people the symbolic life is slowly being pushed out of the collective institutions as such. In the coming age, as Jung frequently pointed out, the symbols must come to birth in the individual soul, in the man or woman who enters on the lonely quest for the Grail within, and this applies to church members as profoundly as to anyone else. It was always in the legends a quest that must be undertaken alone, but it is never achieved without the discovery of objective relatedness to others, as opposed to the all-too-easy unconscious 'mixing', or the 'togetherness' which submerges any true meeting between human beings.

As C. S. Lewis points out in his commentary on Williams's poems, the menstrual blood of women differs from the blood of animals in heat. For animals it is the only time at which they can conceive. In human beings it is the proof of the possibility of motherhood, as in nature, but there is a major difference in that conception can take place at any time. The beginning of the monthly flow at puberty is, moreover, a sign in the body of the psychic split – that is, of the 'Fall' which was the beginning of the conscious 'way of return' for Eve as for Adam. The innocent wholeness of childhood, of Eden, is over. At puberty the longing begins for completion by physical union with the other sex, a longing which continues (symbolically) until the 'stanching' at the menopause. In Plato's image the original human being is a sphere which, being cut in two, forever seeks to reunite with its other half. (See Ch. 4.)

At a later point in the poem Williams hints at the inner identity of the woman's menstrual blood, which tells her that she has not yet conceived, with the blood of the wounded Grail king, bleeding because he cannot bring to life the new consciousness of the Christ, the Self. In some beautiful lines Taliessin speaks of how woman may consciously give birth to the new keeper of the Grail, within herself, and so heal the wound in the psyche.

First, however, Williams speaks of the natural woman living instinctively the One way.

> Women's flesh lives the quest of the Grail
> in the change from Camelot to Carbonek and from
>   Carbonek to Sarras,
> puberty to Carbonek, and the stanching, and Carbonek
>   to death.
> Blessed is she who gives herself to the journey.

Camelot is the city of men, the life of this world, which is entered at puberty – the potentially creative blood begins to flow, and primitive woman already begins her vocation as wife and mother. She cleaves to her man and receives the seed, she gives birth in pain, she is the earth without which the creative seed is sterile. But when this flow of her blood is stanched at the menopause and she must let go of her desire to conceive and give birth to a physical child, then her lifelong experience of 'Camelot' can bring her to that instinctive wisdom which we still may find in old women of this simple kind who have given themselves to the journey – who accept the 'stanching', as they have accepted the pains and joys of motherhood. They come to Carbonek, the place where the 'holy' is glimpsed and from it go on in peace to the goal of death. By the generous, rich living of her feminine nature such a woman is whole, but without knowing that she knows.

Taliessin, making poetry in the Rose Garden, having sung of the quest of the Grail in the flesh of woman – of the blessedness of those who give themselves with the simple diffuse awareness of the natural woman to life's journey, goes on in the next stanza to sing of the blessedness of the conscious woman on this same journey.

> The phosphor of Percivale's philosophical star
> shines down the roads of Logres and Broceliande;
> happy the woman who in the light of Percivale
> feels Galahad, the companion of Percivale, rise
> in her flesh, and her flesh bright in Carbonek with Christ,
> in the turn of her body, in the turn of her flesh, in the turn
> of the Heart that heals itself for the healing of others,
> the only Heart that healed itself without others, when
> our Lord recovered the Scorpion and restored the Zodiac.
> Blessed is she who can know the Dolorous Blow,
> healed in the flesh of Pelles, the flesh of woman;

The philosophical star of Perceval – the image of the wisdom in the heavens, the light of man's soaring spirit – shines on the roads of this world and penetrates into Broceliande, the darkness of the feminine unconscious. Happy the woman, says Williams, who is flooded by this light of consciousness, and who then feels 'Galahad', the new whole man, stir to life within her. We are carried perhaps for an instant into the thought of a woman rising above the earth and *becoming* a sort of female Galahad, but the next line jerks us firmly back to the true blessedness of the new vision for woman. She feels Galahad rise in her flesh; the point is that she feels him *consciously* in the actuality of her feminine nature and so reaches full awareness of the truth of the heart, of the love that is both personal and rooted in the transpersonal life. Her spirit then reaches maturity and 'she knows that she knows'.

Only in the Heart of the Self is the split healed. The use of the word Heart here is vital in our context. As James Hillman has so compellingly shown in his essay on the feeling function, the desperate need of our time is for the discovery of *eros*, of feeling values. Emotional experiences for their own sake and theoretical truths we have in plenty, but true feeling which leads to the perception of the abiding values is still rare in our time. It is for individual, conscious women to lead the way. How difficult it is for men, who are so dangerously exposed in this age to possession by the intellect, by technology, or by their inferior unintegrated femininity, to find the meaning of *eros* without this mediation of true women who do not only live these things instinctively, but 'know that they know'!

There is a letter written by Jung to Aniela Jaffe in 1947, which most beautifully illustrates the value to a great man of a feeling response by a woman who 'knows she knows'. It was written in answer to a letter from her in which she had evidently spoken of his essay on the Trinity. He writes:

I thank you with all my heart for your response to my 'Trinity': I couldn't imagine a more beautiful one. It is a 'total' reaction, and it had a 'total' effect on me too. You have perfectly imaged what I imagined into my work. It again became clear to me from your letter how much one misses when one receives no response or a mere fragment, and what a joy it is to experience the opposite – a creative resonance which is at the same time like a revelation of the feminine being. It is as though a wine, which by dint of toil and sweat, worry and care has finally become mature and good, were being poured into a precious beaker. Without this receptacle and acceptance a man's work remains a delicate child, followed with doubting eyes and released into the world with inner anxiety. But when a soul opens to the work, it is as though a seed were lodged in good earth, or the gates of a city were closed in the evening so that it can enjoy surer repose.[4]

Reading these most beautiful words, how horrifying is the attitude of those many women who are so busy doing things and demanding their rights, personally or collectively, that they reject altogether that 'precious beaker', the Grail of the feminine being which receives the wine of the mystery so that in due time many may drink.

Let us now return to those strange words, 'Blessed is she who can know the Dolorous Blow/ healed in the flesh of Pelles, the flesh of woman.' The so-called Dolorous Blow caused the wound in the thigh of the Grail King Pelles, and bled without healing until the coming of the new man, Galahad. The wounded state of the king was reflected in the sterility of the surrounding wasteland. What lies behind these images? C. S. Lewis, in his commentary, is silent. There is, of course, the obvious connection with what has gone before; the stanching at the menopause of the shedding of blood is a symbol of the making whole of wounded humanity in a natural woman, who, her task of rearing children over, turns towards death with a sense of joy and acceptance during those last years – acceptance which only comes to those who have given themselves freely to the experience of the dark as well as of the light. 'Blessed is she who gives herself to the journey,' says Taliessin. But the second blessing is different. 'Blessed is she who can know' – the meaning of these things.

It is significant that so many modern women suffer acute and painful problems at the menopause both physical and psychic and that it often drags on for years causing all sorts of disturbances. It is beautifully called 'the change of life', but how many women do in fact change their lives – change their attitudes, turn inward to find meanings and to prepare for death, and so enter consciously on the new phase of the journey, from 'Carbonek to Sarras'? Very few; the majority cling desperately to 'Camelot' because they have never fully given themselves to that phase of the journey, and so the energy released by the biological change, instead of flowering into a creative activity of the Logos within her, into an imaginative confrontation with the meaning of death, is eaten up by the unassimilated drives of the 'animus', the masculine component in her psyche which turns destructive instead of connecting her to the spirit within. The wound inflicted by the Dolorous Blow – that is, the split between spirit and flesh, is not healed in such women but bleeds more freely than ever in the psyche. So the wasteland spreads and the heart shrivels. We see all around us the plight of middle-aged women substituting ever-increasing outer activity for the inner life, or searching miserably for a man, any man, or his equivalent, to fill the void by preserving the illusion of youth.

'Blessed is she who can know the healing of the Dolorous Blow.' In such a woman the shedding of blood and its stanching both become conscious sacrifice and are filled with meaning. She is aware of the 'change of life' on every level and embraces it with her whole heart.

These words of Williams, 'Blessed is she who can know the Dolorous Blow/ healed in the flesh of Pelles, the flesh of woman' surely derive from the strangest of all the legends in Malory's *Morte d'Arthur*. As the three knights Galahad, Perceval and Bors approach the end of their quest they are joined by Perceval's sister, who, as has been said, is not named by the earlier writer, but is called either Blanchefleur or Dindrane by Williams. Malory tells of how this 'noblewoman' led Sir Galahad to the 'ship of Solomon', which was later to carry the Grail and the three knights away from Logres to Sarras. Here they found Sir Perceval and Sir Bors waiting, and the lady, fulfilling her role of link to the unconscious, revealed to them the story of the ship, and of the sword which Sir Galahad found there. She was not recognized even by her brother Perceval until she revealed herself as a daughter of King Pellinore. Then all four set forth on the last phase of the quest. (See Ch. 4.)

As they journeyed they came to a castle from which armed knights emerged, who tried to seize the princess, Perceval's sister. There was a battle, but finally the travellers were induced to listen to the reason for the seizure. The lady of the castle was very sick and had long lain in a coma, and it had been foretold that she could only find healing through the blood of a princess of royal descent who was also a virgin; therefore every noblewoman who passed that way was seized upon in the hope that she would fulfil these conditions. When Perceval's sister heard this she said at once that she was both a princess and a virgin and offered freely to give her blood to the lady. 'Who will let my blood?' she said. One of the ladies-in-waiting stepped forward and made an incision in her arm and the blood gushed out into a bowl. So much blood did she lose that she knew she would die, and she spoke to the three knights bidding them not to bury her but to put her in a ship at the next harbour and set it adrift. 'And when you come to Sarras,' she said, 'you will find this ship with my body in it waiting for you, and there you shall bury me.'

And so she died, and the other lady rose from her sick bed and lived. The three knights obeyed her and leaving her body in the ship they came to Carbonek, the Grail city, and Galahad healed the wounded king. From thence they came to the sea and boarded the ship of Solomon, to which the Grail had removed itself; and without sail or oar they were borne over the sea to Sarras.

This legend is the basis of Williams's poem 'The Last Voyage'. In his own recreation of the story he significantly shows us the body of Dindrane, the woman, travelling in the same ship with the Grail and with the three knights – Galahad, the 'alchemical infant', the holy child; Perceval, the star of wisdom; Bors the ordinary practical human being. There is now a quaternity in this ship. All four are carried to the 'spiritual place' where, in the unconscious, two of the knights and the dead woman will remain with the Grail until the time of its rediscovery, while Bors alone returns at once to the world. The ages of growing emphasis on man and his works were ahead – the Renaissance, the Enlightenment, followed by the industrial revolution and our century of technological materialism. This is the great significance of Bors's solitary return, Galahad's intuition, Perceval's inner wisdom and the feminine values of Dindrane are all removed into the unconscious.

Bors is in Williams's poems the husband and father, the

down-to-earth householder, the extrovert. The poet sees him as the guardian of the Grail vision during the coming centuries, but we have watched the gradual eclipse of the simple human values of Bors, in the sterility of intellect and technology divorced from feeling. Now surely the time is ripe for the emergence of the Grail from Sarras – for the resurrection of Dindrane.

Malory's story of Perceval's sister and of her shedding of blood for another and her close connection with the Grail is unique, as far as I know, in the versions of the legend. No one took much notice of it, it seems, until suddenly in Williams's poetry it moves into the centre of that last picture of the swiftly receding Grail.

> Before the helm the ascending-descending sun
> Lay in quadrilateral covers of a saffron pall
> over the bier and the pale body of Blanchefleur,
> mother of the nature of lovers, creature of exchange
> drained there of blood by the thighed wound,
> she died another's death, another lived her life.
> Where it was still to-night, in the last candles of Logres,
> a lady danced, to please the sight of her friends; her
> cheeks were stained from the arteries of Percivale's sister.
> Between them they trod the measure of heaven and earth,
> and the dead woman waited the turn and throe of the dance
> where, rafting and undershafting the quadruplicate sacrum,
> below the saffron pall, the joyous woe of Blanchefleur,
> the ship of Solomon (blessed be he) drove on.

To me these lines are some of the most powerful in the whole cycle of poems; they positively vibrate with meaning, if only we can bring to them a 'total response', in Jung's words.

In Williams's experience of the myth, springing from the hints in Malory, Dindrane is above all 'virgin', one-in-herself, the companion of the poet Taliessin, on all levels – body and heart, mind and spirit; she is the foster-mother of Galahad, the sister of Perceval – the feminine wisdom which is essential to his 'philosophical star'. But Logres, the collective culture of that era, was not ready for the 'new woman' who shines briefly through the story. Woman collectively would remain subject through many centuries to the dominant male, largely unconscious of that which her flesh always knows. Nevertheless the lady, 'mother of the nature of lovers, creature of exchange' had, before her disappearance with the Grail, given her life's blood so that an ordinary woman of this world might carry her life in her bloodstream and transmit it to the future. The sick woman had been in a coma – the 'flesh', the earth, had been too long despised in Christianity. The blood of Dindrane, the whole woman, gave her the possibility of renewal.

> Where it was still to-night, in the last candles of Logres,
> a lady danced, to please the sight of her friends;
> her cheeks were stained from the arteries of Percivale's
> sister.

This lady, dancing in the simple delights of human exchange, carried in her veins, unconsciously in the depths of her being, the life of the 'dead' woman whose 'exchanges' encompassed heaven and the whole world.

> Between them they trod the measure of heaven and earth,
> and the dead woman waited the turn and throe of the
> dance.

She, Dindrane, waited in the unconscious of women for the day when one here, one there, would awaken her from her sleep. She awaited 'the throe of the dance', and a throe means a pang of anguish, and more particularly a pang of childbirth. And the place where she lay in the poem was the ship of Solomon, Solomon whose image carries the meaning of the wise and understanding heart. She is held as in a womb, the fourth in the 'quadruplicate sacrum' of the Grail.

There is one other line which as yet we have not looked at, 'drained there of blood by the thighed wound'. By the use of the word 'thighed' Williams links the sacrifice of Dindrane to the wound of the maimed king, soon to be healed by Galahad. (It will be remembered he had also likened the menstrual blood of the natural woman to the blood of the Grail king in the Rose Garden poem.) The extraordinary interest of this passage lies in the fact that the actual wound of Perceval's sister was cut into her *arm*. The arm is a symbol of creative activity in this world; the thigh indicates male sexual power. The Grail King is wounded, his masculine strength is maimed so that he is unable to beget any new vision. The woman on the other hand is drained of blood from her arm, and her potentially active creativity sinks down again into the unconscious to await 'the throe of the dance' – those birth pangs which have come indeed to woman in the last 100 years. It is immediately after this shedding of Dindrane's blood that Galahad, her foster son, symbol of the whole man, heals the Grail King, but the great vision fails to become incarnate in the world precisely because the values of the whole woman could not yet be accepted. The Grail is withdrawn and with it Dindrane, the 'seeing' woman.

All this may be read as a symbolic statement of the situation in the middle years of this century – when the poet was writing – and also of the inner quest of every conscious woman, whether Williams was aware of this or not. If a woman's true creativity in the realm of Logos is wounded – if her 'arm' activity is used to manipulate instead of create, then man is emasculated. (It is not, of course, fundamentally a matter of cause and effect but of synchronicity.) If, however, her wound becomes sacrifice (the willing death for another which is the giving up of the animus-possessed demands of her ego) there will follow the rebirth. She returns in the 'throe' of the dance, in the true 'exchange' encompassing both earth and heaven, and with her she brings the long hidden Grail.

The human arm is that which distinguishes man from the animal and it symbolizes, as has been said, his relatedness to life. Dindrane gave blood from her arm and life to another. The dancing lady with the blood of Dindrane in her veins was the feminine counterpart of Bors, the husband and householder, who transmitted to his sons, as she to her daughters, the hidden intuition of the Grail, down through the centuries of growing humanism. With the dawning of the age of Aquarius, the age of seeing, which is contemplation, the age of the carrier of the water of life in a vessel, may we not see indeed the awakening of Dindrane, the woman consciously one-in-herself, no longer secluded from this world, but walking the streets of the City of God and mankind. So, in the words of Taliessin in the Rose Garden, she may 'bring to a flash of seeing the women in the world's base'.

Notes

1 C. W. Jung, *Collected Works*, Routledge & Kegan Paul, London, vol. 18, p. 678.
2 C. S. Lewis, *Arthurian Torso*, Oxford University Press, 1948.
3 Spring Publications, Dallas, 1973, p. 52.
4 C. G. Jung, *Letters*, vol. I, Princeton University Press, 1971, 1973, p. 474.

:6:

:SOPHIA: COMPANION·ON THE·QUEST:

CAITLIN·MATTHEWS

We are all involved on a personal quest, of which the Grail is an image, put there, as Caitlin Matthews tells us, 'to make us fall in love with an inner world'. For though the quest is indeed an interior one, it has to manifest in the outer world in order to satisfy our deepest needs, which are by extension the world's. We are all in exile from something: our homes, our childhood, love or God. The Grail shows us that we are also in exile from paradise, which is perhaps all these things, and that the Grail itself shares that state. This is made clear by the nature of the guide and companion who accompanies the Grail knights (and ourselves) on the quest, who shares our exile and seeks to return, through us, to the desired state. So that we see that we are as necessary to the guide as the guide is to us, a truth also applicable to the Grail. As we read: 'to drink from the Grail is to remember Paradise'. This is the experience sought for by all seekers; it should be our greatest source of inspiration.

The Grail quest is in many ways a paradigm of our own spiritual journey. It is a journey upon which we continually find and lose our way as we rediscover and forget what we have learned. The cyclic nature of life ensures that, whatever our achievements, we can never rest on our laurels: we cannot retain that moment of revelation. Whatever our path, this schema holds true. Whether we follow the well-beaten path that others have trod before us, or stride out into new regions of our own devising we meet the same defeats, make the same mistakes, follow the same wrong directions, whether through laziness, ignorance or despair. We embark upon our spiritual journey in a state of primal innocence, like Perceval, that most guileless of knights, when he leaves the womb-like enclosure of the wood where his mother has hidden him from life's realities. From the very first Perceval is hardly aware that he is on a quest at all: mistaking armed knights for angels, he acts unchivalrously to all and omits to ask the important Grail question which will end the Wounded King's pain. But, just as no one who sets out upon the spiritual journey is ever alone, neither is the Grail-seeker left lonely. It is with the identity of one mysterious companion on the quest that we shall be concerned in the course of this essay. She accompanies both the Grail knight and the mystic, and she is rarely absent from any spiritual tradition. In her localized appearance within the Grail legends she is called the Hideous Damsel or Cundrie; mystically speaking, her stature is vast – her ultimate archetype being that of Sophia, the Holy Wisdom of God. However we see her, the task of Sophia is to stimulate awareness or remembrance of paradise; for she is, *par excellence*, the symbolic personification of exile from paradise, as well as showing us the way of return to our original state. Whether we believe literally in the fall of the soul from grace or not, it is clear that, most of the time, we are in a state of forgetfulness – we are divided from our true nature. Sophia, in the person of the Hideous Damsel, fulfils this function specifically for Perceval, and as her role is neglected within the Vulgate cycle, where Galahad is shown as the Grail-winner, I shall be using examples only from those texts which feature Perceval.

Let us meet the Hideous Damsel, then, at the point when Perceval has omitted to ask the Grail question. Peredur (Welsh equivalent for Perceval) is seated with three others in Arthur's court when there enters:

> a black, curly haired woman, riding a yellow mule. . . . she had a rough, unlovable appearance: her face and hands were blacker than pitch, and yet it was her shape rather than her colour that was ugliest – high cheeks and a sagging

face, a snub, wide-nostrilled nose, one eye speckled grey and protruding, the other jet black and sunken, long teeth yellow as broom, a stomach that swelled up over her breasts and above her chin. Her backbone was shaped like a crutch; her hips were wide in the bone, but her legs were narrow, except for her knobbly knees and feet.[1]

She then admonishes Peredur for not having asked the Grail question, in this case why the spear ran with blood; for: 'Had you asked, the king would have been made well and the kingdom made peaceful, but now there will be battles and killing, knights lost and women widowed and children orphaned, all because of you.'[2] Likewise in *Parzival*, where the Hideous Damsel appears as Cundrie the Sorceress. Her appearance is equally hideous, yet she is given an extra dimension of learning, she is termed the Grail Messenger for by her coming is the Grail quest both hastened and eventually achieved.

But who is this ugly hag, and what is she doing in a tale which is an allegory of transcendent spirituality? There are many who would deny her place within the Grail canon at all, for is she not a creature grimed with vile matter and, moreover, a woman? To answer these questions fully we shall have to investigate the origins of the Hideous Damsel and consider the nature of the Divine Feminine. It will be necessary to put aside the mental overlay of dualism which has crept into our appreciation of the spiritual journey and to remember a time when the divine could be as well expressed by female as well as male symbolism. The Grail story has its own female protagonists, as we will see, whose function is as important as that of the Grail knights: their origin lies deeply embedded in the Celtic consciousness and has a direct bearing on our own approach to the spiritual journey. (See Ch. 5.)

Standing in seeming opposition to the Hideous Damsel within the Grail story is the Grail Maiden, she who carries the vessel in the Grail procession. Her description ensures that we do not confuse this lady with the black Cundrie:

Her face shed such refulgence that all imagined it was sunrise. This maiden was seen wearing brocade of Araby.

113

Upon a green achmardi she bore. . . . The Gral . . . She whom the Gral suffered to carry itself had the name of Repanse de Schòye. Such was the nature of the Gral that she who had the care of it was required to be of perfect chastity and to have renounced all things false.[3]

Both she and the Grail Messenger, Cundrie, serve the same end, yet how different is their appearance. The fact that these two figures are in the service of the Grail should give us some clue that they are the same archetype embodied in two guises. Yet this is not at all clear to anyone reading the texts. The nature of the Divine Feminine has been split into two camps: the pliant, acceptable image of sanctity and the threatening image of dark power.

The place of the feminine within the spiritual world and particularly within Christianity, has been ill-defined. The Church, having purged itself of its esoteric or mystical elements (or at least having relegated them to an 'official' position), developed the cult of the Virgin Mary as its only outlet for the feminine principle; stereotyped as the supreme mother, or as lifeless sanctities, the Virgin and the Holy Women, hardly presented fully developed examples of the Divine Feminine. The only 'dangerous' woman within the Christian corpus is the Magdalene, redeemed from earthly concupiscence as the penitent sinner: an archetype for all women to look up to. It was this heavy dualism which depressed the one supreme Goddess to the status of a female demon. As with the Divine Feminine, so with woman: woman was the gateway of the devil, the daughter of Eve through whom came the Fall. Our Hideous Damsel seems at first to partake of this dark image, yet she comes up through deeper levels than the Christian, from substrata which allowed the feminine to assume a fuller prominence than it did during the twelfth century, when the Grail legends were first recorded.

The Grail as vessel of grace is perhaps a familiar idea, but as a specifically feminine symbol it is almost unknown due to the Christian overlay having obscured much of its mysterious origin. The Grail legend existed in one form or another before Christianity shaped its framework and utilized its symbolism. It is perhaps only the greatest symbols which can be so universally applied. Although it seems far from the Christian ethic of Grail as Chalice of the Last Supper, it was once the province of the Divine Feminine to guard knowledge or wisdom. There has been much dismay in some circles that the Grail Bearer should be so unliturgically female: no woman of the time would have been allowed to touch the holy vessels after all. But this argument can be scotched straight away if we look at the Celtic roots of the Grail and its guardian. The Grail and its contents, although subsumed as an apocryphal Christian legend, have no connection with the Cup of the Last Supper and the Redemptive blood at the *earliest* levels of the story: they are directly descended from the ancient and holy belief in sovereignty – the personification of the land whom the candidate king has to espouse.

The ancient rite of kings is deeply concerned with the marriage of the sovereign to the land. This idea has not been totally lost as we can understand if we look no further than the English coronation rite where the monarch is ceremonially wedded to the land with the 'wedding ring of England', at the presentation of the regalia. If we go even further back we may trace this custom to the time when the Goddess and matrilinear descent were the rule; then the king held the land by right of his female relatives. He would often have to undergo a symbolic marriage with a priestess who represented the Goddess for the purposes of the ritual.

In the Irish tale the *Baile in Scaíl*, *The Phantom's Prophecy*, Conn, the King of Tara, stumbles into a mysterious landscape in which he enters a house. He and his companions see there 'a young maiden in a glass chair with a gold crown on her head and a cloak with borders of gold round her. A bowl of silver with four golden corners before her, full of red beer. A cup of gold on the ground. A beaker or cup of gold at her lips.'[4] The maiden is the Sovereignty of Ireland and she gives the bowl of silver to Conn, for it is his descendants who will rule the land. She could well be mistaken for the Grail Bearer, the one who confers enlightenment upon the knightly candidate on the quest; yet she has another face, which is revealed to us in a second Irish tale, that of *Niall of the Nine Hostages*. Here, Niall and his four brothers are serving their weapon training and living off the land. They lose their way and need water. The first brother finds a well but it is guarded by an ugly old hag who will only allow him to drink if he will kiss her. They each go in turn and have the same difficulty: each one returns waterless. Then Niall approaches the hag: he not only kisses her, he embraces her. As he releases her he finds that she has changed into the most beautiful woman in the world. In answer to his question, she replies: 'I am Sovereignty, King of Tara; your descendants will rule over every clan.' And she bids him return to his brothers but to grant them no water until they have acknowledged his seniority over them.

This is a powerful story which tells us much about the early origins of the Grail itself and its guardian. Whether we read of the maiden with the silver cup in the *Baile in Scaíl*, or of the Welsh tale of Ceridwen's Cauldron of Inspiration, or of the hag who guards the well, we may be sure that we are witnessing the ancient Goddess archetype in action.

In the quest for kingship the Hideous Damsel, Sovereignty, cannot assume her proper form nor can the quest succeed, if her ugly form is rejected. The test seeks to discover the one who shows himself more concerned with the land than with the glories of kingship. But what are the implications here for the Grail knight? If we relate the quest for the Grail with the quest for sovereignty, we will see many things in a new light.

We may recall that the result of achieving the Grail is the healing of the Wounded King and the flowering of the Waste Land. From earliest times, especially in Celtic understanding, a maimed or wounded king could not reign – he had to be a whole man. This is the theme of another Irish story when Nuadu, King of the Tuatha de Danaan, loses his arm in the Battle of Mag Tuired. Sovereignty is disputed and bestowed upon another, even though Nuadu is provided with a silver arm in replacement. It is not until his arm is miraculously restored in the flesh that he is allowed to resume the kingship. The implication with the Wounded Grail King is that he is wounded in the genitals or, euphemistically, through the thigh, so that he cannot be joined in union with the land as Sovereignty – therefore the Land is laid waste. The Grail knight's quest, then, is the healing of his king: a fate in which he shares for the whole kingdom suffers. Sovereignty, then, is radically important to an understanding of the Grail legends: not only is the Grail Maiden a reflection of a once-potent image of the Divine Feminine, but so too is the Grail Messenger, the Hideous Damsel. The two faces of Sovereignty re-emerge in the Grail legend as two separate characters; they also may stand for the Land which suffers and is laid waste – as black and unwanted as the Hideous Damsel – and for the healing of the Land, whereby Sovereignty can assume her former condition as the beautiful Grail Maiden.

If the pagan origins of the Grail legends have been over-stressed here, it is only in an attempt to balance the over-emphasis elsewhere on the Christian parallels which are often easier to perceive. The companion on the quest, the Hideous/ Beautiful Maiden, is not peculiar to the Grail quest alone; nor is she solely the province of the pagan past. Before we can see the Grail quest as a type of our spiritual journey, we must examine the mystical tradition – Jewish, as well as Christian – where we shall find our companion in other guises, as well as uncovering a secret tradition which perpetuates the hidden wisdom of the ages.

'Exile chills my heart. May He who numbered the stars guide you in helping us and lead us back to happiness.'[5] says Arthur's mother in *Parzival*. The sense of exile is strong upon us. In every culture there is some legend of how humanity fell out of harmony with God. Among Jews and Christians this legend is found in Genesis, where we follow the Fall of Adam and Eve from paradise: it is an account, in mystical language, of the rupture between God and humanity. Unfortunately, mystical accounts have a way of being interpreted fundamentally, with a view to historicity rather than as allegorical parallels. The Fall, read in isolation, augurs ill for a people exiled from God. But within Christianity the Redemption is a natural concomitant of the Fall which is known liturgically as *felix culpa*, the happy fault whereby Christ came to redeem the world; without the first Adam there would have been no second Adam (Christ) to help us. Logically, following from this, the *ave* of *Ave Maria* (Hail Mary) is a reversal of Eva's name, as Mary also redeems the fault of Eve, the Mother of all living. The Fall is our exile from paradise; we make a Waste Land of the Garden of Eden. The quest is our spiritual journey and the Grail is our return to our sovereign condition as kings and queens of creation. Whatever the orthodox account of the Fall, every culture seems to have developed its own apocryphal explanation of how a part of paradise dwelt among humanity in order to provide a chance of return. The Grail legend is the European response to this exile: but why wasn't the religion of the time deemed sufficiently efficacious?

In his *Flight of the Wild Gander*, Joseph Campbell asks why 'anyone in the Middle Ages should have thought it necessary to embark on such a lonely, dangerous enterprise (i.e. the Grail quest) when the Holy Mass, with Christ himself on the altar, was being celebrated, right next door, every day'.[6]

As we have already seen, the Grail itself does not necessarily derive from Christian origins, although it has been incorporated into its symbolism. The Grail quest incorporates dimensions which are implicit yet not doctrinally apparent within Christianity. It is a necessity for every soul to find its individual return from exile: a return which may pursue or avoid the usual channels of exoteric belief. The fact is that achieving the Grail was not just a parallel experience to that of receiving communion at Mass: it was far more than this. Partaking of communion can be the ultimate knowing – the union of Creator with created – but unless the communicant brings imaginative awareness to the sacrament, the inner and outer worlds run forever on parallel tracks, never to merge as one. The mystery of communion must be actualized in everyday life, not be relegated to some never-never land of spirituality. In its exoteric expression, Christianity fails to give any sense of personal responsibility for one's redemption. Few Christians think beyond the possibilities of free will which is the birthright of humanity alone. It was the exercise of free will which resulted in the Fall; yet why should free will not be exercised positively towards ending our exile?

This question has never been squarely faced within exoteric Christianity: faith, good works and the reception of the sacraments are proposed as the instruments of the Redemption.

Mystically, there is an esoteric quorum within all religions which proposes an alternative and more personally responsible response. Christianity has relegated its esoteric tradition to a 'safe' expression of mysticism; it has purged itself of the Divine Feminine, of a mystery tradition, of anything smacking of private revelation. Yet, despite this, the Grail tradition lived on through an age which saw the destruction of both Cathars and Knights Templar, two different groups whose show of autonomy and grasp of mystical insight, among other things, antagonized the Church. The Grail has never been officially sanctioned by the Church, yet neither has it ever been denied. The Church even had its own Grail story. So popular were Arthurian tales at one time, the Grail legend was turned to good effect by the monks of Glastonbury who took Perceval the Fool and turned him into Perlesvaus: 'He who has lost the valley', recognizing him as a type of Christ, and making the Grail story one of scintillating Christian allegory. So the Grail legend worked on two levels: exoterically as a popular story, esoterically as an alternative path to God, a release from exile.

But what of other traditions? The Jewish conception of the Fall has a distinctly different emphasis. Here the sense of exile is stronger, the urge to return more immediate. In esoteric Judaism, specifically within the Qabala, we see the exile from God expressed in terms of a relationship. The Covenant that God makes with Israel is more like a marriage contract than a legal document. If we follow the esoteric symbolism of Qabala we find our companion once more: not as Hideous Damsel or Grail Maiden, although they share a common imagery, but as Shekinah. The Shekinah was said to reside with God from the beginning of creation; her appearance in the biblical books of wisdom and within Qabalistic texts such as the *Zohar* give us a clear picture of her function in the way of Return.

She appears in this account of the creation from the book of Proverbs:

> The Lord created me at the beginning of his work, the first of his acts of old. Ages ago I was set up, at the first, before the beginning of the earth. . . . When he established the heavens, I was there, . . . when he marked out the founda-

tions of the earth, then I was beside him, like a master workman; and I was daily his delight . . .[7]

It is evident from this account that God and his Shekinah are joined together in a loving partnership. When Adam and Eve eat of the Tree and are cast out of paradise, the Shekinah decides to descend with them; if the unity of God and creation is broken then there can be no union between God and his Shekinah. She goes into voluntary exile with humanity, then; wherever she appears it is as the expression of God's compassion. Yet she is more than an abstract emanation from the Godhead. She inhabits the Ark of the Covenant, going before it in the desert as pillar of cloud by day and a pillar of flame by night: a visible presence of God's dwelling among the Israelites. The Ark, like the Grail, is a relic of great power: it is a piece of paradise. (We will remember that the Grail in *Parzival* is termed *lapsit exillis* or 'stone that fell from heaven'; it is said elsewhere to have been an emerald which fell from Lucifer's crown at the rebellion of the Fallen Angels.) The Shekinah herself is both a personification of that lost paradise as well as becoming associated with the exile from it. She accompanies Israel through the desert until the Ark is eventually housed within the Temple. The destruction of the Temple in 586 BC strengthened the Jewish sense of exile on every level: the Ark was dispersed and its whereabouts became unknown. (But see Ch. 4.) The Shekinah had no dwelling; henceforward she would live in the hearts of her people. By performing such acts which were pleasing to the Shekinah, the pious Jew hastened the return; works of evil saddened the Shekinah and prolonged the exile. For the Jews, the Ark takes on the significance of the Grail – the subject of an interior quest.

The Shekinah is, then, the female counterpart of God; Qabalistic texts go so far as to call her God's wife, for whom he is sundered by the Fall and the continuing sinfulness of humanity. The complexity of the Shekinah is appreciable only if we understand that her imagery stems from that of the Canaanite and Mesopotamian goddess Astarte, or Ishtar, who reigned in heaven supreme with her consort Baal, or Tammuz. Divinity was once expressed by the divine Lord and Lady who ruled as a partnership. The Shekinah is the symbolic descendant of this goddess as well as expressing the feminine nature of an otherwise very patriarchal deity. God's Shekinah was associated with the state of the Israelites themselves who were also the exiled and the promised of God. In the Lamentation of Jeremiah over the fall of Jerusalem we see the city personified as the Shekinah:

> How like a widow has she become, she that was great
>   among the nations!
> She that was a princess among the cities has become
>   a vassal.
> She weeps bitterly in the night, tears on her cheeks,
> among all her lovers she had none to comfort her. . . .
> Judah has gone into exile because of affliction and
>   hard servitude;
> she dwells now among the nations but finds no resting
>   place . . .
> From the daughter of Zion has departed all her majesty.[8]

This is a picture of the manifest Shekinah, the exiled majesty and wisdom of God; personification of a people who have lost their sovereignty. In the biblical books of wisdom, the Shekinah is also called Chokmah, or Wisdom: she who cries aloud in the streets, the one who guards the fountain of wisdom which, like the Grail, brings the soul to its right senses. Wisdom or the Shekinah is the hope of restoration; on the day when the exile is ended she is commanded to:

Take off the garment of your sorrow and affliction, O Jerusalem, and put on for ever the beauty of the glory from God.
Put on the robe of the righteousness from God;
put on your head the diadem of the glory of the Everlasting.
For God will show your splendour everywhere under heaven.[9]

Here the Shekinah as Wisdom is spoken of in her transcendent guise: the one who is no longer in exile but in union with God. For the most striking image of the Shekinah is that of wife, of beloved. The mystic has always dealt in sexual imagery to express his union or separation from the Divine. With the Shekinah the image is extended, by implication, to humanity which is seen as God's beloved. Pious Jewish couples made love on

121

the eve of the Sabbath in imitation of God's union with the Shekinah. Qabalists employed extraordinary techniques of meditation for visualizing this divine union, striving to hasten the return to God.

The symbolism of the Shekinah did not just remain the province of Judaism: the post-exilic period (500 BC onwards) saw the rise of Qabalistic mysticism and the great cross-fertilization of religious concepts within the Jewish, Hellenic and Christian worlds. Gnostic Christianity raised the figure of Wisdom, Sophia, to a position which almost rivalled that of Christ; within their apocryphal gospels they reworked the Shekinah's descent as Sophia's Fall, making her responsible for the creation of the world. Despite the incipient dualism of these texts we find again two faces of Sophia: the fallen Sophia, called Achamoth, who roams the world in sorrow and confusion, and Sophia herself, the transcendent queen of heaven whose union with the Logos (God's emanation or Word) marked the end of creation's exile.

Orthodox Western Christianity may have neglected its esoteric side, but the great mystical texts of the Bible still convey a sense of both Shekinah and Sophia to those mystics who are able to interpret them and comprehend their significance. In both Jewish and Gnostic texts we find the same account of the exile from God, the separation of lover and beloved; Shekinah and Sophia make their appearance among humanity as a way of return, taking on firstly the dark, exiled face as an identification with a lost people; lastly they both appear in their radiant and transcendent guise as saviours. This is most clear in *Parzival*, where the Hideous Damsel, Cundrie, rides to the Grail Castle, where the Wounded King still lies in agony; she goes dressed in a hood of black samite upon which is embroidered 'a flock of Turtle-doves finely wrought in Arabian gold in the style of the Gral-insignia'.[10] She accompanies Parzival to the castle in order that he may answer the Grail question correctly. At sight of her habit, the Grail knights cry: 'Our trouble is over! What we have been longing for ever since we were ensnared by sorrow is approaching us under the Sign of the Gral! . . . Great happiness is on its way to us!'[11] Cundrie's black appearance may have deceived us into thinking her a malevolent witch concerned with obstructing the Grail quest, but we see from her apparel that the Hideous Damsel is sister to the Shekinah and to Sophia. The dove has always been the symbol of divine compassion. It was a bird sacred to the Goddess and it passed into the panoply of the Shekinah where it symbolized God's Holy Spirit. Within Christianity the Holy Spirit's doubtful gender has been obscured by its symbolization as a dove: the promise of ultimate redemption, the perfect indwelling of God. From the beginning of time where the Holy Spirit brooded over the waters at the Creation it is this image of hope which inspires those upon the spiritual journey to continue. However the Holy Spirit is theologically understood today, it stems from its origins as part of the Divine Feminine: the holy Motherhood of God. In this tangle of symbolism Christ has assumed the attributes of Wisdom; he is seen as the expression of God's Word (Logos) and God's Wisdom (Sophia) throughout the New Testament: 'In the beginning was the Word, and the Word was with God and the Word was God. He was in the beginning with God,'[12] just as Wisdom or the Shekinah is in Proverbs 8, Christ is the one 'in whom are hid all the treasures of wisdom and knowledge'.[13] But although there has been a transition of genders the symbolism has been perpetuated within esoteric Christian tradition. The Shekinah is primarily a figure of the Old Testament. The New Testament sees a restatement of both Sophianic and Messianic principles, the manifestations of God's power, investing both in the person of Christ. Christ is male, yet the feminine symbology is not neglected as the Messiah needs the means to manifest. 'The first Adam is moulded from the vile dust of the earth, the second comes forth from the precious womb of the Virgin.'[14] Mary fulfils the role of the second Eve, as well as embodying the principles of the Shekinah. For she is not just a receptacle or vehicle of incarnation for Christ, but she is also a representative of exiled humanity. Her flesh clothes the divinity of the manifest God, Christ. Human and divine meet in a mystical marriage which is birth, death and consummation all at once: this is the experience of communion. In transubstantiation, ordinary bread and wine are changed into the body and blood of Christ: in metaphysical terms, the body and blood of Christ are of Mary as his mother, yet they also represent the inspiriting divinity of the Messiah.

123

(See Ch. 10.) It is not possible to think in terms of the feminine as matter, the male as spirit in this context, for a real union of the two has taken place. The spiritual realities are almost alchemical:

> the heavenly Spirit makes fertile the womb of the virginal font, by the secret admixture of his light, that it may bring forth as heavenly creatures, and bringing back to the likeness of their Creator, those whom their origin in earth's dust had produced as men of dust in miserable state.[15]

Both Sophia and Christ share the Messianic task; both share the exile among humanity, striving to make it remember its likeness to the Creator; both are the means of return from exile.

If we re-examine the Grail legend in this light, we will find startling parallels which are pertinent to our spiritual journey. In the common language of mysticism there is really no conflict between Judaism, Christianity, or any other religious path: these are but means to arrive at a cessation from exile. If the exoteric sides of religion have not been clear enough in their definitions, an esoteric response has always arisen within or parallel to that religion. Within the Grail legend symbolism, both cultural and religious, mingles in a spontaneous and immediate story.

We are in exile, or in a state of forgetfulness. We have lost our sovereignty, our state of union with the divine. Yet the companion of the quest is with us as a potentiality. Perceval is called 'the son of the widow'; an image in which we see ourselves reflected as children both of the exiled Sophia, and Christ, the son of Mary. The Waste Land is our state of exile: the place that is not paradise; it is the violated Jerusalem: whether as the Holy City fought over by Jews, Christians and Moslems, or as the exiled Sophia herself. The Grail is that piece of paradise which remains among us, hidden and transcendent, the cup of sovereignty, of wisdom: a draft from that cup is a remembrance of paradise, a union of soul with God. The Wounded King is the potential Grail Knight himself, a symbol of lost sovereignty; or he is Christ, the crucified King wounded with five wounds, whom each sin wounds afresh. Within the Grail legend we find a mystery tradition which embodies much that is common to

124

the major religions. It is not difficult to see just why it evokes such a popular response wherever it is spoken of.

The awareness of our exile has been blunted in this age. Few people concertedly follow a mystical path which helps them recall the fact that they have a spiritual heritage. We live in a state of forgetfulness. Yet while the major religions seem to decline, there is a corresponding upsurge of interest in the spiritual quest. This often takes some very strange forms. In Steven Spielberg's recent film, *Raiders of the Lost Ark* (1980), we see the goal of the spiritual quest pursued as a physical object. Like the Grail, the Ark of the Covenant is hidden or withdrawn; its power is immanent, not apparent. In the film the Ark is sought by rival interests: on the one hand, evil seeks to use it for its own ends, on the other, the Ark is sought as an archeological treasure. Neither side take into account what can happen if one seeks a spiritual principle as though it were an object. The Ark, like the Grail, is full of power; within the film, the force of the Shekinah reveals itself in such strength that evil is completely overcome on either side, and is replaced by a sense of responsibility. Although this film is a shadow of the real spiritual journey, its universal distribution may have helped awaken some sense of exile, of a yearning to rediscover what is truly our heritage. Stranger vehicles for the action of Sophia have been known. The confusion of an earthly for a heavenly treasure has dogged the history of religion. The heavenly Jerusalem cannot be established on earth; the Wounded King is not a real king, nor is the Grail a physical object. We understand this better if we see these symbols as belonging to the soul itself. The mystique of the Grail symbolism is set there to make us fall in love with an interior world; we must yearn with all our hearts to be there, to inhabit that world and work with these principles. If we apply the Grail principle spiritually, it follows that it will automatically have its reflection in the real world.

The Grail Maiden, the Shekinah or Sophia, is a personification of that holy object; she is the Grail or the Ark, the hidden treasure which symbolizes the union of the soul with the Divine. We find and lose this Grail continually. There is no means to come to spiritual union, to meet the shining glory of

Sophia without we first embrace the Hideous Damsel who is the reality of ourselves. As individuals we cannot embark upon a quest to save the world, without first attending to our own condition. The bitter cup precedes the golden Grail. We are all lost, in exile, out of harmony with ourselves, unaware of the divine spark within us. We all yearn to recover our lost happiness; yet how shall we do this? First of all, by assuming a sense of responsibility towards ourselves: this is not selfishness but common sense. Only those who start the journey deserve to win the Grail; if we wait for everyone else to join our party we shall never begin. It does not matter if we make mistakes along the way. The Grail Messenger, the Hideous Damsel, will soon let us know: we must heed her as the inner voice, the Will of God. Her voice is harsh and its advice unwelcome; but only by knowing ourselves thoroughly will we be able to continue.

As the quest continues, the idea will begin to impinge upon us that we are not searching for a physical object: this is but a symbol of our yearning for union. As day succeeds day, the awful thought grows: there is no Grail, no blaze of glory, no merging into the infinite. Perhaps we will never see the reality of the Grail Maiden, we will be in exile for ever? There is no progress on this path; it is a false assumption that the further on we go the better we become. The path is about forgetting and remembering, and, therefore, ultimately about *awareness*. We need to ask the Grail question. The spiritual journey, our quest, is also its conclusion. We are all on this journey: all we have to do is make the decision to be aware of the fact. We begin to be aware of the suffering of others and their sense of exile from themselves; we begin to realize the compassion of Sophia, our hidden companion, as our own compassion.

Those who are on quest are like those who devote themselves to the Bodhisattva concept. In Buddhism, a Bodhisattva is one who vows never to re-enter Nirvana until 'the last blade of grass' enters first. It is an awesome concept. We begin our quest in seeming selfishness and continue in total unselfishness. We identify with the sign of hope – the exiled Sophia – becoming co-workers with her in seeking to hasten the union of all beings. God, the Divine, is not outside us but within us. While there can be no ultimate universal union yet, we can strive for remembrance of what we really are, unifying ourselves with the principle of quest which we live by. For the essence of the Grail quest is not to disappear into a never-never land of no return; our duty is to return bearing the gifts of the Grail within ourselves, that we might be a cup, a means of regeneration and remembrance to every living creature. We become the Grail that others might drink; for to find the Grail is to become it. Perceval, unlike Galahad, returns from his Grail quest, becoming the king of the Grail castle. The Wounded King finds his sovereignty once more and is healed. The Waste Land and, by implication, the Hideous Damsel, are restored to their former beauty. The Grail itself ceases to be an object and becomes a living reality. Sophia is restored to unity once again, returning from exile in union with the Grail winner.

The two faces of Sophia as Hideous Damsel and Grail Maiden have accompanied us on our quest, the one prompting, the other leading us on. We understand now that the return to paradise will not be bequeathed to us from on high; the reality lies in our hands. Our spiritual journey is after all the return from exile, the quest upon which Sophia accompanies us always.

Notes

1 *Peredur*, in the *Mabinogion* trans. Jeffrey Gantz, Harmondsworth, Penguin, 1976, p. 248.
2 *Ibid.*
3 *Parzival* by Wolfram von Eschenbach, trans. A. T. Hatto, Harmondsworth, Penguin, 1980, p. 125.
4 Arthur C. L. Brown, *The Origin of the Grail Legend*, Harvard University Press, 1943, p. 219.
5 *Parzival, op. cit.*, p. 330.
6 Joseph Campbell, *Flight of the Wild Gander*, Indiana, Gateway Editions, 1951, p. 219.
7 Proverbs VIII: 22, 23, 27, 29, 30. R.S.V. Bible.
8 Lamentations I: 1–3, 6.
9 Baruch V: 1–3.
10 *Parzival, op. cit.*, p. 386.
11 *Parzival, op. cit.*, p. 393.
12 St John I: 1–2.
13 Colossians II: 3.

14 St Peter Chrysologus, Sermon 117, in *The Divine Office*, vol. 3,
London, Collins, 1974, p. 684.
15 *Ibid*., p. 685.

:7:

:THE·WORLD'S·NEED:

·

BRIAN·CLEEVE

·

There are as many arguments about the nature of the Grail as there are about the nature of God: and none are conclusive. Here Brian Cleeve offers a new approach. There are many grails, vessels of grace, both physical and spiritual; but the most important aspect of the matter is not 'What is the Grail?', nor even 'Does it exist?'. The heart of the matter is the responsibility placed upon each of us, to protect the world from the evil we bring to it. In so doing we protect ourselves, as well as our world: both are equally in peril. And if we perform our task as protectors, even while we search for the Grail, then sooner or later it will reveal its most potent message: that the Grail serves us as we serve the Grail. To receive this message we must learn the true meaning of service: a task no more easy than learning and performing the will of God.

The question which I wish to ask, and attempt to answer in this essay, is whether the Grail has any importance for our everyday lives, and in order to do this I want first to consider it as an object, rather than as the subject of various legends. Did it ever have, does it still have, any material existence, and if so, what was it, or what is it? And if it ever existed materially, did it also have any spiritual significance? Finally, most vital of all aspects of the question – does it still have any significance? And not to be mysterious about it, my submission will be – with various qualifications that will become apparent as I continue –

that it did exist, it still does exist, and that it has an immense, an immeasurable importance for everyone.

However, it would be foolish to pretend that anything in the nature of proof could be offered, even on the historical level. Even if perfect evidence existed, if, for example, one could produce a terracotta cup with irrefutable 'provenance', as art dealers express it, tracing it to the Last Supper beyond all shadow of doubt, this would not 'prove' it to be that Grail which by definition has a spiritual significance. All that we can hope to do, if our inclinations lie in that direction, is to examine the idea of the Grail from various angles, and make up our minds as to whether such a possibility seems at all likely. Does it fit in with other things about which we already feel greater certainty? And would it fit in with the general pattern of exist- ence, like the missing piece of a jigsaw puzzle, or would it create new difficulties if we were to try to accept it, by making other desirable ideas seem impossible?

This last question can be quickly answered. The idea of the Grail fits in very well with the general run of mankind's ideas. Most cultures have had some notion of a source of all fertility, of renewal and rebirth, whether it is a fountain of youth, or the Islands of the Blest, or a magic cauldron, or a Horn of Plenty, or a mysterious, symbolic object only to be revealed to initiates, or the potency of the king, to offer some examples out of many.

Moreover, these beliefs do not merely parallel those connected with the Grail, they sometimes converge on them, and even seem intimately connected with them, as in the case of the king's potency as a prerequisite for the land's fertility. Also, the relationship between the king and a magical object, essential to the Grail legends, is a widespread belief, to be found in periods and places untouched by 'our' Grail legends. For example, the pharaoh's divine good fortune was considered to be intimately connected with his afterbirth, always carefully preserved at the birth of a royal prince.

Indeed, the pharaoh's afterbirth was considered to be his 'other self', and was so charged with royal virtue that a mere representation of it in a piece of cloth could convey this virtue elsewhere. Such pieces of cloth were sent by the pharaoh to his distant army commanders to convey his virtue, his good fortune, to them, and bring them success in war. From which practice, so it is claimed, arose the tradition of carrying the royal standard into battle, and the mystical attachment of soldiers and sailors and even civilians to 'the flag'. The king, the monarchy, the state – even if it is a republic – are in some inexplicable, spiritual way not only represented by the flag, but identified with it.

So to think of 'the Grail' as an object charged with magical, mystical significance, with the essence of royalty, and with all that royalty means in the sense of 'right order', of natural and spiritual well being and fertility, and as an object intimately connected, or identified, with a particular king, is not at all strange or inconsonant with the general run of human belief.

Which, of itself, proves nothing, of course, except that the Grail legend or its central idea at least, is compatible with the whole idea of kingship. Perhaps 'the Grail' represents for the world what the royal standard did for armies – a purveyor of good, of virtue, of strength, of Grace. Or rather, not a purveyor, for that would suggest a degree of independence, of separation between king and standard, God and Grail – but a *channel*, a physical means by which the royal or divine virtue might flow from its source to its desired destination.

But, from where did kings obtain their authority, their store of virtue? Only from God. The whole essence of kingship is its divine connection. The king is God's representative, chosen by God, anointed as a sign of God's approval and of the delegation of God's authority. The crown itself represents a divine halo. It is therefore easy to visualize the king and his standard, or any other symbol of his royal authority, as a reflection, or a microcosm, of the relationship between God and Grail.

In the legends, the wounded Fisher King stands for no less a person than God Himself. For the traffic between king and standard is not a one-way affair. The king sends his virtue through and with the standard, but if the standard falls to the enemy, it is not simply the standard that is lost; the king himself is injured – in his authority, in his power to govern. His 'luck', his 'fortune', his kingship itself, have been injured and even crippled. Only the recovery of the standard can cure the king's wounded majesty. Is it therefore too fanciful to suggest that if the Grail is somehow injured by opponents of God, that God may be injured? If you are a Christian this idea will not be difficult to accept, for it is part of basic Christian doctrine that when Christ, God's representative and true self, was crucified, God was crucified in and with Him.

At which point, someone may object that it is the very existence of Christ that makes the idea of the Grail as a source of Grace unthinkable, and unnecessary. Christ, says the Christian, brought infinite Grace into the world, and was all-sufficient in this matter for ever and for everyone. There should be no need of a Grail to do the same work.

The idea that Christ brought Grace into the world for the first time – that until He came no human being could receive the Grace necessary to enter Heaven, is contradicted by the Bible itself. Enoch 'walked with God' and did not 'know death'. Elijah was taken up into Heaven and equally seems not to have tasted death. Abraham, and the Patriarchs, all knew and pleased God. Moses talked with God 'as a man talks to a friend'. Isaiah was accepted by God as His messenger. St John the Baptist, who announced Christ's arrival, died before the Crucifixion and Resurrection. Is one to suppose that these men, not to speak of Samuel, of Solomon, of Joseph, of Gideon, Joshua, Deborah, Heber, Ruth, Naomi, Sarah, and all the other heroes and heroines of the Old Testament, having been approved of and loved by God in their lives, were not welcomed into heaven by Him at their deaths?

If one is to believe in the concept of Divine Grace as the only means of salvation one must believe that it existed before Christ's birth, and not simply after his death, when he 'descended into hell' to liberate the good men and women of the Old Testament.

What Christ did was not to bring a new thing into the world – He did not claim that He was doing so – but to bring a great increase of what already existed, which He makes clear more than once.

Allow then that Grace existed before Christ came, just as it continued to exist after He ascended into Heaven. Was there any need for a physical channel of such Grace? If there was, what was it? And did Christ's coming do away forever with the need for it?

There are only two ways in which Grace might reach a human being: either directly from God, the source of all Grace, or indirectly through some intermediary person or means. And the almost universal opinion of Christians is that we receive Grace through some intermediary; through water at baptism, and the performance of a ceremony by a priest; through the Host at communion and the priest's consecration of the sacrifice; through the laying on of hands at a priest's ordination and so on. Above all, through Christ's physical self-sacrifice on the Cross. Not that He *gave* each of us Grace, but that He made it available for us to receive, if in some way we are made *worthy* to receive it, through our own efforts or those of others, the saints, who are said to earn a surplus of Grace which can be distributed to the weaker, but still deserving, brethren.

That there is still one, central source of Grace is suggested also by the example of Nature. All energy for life on earth derives from the sun – which in turn depends on a long-ago, unimaginable cosmic event. What the sun is to material life, I beg to suggest the Grail is to spiritual life. Or else one might prefer a more homely image, and compare the Grail to a spring of water in the desert, and our world as the oasis around that spring. Grace is the 'living water' of that spring, and the material Grail is the basin, rocky hollow or stone fountain in which the water rises and lies waiting for us to draw from it. God has made the spring itself inexhaustible: but if the desert is to be irrigated we must make the effort to fetch the water. Which, of course, few of us are willing to do.

Christ was the chief 'material' intermediary between us and God during His life and at His death. He was God in the world. Would it be absurd to regard Him as a *living* Grail for that time? A channel through which all Divine Grace entered the world? And if that was so, might there not have been a single intermediary before He arrived to transcend it? And might He not have chosen to leave behind another such intermediary when He returned to be with God and to be God?

Indeed He tells us Himself that this was to be so. The 'Comforter', the Holy Spirit, was to be sent to replace Him, to remain with us always. And before you object that the Holy Spirit is not an object, is utterly immaterial, remember that Christ too was immaterial, as well as material. He was God as well as man, spirit as well as body. Is it possible that in sending the Holy Spirit, God provided It with a material body, or *symbol*? Just as the royal standard symbolizes the royal authority? And not only to represent it, but in a real sense to *be* what it symbolizes? To be the physical channel by which the Holy Spirit, God's Grace and Life, should enter the world, as during the lifetime of Jesus it entered the world through Him? (See Ch. 6, pp. 111–28.)

In the history of God's dealings with us, is there any object which could be regarded as performing the functions of the Grail before the birth of Christ? One object which immediately comes to mind is The Ark of the Covenant. And following the Ark of the Covenant, there is the Holy of Holies in Solomon's Temple, or possibly some object *within* the Holy of Holies, such as the altar stone. (And it will not escape anyone that in some of the legends we are concerned with the Grail is described as a stone.)

The Grail legends themselves offer no single image of the Grail; it is dish, cup, stone, mysterious, unidentifiable abstraction – with pagan echoes of magic cauldrons and even of severed heads that talk and feast with the living. Or else it is the cup of the Last Supper, or Christ's blood *in* the cup, or in a phial.

Either the various legends have no real connection one with another, or they do indeed refer to the same 'reality' but for some reason disagree about its description. Or else that 'reality' varies, so that now the Grail is one object and now another. For our present purpose I suggest that 'our' material Grail was indeed the cup of the Last Supper, and that the confusion about its nature in the various poems and legends concerning it and its story arose in the main from the secrecy that surrounded it. I suggest too, as I have written elsewhere,[1] that the cup was brought to England, not by the Jospeh of Arimathea who helped to bury Jesus, but by his son, also called Joseph, who was a companion of John the Evangelist on Patmos, and to whom John gave the cup.

The cup was eventually brought to Wales, and guarded there by an Order of Knights, whose initiation rituals and ordeals underlie the legends of the 'Grail Quest'. When this Order disbanded, some account of its existence, and of the Grail, found its way into European poetry through the work of the Normanized Welsh poet and prince, Bledri ap Cadivor, identified by J. L. Weston and others[2] with the Bleheris of Wauchier de Denain's continuation of *Perceval* and with Master Blihis of the *Elucidation* etc., who had been a member of the Order. The Grail itself survived, still in secret, and guarded not by a new Order of Knights but by a single family, whose descendants kept it safe from discovery or injury until recent times.

Once in every succeeding century the Grail was removed from its hiding place for a few hours, to be used in a centennial Mass, whose purpose was to release into the world that store of Grace which had been accumulated by the efforts of the good. Otherwise it remained hidden. The actual cup of the Last Supper was not an expensive or luxurious object. It was a cheap terracotta krater of what we think of as Greek design, more like a deep saucer with two handles than our conception of a cup; coarsely decorated, bought in a bazaar in Capernaum for a few coppers. But for such an object to survive unbroken for almost two thousand years, unless it was safely buried for almost all of them, would be next to impossible. So that at the end of its stay in Glastonbury it was encased in gold, as the precious relic it was, and the form the golden reliquary took was that of a chalice. Thereafter, in order to use it there was no need to take it out of its reliquary. It remained like that, hidden from view in its sheath of heavy gold, from that day until early in this century.

Yet if it was physically hidden, its spiritual reality still needed protection. Just as each of us must earn our Grace, so all of us must protect our source of Grace – by the volume and intensity of our united efforts to obtain it.

For those who insist on the all-sufficiency of Christ in this regard there is an answer in the Gospels. He did not say, 'I have done all that is necessary, take your ease.' He said 'Take up your Cross.' He said 'Hard is the way' and 'Many are called but few are chosen.' He made it abundantly clear that we must make tremendous efforts if we are to reach God. But for His intercession, but for God's mercy, even those efforts would be unavailing. But without those efforts, we are warned specifically that the Gates of Heaven will be closed against us. Therefore the concept that we must ourselves protect the Grail, protect our own source or channel of Grace should offend no one.

And, of course, the Grail is not solely a Christian reality. It serves the whole of humanity, and its protection is the duty of all that part of humanity that desires to obey and serve God. The good Moslem, the good Hindu, the good Jew, the good agnostic – for that matter the good atheist, however unwittingly – are among the protectors of the Grail. Just as the bad Christians are among its enemies.

Accepting that goodness in Christ's sense of the word is a rare thing, requiring a life of self-sacrifice, but that it is essential if the Grail is to be protected, the Grail's situation becomes precarious. I suggested just now that it could be compared to a spring of water and the stone fountain in which the water gathers. The oasis that surrounds it depends for its existence on the spring. But the spring in turn depends on the oasis for its protection. If the oasis were to be neglected, if its trees were not watered and its grass tended, they would die. The desert would take over, the sand would invade the fountain and choke the spring.

Imagine now that that oasis was first created by a king, who had the well dug, the basin made out of marble, the trees and grass planted, all for the benefit of a tribe of desert nomads whose lives were in peril for lack of water. 'Here', said the king, 'is life for you. Without me, you could not have created this oasis, because you did not know how. Now it exists, look after it. There is all the water here you can possibly desire. All you need do is come with your water skins to collect it and carry it away, the stronger collecting more to help the weaker and the helpless. And of course you must not pollute the spring with filth, nor allow anyone to cut down the trees for firewood. And you must water the trees and the grass, and maintain the stone wall round the oasis to keep out the sand. Now be happy.'

Unfortunately, being human, most of the tribesmen did nothing of the kind. Few of them would do anything but what was essential for their own survival. So that the oasis grew more and more neglected, the surrounding wall crumbled, the outermost trees withered, the grass grew trampled and brown, filth littered the approaches to the spring, and only the heroic efforts of a few kept things from catastrophe. Day by day the possibility increased that even their efforts would fail, while the many shrugged their shoulders and laughed, saying, 'If this oasis fails, the king will dig us another well and plant more trees for us. It's his job.' But it is not His job. It is ours.

And this is our situation now. The threat has always been there, from the beginning, but it is in the last two centuries that the threat has become mortal. Evil has always existed in the world, and obtained entry for more evil, but in these last centuries the river of evil has become a flood. And just as the source of our Grace, the channel and *means* of it entering our world is the Grail, so the physical means of evil entering our world is the Black Grail, the Grail's counterpart.

To describe the Black Grail, its origin and management, the people who control it and are controlled by it, and the exact use they make of it, would require another essay as long as this one. Here I can only say that it exists. Those who control it are far more numerous and in a worldly sense far more powerful than those concerned with the True Grail – as one might expect. And for the past hundred years, once their power had grown sufficient, their main concern has been to obtain control over the True Grail, and destroy it.

Evil, you may say, cannot destroy good. Indeed. But good must be *created*. As has been said, goodness, true, real goodness, is a rare commodity. If we do not create enough of it to protect the Grail, the Grail, as an object, can be approached and captured by evil. The spirit that gives the Grail its meaning would simply withdraw, as the water withdraws from a choked well. The Grail, from the world's point of view, would cease to exist. And that is the purpose and hope of the evil men who desire to destroy it.

In the late 1880s a number of relevant events were occurring. Various powerful movements dedicated to evil were taking shape and gaining influence. Among them was an apparently insignificant one in London whose declared object was to study mystical systems and practise them. Its true purpose was to obtain and destroy the Grail, at that time hidden in a castle in Wales and guarded by the descendant of the original family of guardians. But this 'guardianship' was of the most nominal kind, mere physical ownership and responsibility. An elderly gentleman who owns a precious object must be said to be its 'guardian', but he cannot hope to guard it in fact against determined enemies. For that he must have help.

Therefore a small company of individuals was formed to give the Grail physical protection, a thing not thought necessary before that moment for several centuries. Secrecy had been regarded as a better protection, for among a number of protectors there is always the danger of including a fool or a betrayer. But in 1889 the matter was urgent. The moment was almost due when the centennial Mass needed to be enacted, the Grail would have to be taken from its hiding place and used. It would be at its most vulnerable. A castle in Wales is not impregnable in the absence of a permanent garrison. The decision was taken to remove the Grail to London, where its protectors could come and go without causing local comment as they could not hope to do in a remote corner of Wales.

In London the essential Mass was celebrated, and there the Grail remained for several years. But eventually the new hiding place of the Grail was betrayed. The Grail, the physical object, of gold and terracotta, was stolen, together with two other chalices, one of silver gilt, the other of silver, a large ceremonial cross for carrying in procession, and three silver book covers for copies of the Gospels. All these dated from the third to the seventh centuries, and had been accumulated at Glastonbury, or in Wales after the Grail's removal there. They were used in ceremonies in conjunction with the Grail, and had received some of its virtue, so that it is proper to speak of them as subsidiary Grails. (Indeed, there are a number of subsidiary Grails elsewhere in the world, under appropriate guardianship, a matter needing further discussion in a moment.)

These particular subsidiary Grails were brought to London by their guardian, with the True Grail, and stolen with it by the Grail's enemies in 1908. Having been desecrated, all the secondary objects were brought to Syria by their new owner, and there they were re-stolen and appeared on the antiquities market in 1910. One of the chalices, now known as the Antioch Chalice, may be seen in the Cloisters Collection of the Metropolitan Museum in New York. What had been the True Grail, or rather its gold reliquary, was melted down, and the Cup smashed, in a final act of desecration.

The purpose of the men who stole the physical Grail was to say a Black Mass with it, and obtain by that means the immense, the incontestable power in the world that they sought. The First World War was approaching. Hitler, born in 1889, not by any coincidence, was growing to manhood, and to an age when he could be of use to those determined to control him. Many other factors calculated to give ultimate power to evil were coinciding. The desecration, the destruction of the Grail by means of a Black Mass, the accompanying and consequent triumph of the Black Grail, would set the seal on these events and on the total victory of evil. And much of what the new possessors of the Grail – or of its physical symbol rather – hoped would happen did happen and has continued to happen, and anyone who reads the newspapers can judge the results, whether or not he agrees with this brief summary of the causes.

But the achievement of those who obtained the Grail was not as complete as they had imagined it would be, for the 'flow' of evil into the world cannot be stimulated by mechanical means, any more than the flow of Grace. Both must be earned, Grace by serving God, evil by serving Satan. To imagine that conjuring tricks and magical formulae, however blasphemous, can 'summon' evil spirits, or control them when they appear, is simply naive. Nothing that the members of the group of 'magical adepts' could do with the Grail would have much positive effect on the flow of evil into our world. Their real effect was negative, or threatened to be so, in cutting off the source of Grace from those who desired it and could earn it. And this, of course, was the sole expectation of the much greater servants of evil who had inspired and directed the group of magicians, allowing its members to delude themselves with dreams of immediate sinister glory.

But even this expectation was not completely fulfilled, for God's mercy is infinite, and while He allowed the physical Grail to be misused and desecrated, He allowed the spiritual Grail, the *reality* of the Grail to remain, and even to return to its place of safe-keeping in Wales. For a spiritual reality, lacking a physical body, can be absolutely without form, mass or appearance, absolutely independent of place and time, as God is. Equally it can, and often must, assume some degree of corporeality, if it is to serve God in time and space. A great example is the series of apparitions of the Virgin at Fatima, in 1917. There, She not only took on a visible form and appearance, that three children could see and two could hear, but She clearly had some degree of physicality for the time of the apparitions. The pressure of Her feet, for example, bent the topmost twigs of the small oak tree above which She appeared, and although She Herself remained invisible to all except the three children, the crowds saw the twigs bending under Her slight weight.

One has in these apparitions parallels to the nature of the Grail that are very instructive. First of all, Her visibility was conditional on the state of mind and spirit of those to whom She appeared. At first the little boy Francisco was unable to see or hear Her, and was mystified by the actions of his sister and his cousin. When he obeyed the instruction to recite his Rosary he was able to see Her, but still unable to hear Her. Later, those who came to the Cova da Iria on the appropriate days saw the effects of Our Lady's presence, without being able to see Her. They could also hear the sound of Her speaking without being able to distinguish the words, which the two little girls heard very clearly.

We therefore have the concept of a spirit capable of being visible to some onlookers, yet invisible to others; audible to some, inaudible to others, and barely audible, 'like the sound of insects buzzing' to yet others. And all the time *detectably* there by the physical effects of Her presence, in much the same way that a breeze is invisible yet detectable by its physical effects.

The parallels with some descriptions of the Grail are too obvious to need underlining. And it is clear that even before the theft of the physical Grail, its effect on those who sought it and found it varied enormously according to their spiritual state. While some would have seen merely an antique gold cup, others would have been blinded by its reality and carried up to a spiritual level where its physical appearance was irrelevant. Those who saw it would have seen what they were fit to see, and of course not many people saw it at all, in any form.

One can pursue this idea of the dual or multiple nature of the Grail in many ways, as I have already attempted to do throughout this essay. Just as abstract monarchy has its physical representative in the king, and the king can be represented by his royal standard, so the papacy has its representative in the living pope. The pope can be represented by his ring, his tiara, or by the granting of papal indulgence. These things can, under certain circumstances, convey his intentions, bring Grace from him to the receiver. In the same manner the devout Moslem, who believes that there is only one God, who is everywhere, also believes that Makkah (Mecca), the physical city, has an especial Grace about it. And within Makkah (Mecca) for the Moslem, the Kaaba, the sacred black stone, is the Grail. Allah's virtue dwells in it, and flows from it. Yet a well-instructed Moslem would no more believe that Allah's virtue in the world, Allah's Grace, depended on the continued existence of a black stone, than we need to believe that God's continued Grace in the world depends on the existence of a terracotta cup within a gold chalice. At the same time, we are physical beings, as well as spiritual ones, and we are not capable of receiving Grace directly from God, any more than we are capable of looking at God's glory with our physical eyes, or withstanding the fire of God's love with our physical bodies. Just as the force of electricity needs a transformer before it can be harnessed for domestic use, so the power of God needs to be diminished and in some way 'insulated', before we can benefit from it. Without that insulation, that physical transformer, we would receive death rather than life from the impact of God's Grace. We are fallen creatures, and need protection even from God's mercy. As was said earlier, we need the water of baptism, the oil of Chrism, the bread and wine of the Eucharist. Even the apostles needed tongues of fire to convey the Holy Spirit to them. Christ Himself needed the water of baptism and the dove. And, as we needed Christ, God become the living man, so we need the Grail, His representative, in its two forms, spiritual reality and physical embodiment.

But, as I have said, that physical embodiment is gone, although the spiritual reality is still localized in a non-physical 'psychical' form. It is as if, to return to our image of the spring and fountain in the oasis, the stone basin had been broken and destroyed. In such a case it would clearly be much harder to gather water from the spring. The oasis would be far more at risk. The spring far easier to choke with debris and filth and sand. One might easily judge the days of the oasis, and of those who depend on it, to be numbered. Evil is very close to a final triumph as far as this world is concerned. The most common-sensible materialist would agree that the risks to our planet and our existence on it are now so great that our chances of long survival are slender. Over-population, pollution, chemical poisoning, nuclear poisoning, not to speak of nuclear warfare, famine, climate changes, the exhaustion of essential resources, and a dozen other global threats, have become familiar to everyone. And familiarity has bred, if not contempt, a resigned indifference.

But for the spiritually minded the threats go far beyond physical destruction. Every man and woman must die, and whether one does so in a day of general holocaust accompanied in death by billions, or alone in bed, the result is the same – one's individual judgment, condemnation or salvation. The real triumph of evil consists not in bringing the world's billions to the point where all of them may die within a brief period – but in bringing them to that brink unrepentant, uncaring about God, disbelieving in the necessity of salvation, or of any effort to obey God, and worse still, utterly complacent in their mortal danger. Even among those comparative few who believe in God, the comfortable certainty has been instilled by false teachers that no effort is required from them, no sacrifice, no devotion, no attempt at sanctity.

We have been allowed to believe that Heaven is like the National Health Service; that everyone has a right to it. That God is like an overworked National Health Doctor, obliged to give us 'sick notes', to let us off work, and to excuse us for everything. And it is in this complacency that the most exquisite triumph of evil exists. We have reached such a pass that the very word evil is taboo, the idea of Hell is laughed at as medieval

142

superstition, the existence of evil spirits is considered unworthy of discussion. Progressing still further in the search for ecumenism, tolerance, broad-mindedness, an accommodation with non-believers, a theology 'acceptable to modern man', many priests have abandoned belief in the Resurrection. Some have even abandoned belief in God. They cough apologetically when obliged to mention such words and look knowingly superior. To talk to them of the war between good and evil would be to bewilder them. They would explain patiently that such subjective terms have no meaning; that for post-Freudian man . . .

But the war between good and evil exists, and the Grail is at its centre. One might visualize it in medieval, heroic terms, a standard set on a little hill, defended by a battered and wounded few, thick beset by a swarming, ever reinforced and superbly equipped enemy. The danger of such William Morris word pictures is that they make the reality seem unreal. The true picture is in the newspapers and on our television screens every day, in our own lives every day. And we are not bystanders. We are part of the battle, however unwillingly, however unknowingly. Everything we do, everything we say, every thought we dwell on, plays its part in the warfare, on one side or the other. And all too often the side on which we find ourselves, however unwittingly, however little we might believe it, is that of evil. It is not only the Hitlers and Stalins, the Idi Amins and Pol Pots and Somozas who serve evil. It may be you and I.

And the Grail? That is what each one of us must find. And when we have found it, we must defend it, to the death, and beyond.

How? By *being* good. By becoming perfect, as the Gospels command us to do. Be ye perfect, as your Father in Heaven is perfect. It is not a question of *doing* good. Few of us know how to. Before one can do, one must become. Really to do good is to affect others by one's own goodness. To act as a lit candle in a dark place. A lamp does not do anything. Yet without it, no one else can see to do anything at all in the darkness. And this type of radiant goodness is so rare as to be rightly called sanctity, holiness.

143

The Jews have a belief in ten just men, whose holiness protects the world. Mohammedans believe in the hidden Imam. Our ancestors believed that Arthur and his knights lay sleeping in a cave, ready to save the world in a crisis. And these legends contain a truth. The world needs its hidden holy ones, to save it from itself, and never more than now. They draw their strength from what is left of the Grail, and give their strength to us. In a true sense they are one with the Grail. For as I said earlier, the Grail has its subsidiaries, as a spring may have many outlets for its water. Some of those subsidiaries are physical. Some are human. And no one could have a higher earthly ambition than to become one of these Holy Ones; to find the Grail, to enter into it, to serve it, and by serving it to serve mankind, and God. The quest leads to what St Teresa of Avila called the Interior Castle, at whose heart the Grail lies.

Notes

1 In *The Seven Mansions*, London and Dulverton, Watkins, 1980.
2 Edward Owen, Cymmrodorion Society, in papers for the Society, and in *Revue Celtique*, 1911, 'A note on the identification of Bleheris'. Also J. L. Weston, *The Quest of the Holy Grail*, G. Bell & Sons, 1913, and *From Ritual to Romance*, Cambridge University Press, and New York, Doubleday/Anchor Books, 1957.

·8·
:THE·DESIRE
OF·THE·HEART:
·
LOIS·LANG-SIMS
·

From the viewpoint of the Christian mystic, to comprehend the truth of the Grail myth one must first ask a question – the same question which, in all the stories of the Divine Vessel, must be asked by the quester before he can penetrate the veils of mystery which surround it. The question is: Whom does the Grail serve? We have already seen that the answer is that it serves everyone – an answer as simple as it is hard to understand. The view expressed here demonstrates that, in the real world as in the mythic, questions almost always lead to acceptance, and acceptance of the truths embodied in and by the Grail leads to a unique kind of fulfilment, one which enables us to do the work which was intended for us from before our birth. In so doing, we ourselves become servants of the Grail.

For most, if not all of us, mention of the Holy Grail suggests immediately two alternative states of mind, each the other's opposite: the one, a sense of bafflement in the face of a tangled complex of strange stories, requiring a lifetime of scholarly application for its unravelling; the other, a single-pointed contemplation of a simple image, that of a gracious chalice, substantial as solid gold, ethereal as the morning mist, seen, as it were, out of the corner of an eye, pregnant with a light that is not of this earth. This simple image seems, we do not know why, to gather up into itself the desire of the heart. We yearn towards it, with a love that is beyond anything we feel for the objects of our deepest personal affection; at the same time it seems to radiate upon us a love that is far beyond any other that we have been privileged to receive (indeed, we feel, there is no 'other' love, none that is not here present, emerging from and returning to this wondrously pulsating source). It – this mysterious 'It' – is the goal of each individual lifetime's quest.

'Quest' and also '*quest*ion' – these two words are keys to the Grail Mystery, and are related in the sense that the quest *is* the question, and when the goal is achieved the question simply answers itself.

There is nothing which need surprise us in the idea that it is laid upon the questing knight to arrive at the place and time where a certain question must be asked. The asking is to be the signal for the moment of achievement, healing and release. The blood of an ancient wound will be staunched. The waters will flow. The earth will blossom. The question is the first step along the path of initiation into heavenly secrets, and the last before those secrets are revealed in the moment of death which is the gateway to eternal life. For what precisely is a question? Rightly understood it is an invocation, calling forth a response. In the realms of reality nothing which has not been called will ever come. Our calling is, of necessity, a question, on account of our ignorance. Conversely, when we are called of God, that too is a question put to us, since God, even God, knows not how our freedom will reply until He hears our voice. *Lovest thou me?* asked the Lord of Simon Peter, whose reply, although it seems to say that the questioner already knew, could not have been given – because the love *in question* would not have been invoked – had not the question been addressed. (We are, of course, assuming that scriptural dialogue on this level represents metaphysical actualities, not the mere phantasms which are all that our habitual 'conversation' has the power to conjure up.)

It is no coincidence that the four gospels – and indeed the whole of our Bible, in common with countless other scriptural writings from all over the world – are sown with questions. (For non-Christian examples, we may turn to the *Upanishads*, the sermons of the Buddha, the dialogues of Plato, and find what amounts to a question-and-answer method constantly in use.) *Whom seek ye? . . . Whom say ye that I am? . . . Why weepest thou? Whom seekest thou? . . .* And from the aspirant, hesitating at the opening up of the path: *What shall I do? . . . How can a man enter a second time into his mother's womb and be born? . . .* In contrast, there are the wrong questions (*Lord, what shall this man do?*), and those which are no more than clever ruses which Jesus answers, or more often refuses to answer, with a fine contempt. The question asked with a pure motive is a sign of readiness, without which no spiritual Master will accept a pupil. The one prompted by scepticism or mere curiosity disqualifies at once. Nowadays children are regarded as being highly 'intelligent' when they ask the sort of questions which would once have been regarded as denoting not intelligence but a lethal silliness. Children seldom naturally ask such questions. A small child, left to its own devices, will ask questions which are either strictly practical or of the kind which arise from and further a quest. Similarly, when the Grail knight, who must have the simplicity of a child, becomes capable, without prompting, of asking for the explanation which will enable him to understand the sublime function of the Grail and his own destiny in relation to it, this is not mere curiosity (as in one version of the story he is misled into supposing it would be) but the correct performance of his role in response to a carefully given cue. The cue, in this case, being the spectacle which has been enacted before his eyes, the procession and the feast.

The first question, in the sense of being fundamental and primary besides being literally the first to be quoted in the scriptural account of the birth, death and resurrection of the Christ, may seem at first glance to be little more than a quavering expression of doubt; however, if we read it so, we are failing to situate it in its proper context within the integrated wholeness of the myth of which it is an essential part.

How shall this be, seeing I know not a man?

The Archangel Gabriel has not told the Virgin that it is incumbent upon her to ask a question. Neither were Perceval and Galahad told what they had to do: it was their business to find out, and it was necessary that they should. The point of such questions is that they must arise spontaneously from the heart, evoking a response. Mary's question, for which Gabriel has provided her with the cue, is not prompted by scepticism. She asks in order that she may be enabled to understand what it is that she, for her part, is being asked to accept. The act of unconditional obedience whereby she dedicates herself – and in so doing receives the Seed of God – is made in the knowledge of precisely what it is to which she is giving her consent. *The Holy Ghost shall come upon thee, the Power of the Most High shall overshadow thee.* It is this Coming, this Overshadowing, in all its fearfulness, that the fourteen-year-old girl accepts when she says: *Be it unto me according to thy word.* So the Godhead is conceived in her womb. She becomes the *Vas Spirituale*, the Vessel of the Spirit.

A great many strange-sounding titles have been bestowed upon the Virgin by the Church. She is described as a vase, a mirror, a tower, a throne, a garden: the procession of images passes before the inward eye as we recite her litanies, reminding us that a single aspect of reality may assume a variety of forms. The forms slide over and under one another like veils, obscuring yet revealing the reality beneath. So the form of the Holy Vase or Chalice is but one manifestation of the Divine Femininity, who appears as Shekinah in the tradition of the Jews, and in the Christian tradition as Mary, Blessed Mother of the Christ. There is a mystical identification between the image of the Grail and those of the virginal womb and the previously unused tomb in which the body of the Lord is laid when it temporarily succumbs to the power of death. This identification is implied in the myth of the two Josephs, described in each case as the Guardian of the Vessel – womb, tomb or cup – which signifies the continuously renewed containment and emergence of the Living God.

In the realms of myth, identity of name implies some sort of identification between the roles of the bearers of the name. There are two Josephs in the gospel accounts of the Sacred Drama of the Christ. The first is Joseph the Protector of the Virgin. This Joseph is espoused to Mary, subsequently discovering that she is pregnant. An Angel reassures him concerning her virginity and the child's miraculous origin. It is being required of him that he should surrender his lawful rights over her womb, leaving her virginity perpetually intact. His wife has been impregnated not by his own seed but by the Holy Spirit. Joseph accepts his allotted role. He becomes the Guardian alike of the virginity of Mary and of her Divine Child. Joseph of Arimathea in like manner surrenders up his rights over the new (or virgin) tomb which he had ordered to be constructed for himself. This tomb, intended to receive his own body, becomes the resting place of Jesus. In the Resurrection Jesus emerges from it into a fair garden. The 'garden enclosed' is an image of the two Marys, mother and lover, reminding us of the Song of Solomon with its strange foreshadowing of the loss and the finding by Mary of her soul's beloved. So the first Joseph presides over the birth, the second over the death and resurrection of the Lord. The womb and the tomb are essentially one: twin aspects of the single Mystery of death-in-life and life-in-death.

Joseph of Glastonbury, who might almost be called the third Joseph although legend identifies him firmly with the second, is the Guardian of the Holy Cup. In one version of his story, Christ appears to him in a vision and presents him with the chalice of the Last Supper, in recognition of his services at that time. More simply, it can be supposed that he came into possession of it in some ordinary way, and used it as a reliquary for a few drops of the sacred blood obtained when the body of Jesus was taken down from the Cross. This Cup appears more than once in the Christian myth. We think of it immediately as the chalice of the Last Supper and so of the Blessed Sacrament. But that same night it plays a duel role in the garden, first as the Cup of Sorrow, of which Christ prays to His Father that if it be possible it may pass from Him; later as *Viaticum*, when Angels minister to Him from what must be the selfsame vessel, source of that spiritual nourishment which is the communication to His human self of His Divine Essence. In many Traditional paintings of the Agony in the Garden, the identity of the two cups, with each other and with that of the Last Supper, is apparent. A similar vessel appears in the iconography of the Crucifixion, held by an Angel who hovers near the Cross to catch the blood dripping from the wounds of the dying Christ.

To understand this image of the Chalice, which in the legend of the third Joseph becomes the Grail, the starting point for the great medieval mythology of the Quest, we should make a mental image of a vessel so pure that it actually becomes one with and indistinguishable from its content. This is the *Vas Spirituale*, the Void that (to quote a Sufic saying) 'is filled with the Light of the Heart of Heaven'. In the First Movement of Creation God withdraws Himself in order to create a Void. Into this Void He projects Himself as Word, returning to Himself as the Third Person of the Trinity, the Divine Sophia, of Whom the Blessed Virgin is a manifestation in time.

Mary herself is not to be identified with the Divine Sophia in an absolute sense. The Church has consistently taught that she is not herself divine, but represents a manifestation or containing form of the otherwise formless Spirit, arising as an immaculate conception in the bonds of time, finally to be deified when, in the Mystery of the Assumption, she is raised into the Heart of God. By her is the Godhead made available *in time* to the children of men. In the liturgy of the Roman Catholic Church she is constantly referred back, by means of the juxtaposition of passages from the Books of Wisdom with her principal feasts, to a semi-divine figure who would seem to be the first emanation of the Divine Sophia (the latter being unconditionally identical with the Holy Spirit). In our meditation on the Grail Mystery, we may consider in particular a passage from this Wisdom literature, which will enable us to form a visual image of the vessel which is one with its contents on account of the absolute purity of both:

> For Wisdom is more moving than any motion: she passeth and goeth through all things by reason of her pureness . . . therefore can no defiled thing fall into her.[1]

A superficial reading of this passage produces an impression of oddness. We wonder, at first, why purity in itself should produce movement; and why it should follow ('therefore') from this that perfect purity cannot be defiled by the introduction of an alien substance. On deeper reflection, however, one begins to see how perfect purity implies an absolute passibility and an absolute swiftness of motion, and how the two parts of the description involve each other as a kind of two-way operation of cause and effect. Any difficulty or slowness of passage must be caused by a two-way resistance. Absolute purity, unmixed with even the smallest particle of material heaviness, does not resist. Conversely, when some alien substance encounters it, that substance passes through it in an instant. From this meditation emerges the idea that the Holy Vessel – Virgin, womb, or Grail – is able to contain the Divine Spirit and diffuse It to infinity, while remaining itself invisible, the form assumed by the Spirit at any given moment.

Another version of the womb-image is the Round Table, with its seating accommodation for the twelve apostles or the twelve knights. In certain medieval paintings (notably the twelfth century French manuscript illustration reproduced on page 44 of John Matthews's *The Grail*) the meaning of this image is made explicit, the circular table with its twelve dishes being clearly recognizable as an ovary studded with the twelve ova which will drop away from it in the course of twelve months. Accounts of this table are visually ambiguous. Were there twelve seats – or thirteen? In general it has been assumed that Jesus Himself occupied a thirteenth seat. But there is a curious fact of geometry which, at least to the kind of mind which moves easily in the realms of myth, points away from this view. To quote from Keith Critchlow's essay on *The Soul as Sphere and Androgyne*:

If we take one complete sphere – irrespective of size – and enquire how many similar spheres can surround this primary sphere it will be found by calculation or physical experiment that the number is *exactly* twelve. Therefore the first complete shell or 'sphere' of spheres surrounding the primary (nuclear) one is precisely twelve, each touching its neighbour and the centre.

It follows – at least if we accept, as any traditionally orientated mind will unhesitatingly do – a mystical significance in this figure according to the laws of correspondence, that Jesus must in some sense represent, or be represented by, the central sphere. A correct visualization of the scene is not easily achieved, because it is not meant to be 'taken literally', and we do not easily visualize something which involves a shifting of images in more dimensions than the three in terms of which

151

we habitually think. A hint is provided in the information that St John was leaning on the bosom of Jesus. In other words they were occupying the same seat. Jesus is waiting for the seat which He knows will be vacated by Judas. The role of Judas in the Sacred Drama is many-aspected and of an inexhaustible significance: here we have one way of interpreting it – as a representation of the ovum which falls away from the ring with the purpose of being born. Judas rises from his seat and goes out – into the night. The central sphere, in this visualization, is temporarily *inside out*, and in this situation it is totally empty and totally dark. It is the world of 'the Fall', 'this world' in the absence of God. It is vitally important to be clear on this point. The world of 'the Fall' is not to be identified unreservedly with *our* world as we normally experience it; for this, *our* world, is the state of being held in a precarious balance between the fall into sin and the redemptive action brought about by the intervention of the Word of God. Christ is that Word, and Christ must be born from the womb, and splayed out (or crucified) upon the bottomless (uncontaining) darkness of the fallen world, in order that *our* world may be restored, in a process experienced by us as *time*, to the heavenly state. Judas is the Betrayer because it is through him – on account of the indissoluble love which unites the Godhead even to fallen man – that the Christ Principle falls into the world and, in doing so, is made subject to death. As the ovum falls into a world which itself must be visualized initially as fallen and dark, it carries with it the incarnating Lord. Judas gives up his seat to Jesus, who first sits upon it, and later, rising, follows in the footsteps of its previous occupant. In the dark garden, the ante-room of death, He is taken by 'swords and staves' (the physiological correspondence is apparent). Again, He takes the place of Judas, who – after all – cannot live, but is destined to perish like the wasted ovum in a 'field of blood'. By this substitution (symbolized in a kiss) the Godhead is made one with death, and emerges triumphant. 'The Void is filled with the Light of the Heart of Heaven.' When we next encounter the circular table of the Upper Room, the vault is passable and through it descends the Holy Spirit. The Cenacle is now the equivalent of

152

the Virgin's womb, and of the Holy Cup containing the liquid fire of the Body and Blood of Christ.

A contemporary ikon by a monk of the Brotherhood of St Seraphim of Sarov (reproduced on page 36 of John Matthews's *The Grail*) provides an exceptionally close-packed statement of the symbology of the three Josephs. Joseph of Glastonbury looks down at the Grail which is enclosed in a cave or tomb from the apex of which sprouts the Glastonbury thorn. The Holy Cup is emitting rays of light which pierce the stones. Behind this feminine symbol rises the altar of the Tor surmounted by its tower; behind the saint is Our Lady's church. St Joseph holds in one hand the leafy rod which is both miraculous thorn and insignia of the Virgin's spouse. (The reference is to the story of the selection of Mary's future husband by means of a sign. Each of the assembled suitors is presented with a rod. A dove flies out of Joseph's rod which is generally shown in pictorial representations of the scene as bursting into leaf.) His cloak is a deep green, colour of burgeoning nature and of the emerald stone which fell from the Crown of Lucifer to become the Grail. (Here again is the image of something falling from its fixed place upon a ring.) He carries over one arm a fair linen cloth, the winding sheet of Christ. This cloth is associated with the Holy Cup in a medieval tradition relating to the various sacred objects which are utilized in the Mass. Visitors to Canterbury Cathedral will find there a twelfth century chalice and paten, the latter bearing a Latin inscription round the rim which being translated reads:

> The altar serves the office of the cross,
> The chalice of the tomb,
> The paten of the stone,
> And the fair linen of the winding sheet.

Honorious of Autun (*Gemma Animae*, Book 1, Ch. XLVII) explains the matter further:

When the priest says *Per omnia saecula saeculorum*, the deacon comes before him and elevates the chalice. He covers a portion of it with a cloth, then returns it to the altar and covers it with the corporal, enacting the part of

Joseph of Arimathea who took the body of Christ down from the cross, covered his face with a sudarium, laid the body in the grave and covered it with a stone. That which is here offered, and also the chalice, are covered with the corporal, which signifies the linen winding sheet in which Joseph wrapped the body of Christ. The chalice signifies the tomb, and the paten the stone with which it was closed.

And Robert de Boron, in his *Roman de l'Estoire dou Graal*, puts these words into the mouth of Christ when he appears to Joseph in prison and presents him with the sacred Vessel:

Thou didst take me down from the Cross and lay me in thy sepulchre, after I had sat by Simon Peter at the meal and said that I would be betrayed. Because this happened at table, tables will be set up in future, that I may be sacrificed. The table signifies the Cross; the vessels in which the sacrifice and consecration will be made signify the tomb wherein thou didst lay me. This is the cup in which my body will be consecrated in the form of the Host. The paten that will be laid upon it signifies the stone with which thou didst close the mouth of the tomb, the cloth that will be spread over it signifies the linen that thou woundest round my body. Thus the meaning of thine action will be known to Christendom for all time, until the end of the world.[2]

The Canterbury chalice has twelve ribbed knobs in place of a stem, and twelve lobes descending to the foot. Although it is, of course, of later date than the vessel used by Jesus, it is an ideal type of the medieval Grail. Chalice and paten were sacrilegiously removed from the tomb of Archbishop Hubert Walter, in the year 1890, by the then Dean and Chapter. At the present time they are being sacrilegiously displayed in a permanent exhibition in return for payment. One imagines how they might be restored to their proper use on the great feast days of the Church; and how in the intervals they might be enshrined in some especially sacred part of the Cathedral, perhaps in the easternmost chapel to which the entire design of the building leads up. Displayed in a correct manner, instead of in one that degrades it to the level of a 'cultural object', this Canterbury chalice could well be, as in a very real sense unquestionably it *is*, the Holy Grail. Every chalice in use at the Communion refers back to, and derives its reality from, the vessel made holy by the hands of Christ. The holiness of that original vessel consisted in its oneness with the Divine Femininity of whom its form and function were a manifestation, as surely as were the tomb in the garden, the womb of the Virgin – and the Virgin herself.

So our meditation links together those two inseparables: the Body and Blood of the Blessed Sacrament and the luminous (because translucent) figure of *Theotokos*, the Mother of God. Mary is entitled to be called the God-bearer because her entire being is surrendered to its function, which is that of bearing and dispensing the Divine Spirit of which she herself is the embodiment. Her own body is invisible save as the form or bearer of the heavenly light. In the same way, the Grail is the bearer of the Holy Blood. In the vessel for use at the Communion, water is mingled with wine to signify the union of the Virgin with her Son. Water is the principal physical manifestation of spiritual purity. It is used in the rite of baptism as the purificatory element. Blood (under the semblance of wine) is akin to fire; but, more profoundly even than fire, it is united with the reality of the Divine Life: poured out, it becomes the Holy Sacrifice by which the fallen world is retrieved from death. The Grail as chalice is, like Dante's Mystic Rose (which has essentially the same meaning) the final image before the falling away of all images in the Vision of Truth. That Vision is vouchsafed to us all, if only for an instant, in the moment of death, holding out to us the possibility of choosing here and now to enter the Presence of God. The Tibetan scripture known as the *Bardo Thodol* describes it as a clear colourless light, unendurable until the soul, having passed through all the stages of its destiny in time, has reached the point of no return.

St John of the Cross, who presumably never heard of the *Bardo*, echoes its teachings when he tells us that 'the soul, when it shall have purified and emptied itself from all intelligible forms and images, will then dwell in this pure and simple light . . . .'

But Plato, writing of the moment immediately preceding that

of the ultimate surrender on the part of the soul, assures us that we shall 'arrive at the knowledge of absolute beauty, and at last know what the essence of beauty is.' That knowledge is (or can be) the last infinitesimal hesitation on the verge of bodily death: the answer to the soul's question can be given only when it voluntarily gives up its clinging to this earthly life.

Whom does the Grail serve? It serves us all in the moment of our dying, performing the function of *Viaticum*, the last thing we see before we see no more, communicating to us the gift of eternal life.

Notes

1 Wisdom, Ch. VII (Authorized Version).
2 *The Grail Legend*, Emma Jung and Marie Louise von Franz – trans. Andrea Dykes, Hodder & Stoughton, London, 1960.

· PART · III ·

◆◆◆◆

MAGIC
AND · THE · USE · OF
IMAGINATION

:9:

:MERLIN AND·THE·GRAIL:

GARETH·KNIGHT

Seen as a magical as well as a mystical experience, the Grail offers a way towards the achievement of unity in all things and all beings. At present we live in an age still largely dominated by a masculine impulse. Through the recognition of the part played by the Divine Feminine in all of Creation, and the way in which the resultant energies of balance and polarity can be harnessed to help the survival of the human race, Gareth Knight explores the intrinsic power of the Grail as a vessel of divine grace and magical inspiration – two poles which to many seem far apart, but which time and events will show to be merely two faces of the same coin.

The Holy Grail is pre-eminently a *mystical* experience; that is to say an experience pertaining to a vision of God and the uncreate realities of a different order of being. Yet in the background there is to be discerned very much a *magical* approach to these dynamics. That is, a technique of so ordering the immediate powers behind physical existence that the mystical experience is likely to be the more readily available to the questing soul. This is very much the province of Merlin, the archetypal magician of the Matter of Britain.

In Celtic mythology, which like all mythology, tends to the *magical* rather than the *mystical* dynamic, the prototype of the Holy Grail is to be found in the form of a cauldron of inspiration, bounty and regeneration. As such it is in the keeping of the

159

goddess Ceridwen and is tended by nine maidens. These have analogues with the nine muses of classical mythology; and with the Qabalistic Tree of Life where there is a clear link with the *ninth* Sephirah, Yesod, the Foundation, which, amongst other things is designated a Treasure-house of Images.

In its bountiful, regenerating aspect, the proto-Grail is associated with the Dagda, chief of the Tuatha de Danaan (the children of the goddess Dana), and with Bran the Blessed, who used it to feed his men and to restore those killed in battle. As such it forms one of the principal treasures of the Tuatha de Danaan, together with the Spear of Lugh Lavadha, the Sword of Conary Mor, and the Lia Fail, the oracular stone that identifies rightful kings. Slightly modified in form, these treasures are still to be found in the traditional magical weapons of the four quarters of a magic circle – the Sword of Air in the East; the Lance or Rod of Fire in the South; the Cup or Cauldron of Water in the West; and the Stone, Disk, Coin or Shield of Earth in the North. Much the same symbolism is found in the four suits of the Tarot from which the suits of our modern playing cards derive.

In the earliest times there is a close relationship between these symbols and the Principle of Sovereignty, which is identified with a *female* figure, Eriu, the Sovereignty of Ireland, who gave these treasures. She was dual aspected. Sometimes she appeared to be beautiful and at other times to be loathly. This is a characteristic that is shared with other great goddesses of antiquity, who are each in their way aspects of the Isis of Nature. It is also to be found in the Grail messenger or maiden.

However the final balancing and acceptance of the divinity of the feminine (in safely disguised form) is to be found in the peace giving, integrating fulfilment of the 'New Jerusalem', adorned like a bride. Of course, the 'scarlet woman' is something that must be come to terms with, rather than dissociated from. It indeed is the acceptance of her or the energies she contains through an all-encompassing love that will transform her into a bright healing figure.

One does not have to research far into this symbolism to realize the great complex of images that form parts of the Feminine Principle. In it is embraced the whole principle of Form and thus of the world, the Earth, the mass of humanity in general, all forms of container and containment; cups, cities, houses, countries, bodies, as well as the female of each and every bi-polar species. Indeed the Feminine is one half of a great dichotomy of creation. All that exists is formed by the union and intermarrying of the masculine and feminine principles, which appear in the various metaphysical philosophies as the *yang* and the *yin*, the *ida* and the *pingala*, the positive and the negative, the male and the female, the force and the form, the two pillars Jachin and Boaz that stand before the portal of the Temple of the Mysteries.

These two principles are fundamental to the meditational operations that form part of the various yogic practices and their Western equivalents. In these days they are also to be found in the context of various psycho-therapies. In their fullest understanding, however, there is more to them than psychology admits. They fall into the province of magic – of which the archetypal Western practitioner is Merlin. Magic is a skilled and objective use of the imagination, as organ of perception and action. Its dynamics are the two poles of a 'horizontal' polarity, so to speak, that by their equilibration and balanced use, provide vehicles for forces to indwell. Conversely, forces can be released from their involvement in these vehicles. In their profounder aspects, these are the mechanisms of birth and death – and also of all making, manufacturing, artistic or other creation, and the forming of organizations or social groups, whether permanent or ephemeral. All are the interchange of horizontal polarities, that by their manipulation may allow a 'vertical' polarity to take effect.

The vertical polarity is the manifestation of life upon various levels of expression. To a higher force, the form in which it is going to express itself is relatively feminine; and to a lower form, the force that is to indwell it is relatively masculine.

In ultimate terms the vertical polarity is a *mystical* dynamic, for by this direction of flow the uncreate realities enter the worlds of expression. The horizontal polarity is a *magical* dynamic, for although it serves the mystical intention in its highest and proper use, its *modus operandi* and prime material is entirely in the structures of the worlds of form. At lower levels of magic this is in terms of effecting changes in the material world. At higher levels it is expressed in a technology of ideation and imagination. At an even higher level, and more powerfully, it is the formulation and manipulation of intuitions and a preparation for their ultimate expression 'down the planes'.

Although this is expressed in terms of magic, we should also keep well in mind that this is the perfectly natural expression of *all* thought processes that come to physical fruition. There is no gulf or barrier between magic and the ordinary world. We all use magic in order to live our lives; just as we use prose to express ourselves – without necessarily being consciously aware of the fact. The alchemists tried very hard to express this fact by asserting that their prime material was everywhere to be found and yet commonly ignored and taken for granted. Their principles of *solve* and *coagule* – solution and coagulation – are not great hidden secrets reserved only for the few; they are basic life principles, used naturally and instinctively by all, in various ways: distillation, precipitation, calcination and the other chemical laboratory operative terms used by alchemists are all precise definitions for various 'processes' of consciousness.

The results of our unconscious magic or taken-for-granted alchemy is the world that we create around ourselves. Magic or alchemy is therefore not something that can ever be banned; without it nothing would exist. One might as well try to outlaw perception or metabolism. The only point at issue is how consciously it is used, for an increase in faith and intention renders its operation more effective, just as a forced draught will enhance the powers of a natural fire, or turn a domestic hearth into an alchemical furnace, so to speak.

In the profoundest magic the extent of the vertical polarity is from the uncreate spiritual source, beyond form, beyond even the formless, to the physical world of objective appearances. This is rare, for most who are consciously perceptive of the world through being incarnate in this particular planet at this particular time are, by that very fact, not able *consciously* to be aware of the higher levels. Even the intuitional realms are closed to many.

Materialist thought, of course, tries to seek causation on the plane of effects – which is why it is ultimately so deadening to the soul and spiritually barren. A few short-term technological advantages have accrued from this perverted view, but the world simply rushes the faster like a train down a concrete tunnel with a dead end. What began as an adventure of the mind heralded by Francis Bacon in his *New Atlantis* now shows signs of an impending catastrophe of global dimensions in eco-logical exploitation and nuclear destruction.

The rare event which could prevent this rush to global destruction might well be termed a manifestation of the Holy Grail. The pure mystic and the Christian Church of the West might say that 'the spirit bloweth where it listeth' and that all that mankind should do is to have faith, and pray, awaiting the Will of God. However, whilst one cannot dictate to the Holy Spirit, our human powers and free will are meant to be used. Indeed they are already being used in a misguided and evil fashion, so some personal effort at making the ways straight is required from those who have the knowledge, the will and the ability. Were this not so there would have been no point in the Quest of the Holy Grail to which the whole of Arthurian knighthood was committed. The knights could simply have stayed at Camelot and prayed that the Grail would come to them.

Behind all of this we find Merlin, the Arch-Mage, with his consort the Lady of the Lake, who prepared the flower of Knighthood for this supremely important Quest. There is a certain ominous relevance to our present times in the tradition that the original Merlin was a survivor of a fiery holocaust that sank a previous civilization beneath the waves; that is, the legendary lost Atlantis. It will be obvious that we do not place the origins of the Arthurian Tradition in the 5th Century AD – although the Romano-Celtic *dux bellorum* beloved of contem-porary historians formed a certain focus about which ancient memories could crystallize. The real roots of power in the tradi-tion go much further back, with the builders of the megaliths of Western Europe.

Here, the tradition has it, the neolithic builders of these ancient sites were guided in the first instance by colonists of the Far West, who built important centres along the Western seaboard of the continent of Europe, in Ireland, Scotland, Wales, South-west England, Brittany, the Iberian peninsula and into the Mediterranean basin in island centres such as Malta. Most of these areas are lands now associated with the Celt whose culture is, however, an overlay on that of the original inhabitants, for the Celts absorbed and preserved the traditions and folk memories of the bronze age and neolithic cultures that they displaced.

So the deeper dynamics of the Arthurian and Grail legends are to be found in Celtic mythology. These concern Merlin's attempt to establish a new dynasty by genetic engineering; aided by the Lady of the Lake, and magically hindered by Morgan le Fay. The native aristocratic line, represented by King Uther Pendragon, was to be merged with the line of ancient Atlantean priestly aristocracy, represented by Igraine who, according to tradition, was an Atlantean princess who had found refuge as the wife of one of the chiefs of the Cornish peninsula – Gorlois of Tintagel.

The old Atlantean line was based upon principles of inherited clairvoyance through a particular quality of the blood. This is the basis of the *sang real*. Those possessing this clairvoyant gift had access to inner powers and knowledge denied to ordinary mortals. The system is that which also pertained in Ancient Egypt almost until the time of Alexander; and it forms the ancient root of the aristocratic and royal tradition. Its problem, as with all forms of highly selective breeding, is that it can lead to degeneracy, particularly if the pool of available blood stock becomes too small.

The matter remains an important issue and has had its effect upon modern history, particularly in relation to the institution of monarchy. The 'divine right of kings' is a concept deriving from it and one that is particularly deeply impressed upon British racial memory through the execution of Charles I. A popular seventeenth-century print shows him kneeling at an altar, putting aside his earthly crown for the heavenly crown of a martyr. Any cause receives immense power through a voluntary sacrificial death, and particularly so in the case of a sacrificed king for in ancient times the divine king of the tribe was a voluntary sacrificial victim also, for the welfare of his people and the continuance of the cycles of nature. Despite the spread of republican democratic institutions over the last century or so there is a romance of royalty that catches the popular imagination as is shown by newspaper coverage the world over. Aristocracy is no longer a psychically gifted elite whose power derives from an ability to discern 'the will of the gods' or the flow of supra-material powers but the institution survives so long because of its origins in such a potent psycho-spiritual dynamic.

In historical terms the link between the traditional *sang real* and the Holy Grail, as representative of the Feminine Principle, might be discerned by examining the effects of the Queens of England, and latterly of Great Britain, upon her destiny. Not only the great queens such as Elizabeth I or Victoria; or important transitional figures such as Mary I, focus of Catholic reaction, or Anne, who presided over the Union, but also the important consorts such as Eleanor of Aquitaine, queen of Henry II, who, like certain other queens, brought links with tracts of Western Europe (finally lost under Mary), which reinforced ancient esoteric and prehistoric links.

Eleanor is particularly relevant to studies of the Grail and the Matter of Britain in that she was a patron of the Courts of Love and troubadour minstrelsy that form a vital strand in the literary formulation of the ancient oral Arthurian and Grail legends by Chrétien de Troyes and his successors. She was also mother of the charismatic Richard the Lionheart, and his brother John Lackland, who play dark and bright roles of evil usurper and absent once-and-future king in the great nature cycle of ballad legends of Robin Hood.

In much of this we can only hint at possible fruitful lines of thought and research. There remains, for example, much to be done by way of scholarly research into the inner activities of the Elizabethan magus, mathematician, geographer and bibliophile Dr John Dee. Dee is, in a sense, one upon whom the mantle of the legendary Merlin falls – and this is no light burden. Dee has suffered from the slip-shod preconceptions of the post-Renaissance academic world, which is the lot even of great spirits such as Newton, whose alchemical and other

esoteric pursuits have been ignored by an intellectual establishment woefully unqualified to understand their importance.
They have not even been considered worthy of denigration. We
now await a generation of scholars adequately equipped to do
justice to the treasure-house of esoteric studies undertaken by
the great seventeenth- and early eighteenth-century men of
science, before the Enlightenment (an ironic mis-use of terms)
discouraged men of science from involvement in anything but
material observation.

On a practical level it was to Dee's library that Drake, Raleigh
and the other great navigators of the time went for guidance;
just as Merlin gave practical strategical and tactical advice to
Arthur and his allies. Dee was as learned in the Renaissance
kind of magic as was Merlin in the pre-Druidical methods. He
was known at the major courts of Europe, and was an influence
within them, just as Merlin wandered about the kingdoms of
ancient Logres – Cornwall, Lionesse, North Galles, and so on.

Finally just as Merlin had a grand strategy for the country of
Logres so did John Dee, with his concept of Empire, which was
the logical extension of his cartographical expertise.

It may be that the concept of Empire has passed its time,
along with the preservation of the blood royal as a means of
governance, but the dynamic behind it is one of service to the
group soul of the race which in its turn expresses, however
misguidedly sometimes, a leadership of other nations. The idea
of Britain being a leader of nations may seem dated and foolish
to many contemporaries of an internationalist turn of mind but
it is an important archetype that goes back to the very mists of
time when the British Isles was the religious centre for the Celtic
world. The Roman historian Pliny indeed credits the religious
genius of the British as being capable of instructing even the
Persians – the great priests and holders of the starry wisdom
in the ancient world.

This derives from the tradition of the lost continent of Atlantis
which, even if denied a physical existence by contemporary
science, is an imaginative vision of very great power that sent
early navigators such as St Brendan in search of the Isles of the
Blessed. The power behind this vision is so powerful because
it represents racial memories of a golden age which is part of the

the experience of human consciousness in previous conditions of cognition. Such concepts are not easy for the modern analytical mind to grasp but they are explained in some detail, together with methods for their investigation, in the writings and lectures of Rudolf Steiner on 'spiritual science'.

To the ancient world of pre-Roman times wisdom came from the West. The British Isles were a centre of great religious culture and knowledge and particularly the western areas, especially Ireland. Anglesey was still a great Druidic centre of teaching when the Romans conquered it. Later, the culture of Celtic Christianity also spread eastward from Ireland to keep alight the torch of learning in the Dark Ages. These are but later reflections of the earlier spread of neolithic culture from the Boyne Valley (with its important sites such as Tara and Newgrange), to the mainland of Britain.

Thus we have the traditions of the group soul of the various tribes and races that have successively inhabited the British Isles, and who constitute, in a sense, the human consciousness of this particular tract of the Earth's surface. These traditions look westward for wisdom. Also, the British Isles themselves, as the most western part of the European land mass, lay claim to being the first repository of this wisdom – and a wisdom so great that it contains the destiny of nations.

Something of this conception is symbolized graphically by Charles Williams in his poetic Arthurian cycle *The Region of the Summer Stars* and *Taliessin through Logres*. In this, his hero, the bard Taliessin, meets Merlin and the Lady of the Lake (here called Brisen) in the fringes of the enchanted Forest Broceliande. The power of the magic is so profound and strong that Taliessin can only watch it in vision. In this Merlin invokes with mighty conjurations the powers of the stars whilst Brisen, identifying with the Feminine Principle, merges, naked, with the landscape of the whole European and Middle Eastern land-mass. In this great symbolic at-one-ment with the land various parts of her body correspond with important centres of culture and civiliz-ation, the Vatican; the University of Paris; the cosmopolis of Toledo; Jerusalem; the Caucasus; and most significantly, her brow, comprising the mind and intuitive awareness of what should be and what is to come, are centred upon Logres as she sets her gaze out into the Western Ocean wherein, in its margins with the enchanted forest, the Castle of the Grail may be found.

The Grail Castle is a condition, within the forest (equated broadly with the unconscious mind), which corresponds to the main centre of religious aspiration, the capital of the symbolic Universal Empire, at Byzantium. This mythical empire capital, which is placed at the same location as the historical Byzantium, and at the navel of the All-Woman All-Land Brisen, is the goal of all prayer, of all formal religious aspirations. The vast bulk of humanity are enjoined to aspire to make a direct pilgrimage there rather than to venture the hazardous tracks of the Western Forest of Broceliande, the haunt of strange wonders and monsters, and entered into only by poets, lunatics and lovers – although psychic researchers, psycho-analysts and practitioners of the occult arts also have their abode there. It is said that no one ever enters the Forest and comes out unchanged. The subconscious underworld forces always leave their mark. In another aspect they are also the forces of death and rebirth.

Beyond a certain part – and only a certain part of the Forest – may be found the Castle of the Grail. Those who lose their way can even find themselves in the environs of real evil, amongst the tentacled minions of the obscene headless emperor of Po-Lu. However, what is this Grail Castle within this dangerous forest? It is the Feminine Principle of God inherent in the deep consciousness of matter itself.

Here is a profound secret of ancient initiation and of alchemy. The Rosicrucian alchemists enjoined the student in an acrostic based upon the universal solvent, VITRIOL, to visit the interior of the earth, there to discover and rectify the hidden stone. (*Visita Interiora Terrae Rectificando Invenies Occultum Lapidem.*)

In another important Rosicrucian alchemical manuscript *The Chymical Marriage of Christian Rosencreutz* the Feminine Principle appears in an underground tomb, as the sleeping form of the naked Lady Venus. This is the Isis of Nature; or Godhead as expressed in manifestation as a power centre of cosmic feminine force. Whoever dares to wake the sleeping Venus, assuming he can find her secret chamber (which is through a symbolic copper trap door), will discover that she has given birth to a King.

It is little realized that it is the *discoverer* of the sleeping Venus, or Isis of Nature, who will himself be the new-born king that she bears. By the personal discovery of the real nature of Nature, man is transformed into a spiritual being in command of his destiny. He now 'knows' even as he himself is known. This is the knowledge of the Gnosis. He is aware, beyond *natura naturata*, of *natura naturans*. This process, extremely difficult to formulate intellectually, is best described in Owen Barfield's constructive analysis of Coleridge's underlying philosophy: *What Coleridge Thought* (Wesleyan University Press).

This alternative Path to spiritual illumination is one hardly to be welcomed by orthodox ecclesiasticism, which can barely cope with or tolerate the attainment of spiritual revelation through the broad way of divine mystical experience, as represented symbolically by the great imperial roads to Byzantium. How less can it cope with or tolerate those who go by even stranger ways? Who find illumination in the Feminine rather than the Masculine bias of Judeo-Christian-Islamic theological preconceptions? Who seek within matter for illumination, rather than through ascetically denying it?

Yet the way is there, spelled out even in the Christian mythology. The child Jesus is found in a stable or cave, surrounded by the most earthy beasts – the donkeys and the cows – cradled in the arms of his mother. At the end of his mission the Resurrection takes place after his body is buried in a cave, and thence he proceeds even down into Hades. Even in Dante's great epic of medieval Christianity the way to the Heavens is first down through the centre of the Earth. Hell may be there, but without passing through it, the redemption of Mt Purgatory and the blissful experience of the journey through the Heavens would not have been experienced.

Perhaps the way of the many is to await the coming of a Redeeming Saviour, and to be shepherded by a caring church in the meantime. However, this does not mean that there is no other way that can be trodden by the pilgrim soul. In the East it is the way of Mahayana Buddhism, whereby enlightenment is sought by personal effort in order to lessen the weight of ignorance in the worlds of sense, desire and form. It may seem presumptuous to a Western Church for any to aspire to become a *boddhisattva* or 'saviour', but Christ's enjoinder 'be ye therefore perfect as thy father in heaven is perfect' is surely an invitation to the aspiring soul; and the parable of the talents must also have relevance. The church should avoid the error of denying souls the opportunity of using their talents.

The way to the stars being via the centre of the Earth is also reflected in the legend of Merlin being enchanted by the Lady of the Lake, Nimuë. According to this he was besotted by her beauty and she, learning his magic, wove an enchantment round him so that he became imprisoned in a hawthorn tower that seemed to him like a prison, so that he was unable to continue his work of assisting Arthur and the Round Table Fellowship.

Clairvoyant investigation of certain ancient tombs suggests that this legend embodies a memory of the voluntary entombment of a priest-king or leader in order to merge with the Earth, and with his ancestors, on behalf of the living tribe. It is conceived also, contrary to our own assumptions, that the starry heavens and their powers are within, not without, the Earth.

This is a difficult concept for a modern Westerner to conceive, but the powers so generated have left their traces in a pattern of psychic stresses interlinking founts and pools of stellar powers brought down (or 'out' according to viewpoint), that are detected in piecemeal fashion by those who research into 'ley-lines' and similar matters today. The tradition of the Holy Grail being buried in a secret place for future discovery is also another expression of this complex of magical energies.

In the story of the Quest of the Holy Grail as it has come down to us, from Sir Thomas Malory (who used as a principal source the Cistercian version of the story which centres on Sir Galahad), the Arthurian Quest was at best a partial success.

Galahad the Grail-winner never returned to Earth. His one wish was to proceed onward to heaven. This one-pointed idealism has its merits; but its abandonment of the realm of Logres and its worldly setting is narrowly monastic in religious idealism. In terms of Tibetan Buddhism, which has an odd correlation with the old Celtic mysteries, Galahad seems one of the Hinayana rather than the Mahayana Vehicle. That is, one concerned more for his own soul than one embodying compassion for all sentient beings and forgoing *nirvana* until all are ready to share it. In this conception the best of the Christian and Buddhist traditions meet, and this final assumption of all into heaven will be the time when East meets West, as foreshadowed in the Wesak Festival, an August moon celebration of the Buddha and the Christ in harmonious co-operation.

Such an achievement by Galahad may not have been without due merit and effect upon the planes of form but the Grail was never brought back to shower its blessings on Earth. Galahad's companions, Percivale and his sister, likewise never returned; although significantly the latter died that another might live, giving her pure blood to a chronically ailing lady.

It was the comparatively unsung Bors who returned from a successful Grail Quest to tell the story of what had occurred. Bors was a family man and man of the world, although the monastic chroniclers with dirty-minded holy intention criticize the fact that he has a son, and consider it a lapse from grace. Without the testimony of Bors we would know nothing of the inner history of the Holy Grail; it would have disappeared without trace in a holy mist.

However, the time is approaching when the Quest shall be renewed, and in a form that reflects present needs. Both scientific and religious establishments need radically to review their positions, which are in equal disarray since the disastrous split between the two that came about through the development of the scientific method in the seventeenth century. The break between them was bridged for a time by men of vision, to a greater or lesser extent, according to method and ability. These included famous names such as Robert Boyle, Johannes Kepler, Elias Ashmole, Isaac Newton; others who have lapsed into comparative obscurity such as Michael Maier, Robert Fludd, Athanasius Kircher; and some who retained anonymity such as the Rosicrucian Brotherhood. With all this is linked the parallel expression of the crisis of the *sang real* in terms little understood at the time, or since, except by a few, in the civil war and sacrificial death of a king, and the later restoration of the Stuart

line. The masonic and Jesuitical intrigues and their inner relation to a deep crisis within the human soul, particularly within
the crucible of the land of Britain (Merlin's Enclosure), and the
later continental and imperial offshoots, have never been fully
realized or recorded. These are outcroppings of a deep magic
beyond most realizations of the nature of the art.

The split between science and religion has now become a
chasm of disastrous proportion so that the future of the human
race and the habitability of the planet by higher forms of life is
now at stake. Hope comes in the fact that in certain disciplines
such as physics the boundary of false conception has been met,
and in new disciplines such as ecology some moral responsibility is being realized as an essential for survival, preventing
the continued rape of the Earth.

The way ahead lies either in nuclear holocaust, following the
way of legendary ancient Atlantis, which sunk under the weight
of its own sin, pride and violence; or in a re-assessment of
man's own spiritual destiny upon a small planet. The latter is
a magical way, for it leads directly into conscious co-operation
with 'inner' or 'occult' forces. It becomes mystical in that these
forces become channels for an ultimate reality of God expressed
in form – which is best resumed in symbol as the Vision of the
Holy Grail. This is a cup formed by the realizations of men and
women incarnate in physical bodies of the substance of the
Earth, each a miniature Grail, containing within themselves the
blood of the Holy Spirit, the expression of their own true
essence. Thus in a special way man becomes God, incarnate
upon Earth – a concept at present heretical to the church and
ridiculous to the materialist scientific establishment.

However, those trained to see the inner tides see them rolling
in, and great will be the changes in the sand-castles of the
intellectual assumptions of mankind. The hope for the future
has many ways in which it may be expressed. The Vision of
the Grail is one form of symbolic expression, capable of almost
infinite expansion of realization in that it is synonymous with
the spirit-in-form; or heaven-on-earth; and may also be
discerned in terms of the ancient Mysteries of the Feminine; the
Assumption and Coronation of the Blessed Virgin Mary; the
Passion, Resurrection and Ascension of God-made-Man; the

Divine Priest-King-Victim of pagan antiquity; the Tantrik Path of Mahayana Buddhism; the Building of the Temple of Solomon; the Blooming of the Rose upon the Cross; the Alchemical Process; the Gnosis as revealed to the Magdalene: or the host of other ways wherein the sanctity of form and its redemption from a fallen condition (which largely results from a fallen mode of perception) is expressed in the consciousness of an aspiring humanity.

:10:
:THE·GRAIL·AS BODILY·VESSEL:
·
BOB·STEWART
·

The themes of renewal and restoration which are such a crucial part of Grail literature all point towards the supreme example of the Vessel expressed in human terms – the Virgin who bears the body and blood of the Saviour within her own body. Here the image is taken further, into the realm of genetic manipulation, and though the author's own statements make it clear that we must be wary of placing too much emphasis on the words, an abiding truth can be found in the statement that 'the physical vessel of the body is also the spiritual vessel of renewal.' For here is an essential matter of the Grail: that within the symbolic vessel is a reality which transcends physical fact, and that within each person who succeeds in the quest a spiritual alchemy must take place.

I

Among the many obscure and fascinating documents relating to the Grail, the diligent reader may find references to two lesser vessels: 'And when our lorde in the dendony was drest, This blode in two cruettes Joseph dyd take' (*The Life of Joseph of Arimathea*); 'Joseph has with him in his sarcophagus two white and silver cruets, filled with the blood and sweat of the Prophet Jesus' (Maelgwyn of Avalon: *Historia de Rebus Britannicus*). We shall return to these curious statements later, as they form part of a persistent oral tradition which manifests to the present day.

174

The main proposition of this analysis of certain aspects of Grail lore is not, as one might expect, identical to the subject suggested by the title. Before the reader accuses the author of false pretences, and tears the pages from the book, this use of the stump of tradition as a peg upon which to hang the shield of reflection must be explained.

The external appearance of any subject is seldom sufficient to prove its origin and identity, and this is especially true when we examine ancient and obscure traditions, tales, legends, songs and accumulated expositions and commentaries upon such lore. In several portentous and wonderful publications that have appeared amidst loud fanfares in recent years, tradition has been represented as an occult and political conspiracy. The message of the following pages is that tradition is neither a material conspiracy to be unravelled by television documentaries, nor a reliquary of eccentric old gew-gaws, but a catalytic mode of alteration of individual and group awareness. In this respect, tradition may be passive, as the group vehicle of inter-related symbols preserved and passed on through time by various means, or it may be active. The activation occurs through an enlivening of the basic symbols within imagination, a process which we shall refer to again when considering symbols from the Grail lore itself.

Any writer who makes such a suggestion stands as a helpless guardian of the entrance to Tophet, the burial place of forbidden and cursed gods. It was customary for the Hebrews to spit at the very name of this place, which is identical to the Celtic Underworld of Annwn in many respects, the same place in which the Grail may be found. Why helpless? Because the steady stream of pseudo-academic looters that bustles back and forth does not consider such a theory worthy of their spittle; it 'proves' nothing.

The Grail is a vessel of the Underworld, no matter what upper route it has travelled in the hands of exalted intellects. Qabalists may understand this paradox instantly, but it will be more difficult for orthodox Christians or those who follow eastern paths adapted for the use of westerners.

Familiarity with the source material is essential, and the suggestions offered are meaningless unless related to the early and basic 'Grail' texts, or other sources mentioned in context. The main source is *The Quest of The Holy Grail* (translated by P. Matarasso, Penguin, 1976). No amount of restrospective commentary can replace the actual legends themselves; they are the vehicle of a living, powerful, and ultimately undeniable inner transformation. As tradition implies, this transformation ferments from within to express itself outwardly, and not in any mere political or religious or ephemeral form.[1]

One of the hallmarks of a great symbol, such as the Grail, is that it may manifest in a number of different ways to human perception, yet each manifestation will be attuned to the nature of the original. Such a definition is not identical to suggestions that the Grail is 'all things to all men' or that it may be 'whatever we wish it to be'. A great symbol or key to altered awareness has limits, even if we cannot perceive them, and we may presume that the Grail is no exception to this rule.

The activation of a great symbol, or arch-symbol, can cause numerous effects within apparent serial time, all of which are analogous to their original, albeit with different modes of expression. The relationship between such manifestations cannot be deduced by mere lists of their correspondences, but by a deep realization that they are simultaneous expressions of one original model.

Careful consideration of this process suggests that whereas the ramifications of a great symbol may indeed be countless in expression, no one of these units alone can be true to the original. To be defined by material expression involves limitation, but we should not blandly assume that if we patch all the limited expressions together the resulting whole will be a sum of all parts! When this mechanical approach to symbolism is attempted, the potency and clarity of the original is inevitably lost.

Paradoxically, perhaps, it is one of the major operational laws of magic that the whole may operate through one part, even though the total accretion of parts can never make the whole. Understanding of this simultaneous diversity in unity was common to the philosophy, metaphysics, and ritual of the ancients; it is currently undergoing a considerable intellectual revival.

The pagan and early Christian symbolists were eminently practical. They expected, even demanded, that their most potent symbols should manifest through the physical body. It is in this context that we shall consider the Grail, always bearing in mind that its manifestation as a bodily vessel, a human being, is identical in essence (but not in mode of expression) to manifestation in any other consensual form.

The most dramatic and far-reaching religious variant of this potent manifestation may be found within orthodox Christianity, modulated through the individual preference for cult expressions of the primary original faith. The Christian Incarnation was founded upon a well-known and widespread system of magic, available not only to so-called 'initiates' but also to everyday common folk.

While adherents of esoteric Christianity will dispute that the Incarnation was of a higher order or degree than those of similar pagan rituals, they cannot reasonably suggest that the symbolism of virgin birth was not of long standing and well established before, during, and after the appearance of the Saviour. Orthodox religion, of course, does not allow such considerations at any price, even in the light of factual historical evidence such as classical literature, archaeological proof, or comparative religion and mythology.

Of particular interest in our present context is the repeated evidence that such an ancient system may still operate today, or rather that people believe that it still operates. Whether or not such a system is in any way effective or valid for the twentieth century is a separate discussion.

Within the popular revival of interest in ancient and racial lore, a revival which occurs with almost every generation, acceptance of the Grail as a Celtic and early Christian symbol has become commonplace. Despite the ever-increasing mass of literature that examines the manuscript and folklore evidence relating to the subject, there are several curious aspects of what might be termed 'Grail lore' that spill over into British tradition, and these should be considered within the broader context of magical practices and both pagan and Christian symbology.

While our analysis will revolve around one brief and specific tradition, it will not be limited to that subject alone, and will not adopt the typical approach of literary comparison, or semi-scientific folklore. Much of the material offered will probably be familiar to the reader, but some of the conclusions may be startling.

The tradition from which we begin is pleasantly short, appearing in literary form early in the thirteenth century, in the work of Robert de Boron. The reference, to two vessels or 'cruets' associated with the Grail, is a feature of the familiar tale of Joseph of Arimathea, and his association with the holy ground of Glastonbury. The endless argument about the origins and validity of this material is well known, but the absorption within popular and esoteric tradition is worthy of close examination. (*Joseph d'Arimathie*, Robert de Boron, c. 1200.)

No better way can be found to emasculate old traditions than to find a 'proof' of their origins. What is seldom grasped by the pernicious peddlers of 'proof' is that many apparently fabricated traditions find their way into the common imagination, and are openly accepted for centuries after the originators (or presumed originators) are dust.

Before proceeding any further, we must make clear to the reader that we have no intention of 'proving' anything. It is unnecessary to prove traditional lore; if it could be proven it would be valueless. We are concerned only with the undeniable fact that a tradition exists, and that the many branches of that tradition (literary, folklore, and esoteric) all offer similar information, though in confused and fragmented forms.

To treat such material as a mere detective problem, to suggest that there were or are actual secret 'orders' preserving lore into the present era for purposes of world domination, is to utterly degrade the value of traditional lore, and effectively reveals the petty mentality of the authors of such theories.

One cannot 'own' the Grail; nor can one 'prove' a Tradition.

Sources for the pattern of tradition under analysis are numerous, and references may be found within:

1 orthodox Christian teaching and scripture. Old and New Testaments;

2 pagan parallels to Christian mythology;

3 folklore parallels, in native British and European tales, songs, ballads and games or ritual dramas;

4 the main body of Grail literature from the twelfth and thirteenth centuries, which offers heretical Christian and pagan traditions in profusion;

5 esoteric traditions, as taught in European and British schools or systems of magic. These include the so-called 'inner-plane' teachings, devolving from sources not of this world, but are well represented in oral teaching, ranging from revived witchcraft through to various forms of Qabalah.

Once again we should state, at the risk of being repetitive, that the following pages are not offered as a 'proof' of anything whatsoever; nor do they necessarily constitute a statement of belief or practice on the part of the author. The true value of esoteric or symbolic lore is not found within its content, but through the effect of that content upon awareness.

Setting aside the matter of social or historical, or even literary, validity, we must consider the power of traditional material to shape and develop individual and group consciousness. In certain cases, that power acts suddenly, dynamically, and irrevocably.

Eastern systems of altered consciousness have gained considerable attention, and the use of certain tales and sayings, such as the famous Zen 'koan' are now well known. Keys of this sort work by jolting the awareness of the individual into new and previously unexperienced modes. This catalytic power may be experienced to very deep levels through the Mystery of the Grail.

Within the overall Mystery, there are a number of lesser but significant mysteries which devolve from it, which we might call sub-symbols. Such sub-symbols are useful means of approach to the greater symbol, and often act as short-cuts or secret ways to understanding, by-passing corrupted or authoritarian routes.

It is within such a context that we should consider the esoteric traditions that suggest possible physical descendants of Jesus Christ. Such traditions are not required to be factual, though they may very well be so, and are utterly prostituted when treated as seamy press scandals.

They are, in fact, operative as 'koans' or as parables. The realization of a traditional genetic inheritance, a magically activated bloodline, was intended to shock the awareness of the

179

initiate into new modes or realms of reality. The initial jolt may have been great indeed, in the face of stultifying orthodoxy, but the process of association and absorption resulting from the first shock attunes to a level of awareness that runs under religious propaganda, and provides a continuing tradition.

More significant, from a practical approach, is that the potent catalysing effect is not triggered by mere verbal or literary analysis; it comes as a surprising and inward certainty, through participation in the symbolic language of the Grail Mystery. To this end, popular works aimed at earning money from bowdlerizing tradition and esoteric keys may not, in fact, do as much damage as one thinks.

During previous centuries, however, the realizations under discussion were regarded as secrets, not in themselves, but in their linking or bridging function between esoteric practices and the mass, group, or racial consciousness. These secrets, which were punishable heresy to preach, were regarded as games, jokes, and silly tales. The myth-historian Geoffrey of Monmouth, for example, went to great lengths to tell us repeatedly that his material was full of puns, even at the risk of being accused of mocking his noble patrons. The Grail legends, however serious in their intent, contain this same child-like accumulation of traditional lore.

The precedents for such an approach are ancient indeed, and are firmly stated in Luke XVIII: verse 17. 'Verily I say unto you, Whosoever shall not receive the kingdom of God as a little child shall in no wise enter therein.'

While there is no firm evidence of coherent or secret teaching being perpetuated through the centuries, there is evidence of a recurring tradition which is protean and indestructible. From a magical standpoint, and even from the grossly materialist suppositions of modern psychology, we find that lore connected to 'genetic magic' arises spontaneously through contact, real or imagined, with certain branches of the Western Mysteries.

It is lore of this sort that advises that the 'cruets' mentioned by de Boron were offspring of Jesus of Nazareth; male and female vessels of seed and blood. In both orthodox and esoteric symbolism, 'water' is a euphemism for seed or semen in certain contexts.

This esoteric tradition may be communicated by word of mouth, and may also occur as a 'communication' from non-physical entities, who teach a coherent and applicable body of lore combining pagan and Christian enlightenment within a physical Mystery framework, aimed at manifestation through human reproduction and reincarnation.

The validity of this teaching is of no importance, but its repeated occurrence within individual and group awareness even to the present day is of great significance. It shows the operation of certain symbolic modes of consciousness through the interpretation of the emotions and the intellect into physical expression.

This same 'mystery' has occurred for thousands of years, and has many variant expressions in the main body of Grail lore. It may be fashionable from time to time to 'prove' that the mystery has been faked or forged, or that it is real and exists through the occult activity of secret organizations. The truth may be more simple, rooted in the regeneration of such concepts within group awareness. That which does not regenerate is not the Grail.

The European development of symbolism expressing a vessel of regeneration may be traced to famous manuscript references, reporting ancient Celtic tradition. These in turn compare favourably with classical references, and with remains from the Roman-Celtic period as early as the first century AD. Sites such as Aquae Sulis, with its Celtic-Roman Temple of Sul Minerva, offer practical working models of pagan belief in regeneration within the Underworld or Otherworld.

This regeneration motif is present in folklore and folksong collected from oral tradition during the twentieth century, though references are widely diffused, and the word 'grail' never occurs.

The heretical Grail lore of the twelfth and thirteenth centuries binds pagan and early Christian beliefs with a strong thread of monastic influence in interpretation. This interpretation, which is not always orthodox, acts as a cement that enabled the pagan and rather 'dangerous' native lore to hold together. Whereas in the work of Geoffrey of Monmouth, the various mythical traditions were combined upon an old 'after the cataclysm' model, in 'The Quest Of the Holy Grail' such traditions are linked by a 'redemption of the world' model.

We know from sources which noted Welsh lore in the Middle Ages that the Celts believed in a Cauldron of Immortality. This vessel restored dead men to life, though they were sometimes dumb, and renewed pork joints from old bones. It was part of the sacred feast of the dead ancestors, and was employed in a ritual which was aimed at conferring divine knowledge and immortality. This theme was also found in Greek mythology and ritual.

The magical vessel had its home underground, and all wells, springs and lakes were regarded as Gateways to the Underworld. A much-quoted Welsh poem, *Preiddeu Annwn* records a magical raid upon the Underworld by a band of heroes and this theme of theft from the depths recurs in various forms throughout folklore, magic, and religion. The poem is likely to be an early example of the Grail quest.

The foundation of belief in a vessel of power, and its place in the Underworld lay in the pagan concept of exchange between the human and otherworlds, a concept still important in ritual magic today. Duality of death and life was unknown, they were manifestations of one power, not entities in conflict.

A most obvious vessel for magical power in the outerworld is the human being, and this is reflected in the constant belief in exchange found in period inscriptions from the Celtic-Roman culture, and from classical accounts of the Celtic attitude to physical death. Humankind bargained with the Underworld.

It is in this context of exchange and interplay between human and otherworld powers that practices of human sacrifice arose. Such practices were inseparable from systems of controlled birth or potential reincarnation.

Although this system is generally bandied about in modern works on magic, and much of the material concerned is vague and nonsensical, there is a strong suggestion of its continuity in esoteric traditions and in folk or rural magical practices. The modern revival of witchcraft, although essential and praiseworthy in its attempts to recapture a fresh relationship with nature powers, has tended to cloud perception of the magical systems concerned by claiming traditions without recourse to the metaphysics which underpinned their operation. While the Christians attempted to use the conceptual models of the ancients without allowing the generative magic that gave such models life, the modern pagans have picked up the cast-off generative organs without considering that they are fallen from a great and divine body of wisdom. Little wonder, in the face of such a conflict, that the prototype of the Maimed Fisher King should have been pierced through the thighs, losing his ability to reproduce. This type of symbolism refers not only to spiritual imbalance or sickness, but to actual physical illness and reproductive processes.

In its simplest form, we have a story of heroes who raid the mysterious otherworld to gain a great prize; in its most complex form we have the quest for the Grail. In both cases, there is a powerful motif connected with fertility; not fertility in a merely sexual reproductive sense, but a through line of fertility, reaching from the Underworld, to the physical body, to the mental, emotional, and spiritual fertility of the individual and of the tribe or race.

That which does not regenerate is not the Grail.

Celtic practices of ancestor worship (the cult of the dead) involved the spirit passing into the otherworld or underworld, and then communicating with a seer or seeress who still lived in the outer or human world. This system was so widespread in the ancient cultures that it merely needs to be mentioned here, as the reader will have access to numerous works which speculate upon it in great detail. The esoteric practices of controlled fertility and timed conception were aimed at specific reincarnations of certain ancestors. Over a considerable period of time, a theoretical reservoir of illuminated souls became available to the mysteries which operated in this manner. It was believed that any particular king was literally the vehicle of all his ancestors, and this is reflected in examples from Irish tradition.

The widespread pre-Christian system, often called the rituals of the sacred king in modern literature, permeated through orthodox religion well into historical time, and much of its subtle practical operation is enshrined in the Grail legends. This enshrinement takes two forms; as specific almost offhand examples of apparently unrelated incidents, and as a continual theme reflecting upon the value of divinely given qualities of nobility.

We should not be surprised, therefore, when one branch of this material suggests that actual children were born to Jesus of Nazareth, and that they should be of the blood of the dark myth-woman of Christianity, Mary Magdalene.

The type of tradition outlined may be horribly unorthodox in the crude authoritarian sense, yet it harmonizes with some deep and persistent myth that is rooted in the group consciousness expressed within the Western Mysteries. The physical vessel of the body is also the spiritual vessel of renewal, either in the timeless experience of inspiration, or through numerous rein-carnations, depending upon the will, beliefs and culture of the individual.

In Celtic imagination, there is little to separate the dead, the ancestors, the fairies or otherworld powers, and those about to be born. Similar beliefs were held by many pagan cultures, often refined to great sophistication and complexity.

All such arbitrary selection of lore might indeed be regarded as superficial, were it not for several undeniable facts that support our curious conclusions, without ever proving them. The most important indication is the persistence of certain themes both in and out of manuscript or print, particularly as folklore or as esoteric teachings, maintained by oral traditions.

The second significant element is the relatively modern science of genetics. Knowledge of this field may have been applied by the ancients, but based upon a rather different primary model to that of deductive and experimental science.

If we dare to encapsulate this complex subject, we might define genetics as one of the major factors in the construct that appears as a 'human being'. Genetics form one of the matrices that enable the entity to operate through many levels of function in manifestation. Specialists are still researching the relative values of genetics, environment, conditioning, innate response and so forth, but the genetic inheritance is as proven as any workable scientific theory, and new applications are constantly being discovered for genetic theories.

In short, science instructs us that we inherit something of our

ancestors, as was common knowledge to the ancestors themselves. Such a concept is central to the practice of ritual magic;
orthodox authority was able to charge pagans and heretics with
necromancy. Geoffrey of Monmouth tells us that the British
King Bladud 'spread necromancy throughout the land', which is
merely another way of saying that his forefathers were ancestor
worshippers. Both archaeology and classical sources confirm
Geoffrey's statement.

The Celtic lore in Geoffrey is only superficially concealed, and
the reader will find many parallels to the later Grail legends in
The History of the British Kings (translated by Aaron Thompson,
1718, or the more modern translations, such as that of Sebastian
Evans). While Geoffrey used to be popular as a 'source' for the
Grail legends, as his work 'predated their appearance', scholars
now suggest that all such material may be derived from general
sources within oral lore . . . a concept which has always been
understood by teachers of esoteric traditions, and by modern
folklorists.

It is significant that Geoffrey applies a genealogical proof to
his post-cataclysm mythical history.

How is the genetic inheritance communicated? Through the
interaction of male and female characteristics. In magical
language these factors have long been expressed as The Seed
and The Blood. The Celtic obsession with genealogy is not
entirely a claim for social superiority. In the not too distant past,
it was the equivalent of the modern genetic chart; a statement
of direction with respect to the future, confirmed by the records
of the past.

Readers who are familiar with the Christian Bible will
remember the two distinct genealogies offered for Jesus Christ,
by Matthew and Luke, in their opening chapters. Matthew
gives an orthodox male line of inheritance, whereas Luke shows
a female line, including miraculous births of both Jesus and
John the Baptist brought about by the mediation of the Archangel Gabriel upon the 'daughters of Aaron', Elisabeth and
Mary.

In many ancient cultures, the matrilinear line is primary in
the definition of race, tribe, inheritance of property and other
matters, and this emphasis is found in a great deal of Celtic

folklore. Although modern revivalist pagans often take this, perhaps rightly, as evidence of a once dominant Goddess culture, it also reflects the magical and metaphysical concern with genetic lines.

Many of the clearly emphasized incidents within the Grail cycle involving female lines of descent, blood, and mysterious conceptions should be analysed in the light of modern genetic science. They are likely to be a magical analogy or operative model which uses a different vocabulary, but relates to the same processes as the modern expositions. This comparison should not be taken too literally, however, for the magical or metaphysical models were concerned only with the inheritance of otherworld power through the physical body, and were based upon long cycles of observation and correlation linked to seership. These are the very cycles that are referred to in both genealogies of Jesus, and which appear again in the replication of Christ in the form of Galahad.

The special role of Jesus in replacing the hero who raids the otherworld is emphasized in several ways in Celtic Christian mythology, the earliest form of Christianity native to Britain.

Scottish Highlanders retained the ancient tradition that Jesus was fostered by the native goddess Brigit, the most powerful beneficial goddess of the Celtic pantheon. In early social structures, the foster mother and midwife were as important as the blood mother; in magical terms that which brings a child from the womb will powerfully affect the outer life of that child. The birth of the Saviour was associated with the blessing of the most important culture goddess of the pagan world, Brigit to the Celts, and Minerva to the Romans, patroness of so many heroes who plundered the dark powers of the Underworld, slew monsters, and brought special aid to their people.

As a result of this significant midwifery, which may be interpreted in several ways, Jesus fulfilled his expected duty by the so-called Harrowing of Hell – his journey through the Underworld. It would have been unthinkable that such a divine hero might pass from the outer world without reproducing his line, the blood line carries the message of the experience of his role as Mediator and Saviour. The power is passed *directly* through the body, bypassing all other mental and emotional routes.

It is not surprising that this heretical aspect of early Christian belief should be rigorously suppressed – the aim of the later church was to control and suppress the power, not to scatter it broadcast as a universal seed. Esoteric tradition advises us that sensuality may be a snare, but that specific reproduction along certain special lines may be beneficial to us all. Concepts of this sort are subject to considerable abuse, and historic manifestations up to and including the present century have frequently been of the worst possible nature. The abuse comes through literal attempts to 'prove' the system by 'purifying' human groups, a quite absurd and impossible venture, which utterly ignores the complex time-scales inherent in magical work, and wilfully rejects the spirit of true grace and enlightenment which blows where it will.

Despite the obvious abuses, against which we might choose to weigh the appalling career of the orthodox churches in their abuse of humanity at large, we may indulge in a few (idle) speculations. If Jesus of Nazareth had been initiated in the ancient mysteries, or as an Essene, or during his traditionally avowed youth in Druid Glastonbury, he would have had a clear understanding of the magical lore of sacred breeding and reincarnation. Indeed, the fragments of the suppressed Gnostic gospels suggest that he tried to apply this knowledge in rather specific ways which aimed at removing the enlightened from the physical matrix of consensual reality through the practice of magical chastity. We will return to this disappearing act shortly, in later and lesser variants.

It might not be too wildly imaginative to suggest that there could be no better way of perpetuating a spiritual revolution in a fallen world than to plant its seed within the blood of following generations. Such is the esoteric tradition which deals with the two Vessels or Cruets associated with the Grail.

II

It is difficult for the retrospective analyst of folklore or of period embodiments of tradition in manuscript to decide exactly what the true nature of the subject matter may be. This is why we gain such endless occupation in the study of early literature and of oral tales and songs.

Material may be classified into units of local, national, and even international currency as motifs, but this does little more than show a crude statistical summary, a preliminary organization which tidies up the sweepings ready for real examination.

Ultimately it is the personal belief of the student of any school or body of lore that enlivens and colours interpretation. Some modern writers regard all ancient lore as nothing more nor less than the inevitable product of economic and social struggles; many folklorists insist that apparent evidence of early magical or pagan lore in modern folk sources is either an illusion on the part of the interpreter, or an intrusion culled from nasty literature. Regrettably, they are often correct in their insistence.

During our analysis, we have made the monstrous presumption that a great deal of ancient matter is incorporated within oral tradition and that this matter is available to the present day, in numerous though attenuated forms. We have capped this presumption with an even greater one; that a careful comparison of standard folklore and song, magical symbolism and pagan philosophy will reveal many practical insights into the Grail legends.

Any student of magic who reaches beyond the superficial levels so profusely available in publication will have realized that magic is somehow concerned with 'genetics'. Our ancestors, from whom we inherit our magic as well as our physical characteristics, were most concerned to perpetuate certain blood lines that held special abilities. If the Grail legends are considered in this light, they are found to be replete with indications of genetic magic, especially aimed at spiritual regeneration attuned to physical regeneration.

As we mentioned above, *The History of The Kings of Britain* assembled traditional magical and religious motifs upon a mythical 'post-cataclysm' framework, a rationalization of myth in the classical form of the fall of Troy, and the flight of a band of heroes. The Grail legends, on the other hand, deal with the Fall and Redemption. By the time alchemical works had begun to appear, based upon the common symbolism found within the Grail and pagan lore, and later refined by the great hermetic philosophers of the fifteenth, sixteenth and seventeenth centuries, the esoteric tradition as a whole had begun to concern itself with the redemption and regeneration or restoration of the Fallen World. It is in this atmosphere that the monumental works of Christian metaphysics allied to magical practices appeared. The perceptive reader may detect a similar cycle, expressed in different modes, from the eighteenth century to the present day, distributing the three phases over a shorter time scale.

A few obvious examples of genetic magic within the 'Quest' would be:

1 Lancelot, whose excellence is the product of his breeding and not of his own inward efforts. He falls into sin and despair through the squandering of his natural gifts, and suffers considerable hardship before he attempts to develop his spiritual essence or true nature and attune his physical inheritance and prowess to its proper end. A believer in reincarnation might suggest that Lancelot lives off the capital of previous lives, without fully becoming aware of his function in the present life. He is, in this sense, an example of everyman, though a highly amplified and noble example in many respects.

2 Galahad, the product of a mysterious liaison between Lancelot and a maiden. Galahad seems to be a model of perfection, so much so that his father asks why he does not aid him in his spiritual plight.

The esoteric answer to this question is that if Lancelot and Galahad are to become spiritually free, each to his own degree, then they must transcend the old genetic cycles of magical work, and realize a truly spiritual inspiration.

3 Arthur, the offspring of a union arranged by magical illusion, and traditionally said to be under the protection of the enchanter Merlin during his childhood.

Most important of all, however, is the master model that explains many of the lesser examples and characters in the Grail legends, so we will move straight to this without listing further individuals, especially as such lines may be found clearly stated within the 'Quest' itself.

The major key is, of course, the tale of the 'Tree of Life', which clearly offers the salvation of humankind through the action of the power of woman. This tale should be studied in detail, and compared to topological models such as the Qabalistic Tree of Life, a mathematical structure which shows the interrelationship between metaphysics and human energies through various conceptual worlds. It also shows the pattern of genetics and relationships which have been 'discovered' by modern science and psychology.

Of particular relevance to our suggestion that the Grail may manifest as ancestor worship or necromancy is the action of Solomon in the legend of 'The Tree Of Life'. Through meditation upon the quality of womanhood, Solomon, the model or archetype of wisdom, achieves the revelation that 'there shall come a woman through whom man shall know joy greater an hundred times than is your sorrow; and she shall be born of your inheritance.'[2]

Delighted by this knowledge, Solomon studies 'every sign according him, whether waking or in dream, in the hope of coming at the truth of the ending of his line'.

Finally, having discovered that The Virgin shall be his descendant, and that the last male of his line shall be even more valorous than Josiah, he decides to send a message through time to his descendants.

The resulting magical ship, needless to say, is devised by his scheming wife, who uses the three sports of the Tree of Life in its symbolism; Red, White and Green. While the male struggles to send his knowledge through time, the female provides the means whereby this might be realized, and a third and mysterious power activates the vessel and casts it off upon the ocean of life. (See Ch. 4, p. 83.)

The entire venture is a simple restatement of the Celtic application of ancestor lore, magical genetics, and divination; science-arts which were held in common by the advanced peoples of the ancient world, and which persist to the present day in diffused forms.

One factor which is easily overlooked in consideration of the Grail legends is that their originals were from an oral tradition; the reader of, or rather the listener to, the Grail stories would have been comfortably able to relate their content to a large store of similar tales, songs and entertainments which were widespread in all levels of society.

It is only in relatively recent years that an understanding of folklore has enabled scholars to realize the nature of the Grail material; it is combined and edited from a common stock of lore, and doubtless contains innumerable cross-references, themes and motifs which the modern reader cannot glimpse, or which have been lost.

Such themes, however, cannot be 'traced to originals', for they are the currency of communication in the dream-like process of the group imagination. It cannot be over-emphasized that Grail lore was intentionally fused from parts in common regular use in the general imagination; it cannot be denied that this fusion created a new and powerful imaginative entity that works as a vehicle for transformation when activated. The works of Homer are directly comparable.

In modern jargon, we could suggest that the Grail legends, and the related works such as *The History of the Kings of Britain* and *The Prophecies of Merlin*, are models of the racial psychology; but they are also maps of the magical physiology of the relationship between the Ancestors, the Land, and the Underworld.

Primitive examples of this type of symbolism were operative as rituals during the early part of the twentieth century, and a few still persist today. A list of such examples from folklore would be long indeed, but one of the most famous examples, 'The Cutty Wren', involves a ritual hunt for a mythical bird (represented by a real wren), and its cooking in 'a bloody great brass cauldron'. The remains are so large, that the poor can be fed with the spare ribs alone.

Promoters of the theory of sacrificial kingship often use this folksong and ritual as proof of survival, but setting such a complex argument aside, we can observe identical motifs to those of the raid upon the Underworld in the poem *Preiddeu Annwn* mentioned above. For while the gap in time between the two is many centuries, the message has been sent down through time in the vessel of the common tradition.

The genetic flow, or pattern of communication with the ancestors in the otherworld, is intimately linked to the persistence of a common tradition which expresses itself in song, story and ritual, carrying material that appears to be retained from ancient cultural and magical sources. We would emphasize the apparent or superficial nature of this similarity, which is more likely to be the result of a deeply regenerative power of group consciousness than of active preservation and policy.

The legend of the 'Tree of Life' also gives an insight into the nature of magical or spiritual virginity, an esoteric under-standing which greatly pre-dates the Christian emphasis of its appearance in the Grail lore. Maidenhood, we are advised, is a mere physical circumstance, but virginity is a state of awar-eness, a mode of consciousness. The collator of the Grail stories is intentionally stating a central and powerful magical law – something which must be fully realized before any type of magical work becomes truly effective. It has very little to do with morality and physical chastity, and a 'virgin' in ancient terminology need not be a 'maiden'. This applies equally to males and females, as the Grail legends repeatedly state.

Virginity is a primal or spiritual state, whereas maidenhood is the physical mirror of that state, which occurs through renewal of the body in reincarnation. Conversely, a maiden may not be virgin, but maidens who are not virgin are of little use in magic, contrary to popular opinion and fiction.

This metaphysical law was clearly stated by Jesus: 'But I say unto you, that every one that looketh upon a woman to lust after her hath committed adultery with her already in his heart' Matthew V: verse 28. Regrettably, subtle magical laws of this sort have been deliberately poisoned and misrepresented, leaving modern men and women with a dismal heritage of separation from their true power of relationship.

When we are advised that both the mother of Jesus and the mother of John the Baptist were 'the daughters of Aaron' and conceived as virgins, we are experiencing a mythical reworking of the magical rituals common to the pagans, whereby special breeding was aimed at bringing forth certain powerful ancestral or otherworld beings by the purity of the male and female partners, synchronized to specific times and places. Such a suggestion, however, in no way challenges or lessens the reli-gious or spiritual power of the Virgin, as She is the essence, the Virgin of all virgins, and the human manifestation of the Grail.

With this point, we have come full circle in our argument, and repeat that a great symbol, such as the Holy Grail, may manifest in several different modes simultaneously. The difference is actually in the perception or level of consciousness of the recipient, as is clearly shown at the conclusion of the 'Quest'.

Although we have found a convenient circularity in the exposition, it does not suggest that all Mysteries are identical in operation or results, even if they use identical methods and key symbols. In the case of 'genetic magic' esoteric tradition supposes several sources for magical lines of descent, initiation, and communication from otherworld beings. These vary from widely published (but little understood) sources such as the lost continent of Atlantis, to quite obscure individuals with utterly localized traditions. Royal and noble families are often included, though pedigree is no guarantee of magical and spiritual power. As a mere aside, the perceptive student of history will have realized that most, if not all, of the ancient European blood lines have been usurped.

To express the matter crudely, not all members of the Mysteries are descendants of Jesus Christ, but there is a symbolic tradition that implies that any one of them *might be*. The corollary, that any one of us might be a descendant of some lesser divine hero or sacred king, is almost equally important.

It is this imaginative potential that acts as the super-catalyst to fire the consciousness into new realms, and the resulting changes will be shaped by the matrix which contains the imaginative energies at the moment of transition or translation. This method is radically different from the standard concepts of prayer, faith, or even of meditation, and is one of the true magical or esoteric 'secrets' handed down to us by our native tradition. An understanding of this pattern of human consciousness, this method of transformation, enabled the early Christian authorities to sink certain programmes of control very deeply into the group mind, by tapping the collective symbols and merely re-connecting them in a slightly, but deliberately, confused manner.

If, as genetic science informs us, there is a set of co-ordinates that defines the physical entity derived from our ancestors; if, as modern psychology suggests by vaguely plagiarizing the philosophy of the ancients, there is a deep fund of group or racial memory, how may we awaken this knowledge, wisdom and understanding, locked within our very cells and our hidden depths of consciousness? Might not the deep memories and the bodily pattern be one and the same thing?

Magical tradition avers that this is indeed the case, and offers a full and effective method for such an arousal.

Folk tradition supports this with accounts of certain persons who made trips to the otherworld while still in bodily form. Some of these returned as seers or seeresses, while others remain lost but not dead. One typical example of this class of magical disappearance is the Reverend Robert Kirk of Aberfoyle (1644–?), the first translator of the Bible into Gaelic, and collector of an early set of examples of fairy lore and the Second Sight. People were still attempting to rescue Kirk from fairyland only a generation ago, as the result of a local tradition that had continued for almost three hundred years.

Religious tradition offers us the example of Enoch, who walked with God and 'was not', and, more relevant to the Grail, the Roman Catholic belief in the physical ascent of the Virgin into Heaven.

Similar examples might be enumerated at great length, but their significance in our present context is that the belief was attached to historical persons, such as Kirk, Thomas of Ercle-doune, and others within British or Celtic tradition. It is this demanding of literal physical manifestation (or perhaps we should say un-manifestation) that is close to the inmost heart of Western magic; this same deep intuition that the divine powers must flow through the body has led to popular misconceptions of the work of the alchemists, magicians and metaphysicians of past centuries. More subtly, it leads to the common complaint against 'magic', that the art does not work, for the experimenter had no physical results to be observed or experienced.

The demand that magic work upon the outer matrix or physical world is no mere puerile materialist plea; it runs ancient and deep, and is actually the result of our most potent collective intuition about apparent reality; that it can be changed.

Firm attempts to combine magical power, blood lines, and temporal power have frequently appeared in history, such as the foundation of The Order of the Garter, based upon Grail symbolism. Such organizations, dependent upon hierarchies of beings similar to those of the orthodox church, inevitably fail.

The true value of such traditions as those outlined briefly above lies in a full absorption of the symbolism, and its subsequent activation to create a revolutionary alteration of awareness. This revolution is not limited to politics, religion, or even personal mental activity, but runs through each and every aspect of the human entity, manifesting through the physical body, and transforming utterly. No hierarchical authority can exist or function against the blowing of the spirit.

One final suggestion, which seems inevitable, is that the subsequent destruction of the kingdom, in which Arthur and his knights are defeated after the quest, is the result of their seeking the Grail. That this destruction should arise through Arthur's own seed in the form of his magically inspired offspring of incest is hardly surprising, if we follow the concepts of genetic magic through carefully.

The willed pursuit of the power of the spirit brings breakdown and change (Matthew X:34), and in the earliest version of the Grail quest, the vessel was stolen from the Underworld, the realm of seething, ever changing energy. Unless this energy is contained by perfect balance and purity within the outer world, it will rotate according to cycles of creation and destruction, the only way in which its essential nature may be expressed in manifestation. This cyclical pattern of ancient lore repeats itself in the Grail legends, despite the higher order of Salvation offered by the Saviour.

We are promised, however, that Arthur is not dead, but merely sleeping or waiting within the otherworld for the correct time to return. Not wise, indeed, to seek the grave of any of our true kings, virgins or heroes, for they live on within each and everyone of us, waiting to be aroused by the power of the spirit, the regeneration offered through The Holy Grail.

Notes

1 For those who seek academic cross references, such delights occur in abundance in the footnotes of any good research work upon medieval or traditional tales. For the present a short list of works is here appended. All have been used extensively in the preparation of this essay. P. Matarasso, *The Quest of The Holy Grail*, Harmondsworth, Penguin, 1969 (translation). J. Cable, *The Death of King Arthur*, Harmondsworth, Penguin, 1971 (translation). J. Gantz, *The Mabinogion*, Harmondsworth, Penguin, 1976 (translation). Rev. C. C. Dobson, *Did Our Lord Visit Britain?*, London, Covenant, 1974. H. Jennings, *The Rosicrucians*, London, George Routledge, 1907. Rev. R. Kirk, *The Secret Commonwealth*, ed. Sanderson, Cambridge, N.J., Brewer/Rowman & Littlefield, 1976. A. and B. Rees, *Celtic Heritage*, Thames & Hudson, London, 1978. A. Ross, *Pagan Celtic Britain*, Cardinal, London, 1974. A. Ross, *Folklore of the Scottish Highlands*, Batsford, London, 1976. H. M. Porter, *The Celtic Church in Somerset*, Morgan, Bath, 1971. E. Pagels, *The Gnostic Gospels*, Weidenfeld & Nicolson, London, 1980. R. Steiner, *The Occult Significance of Blood*, Steiner Publishing Co., London. G. R. S. Mead, *The Hymn of Jesus*, Watkins, London, 1963. L. C. Wimberley, *Folklore in the English and Scottish Ballads*, Ungar, New York, 1959.

2 Matarasso, *op. cit.*, pp. 222–35. The position of this legend relative to the other material of *The Quest* is interesting, for it comes almost as a retrospective key to many of the events and relationships in the preceding adventures. In this key explanatory role, it prepares the reader for the revelations that are to follow.

:11:

:THE·PATH TO·THE·GRAIL:

·

DOLORES·ASHCROFT-NOWICKI

·

The interior journey of the soul in search of wisdom must always be for the individual. As the author of this essay says in her introduction, the seeker after the Grail 'is forever set apart from those he serves'. Reading the Grail texts can itself be a rewarding experience, but this need only be a beginning. The images and the words have a reality far beyond themselves. In the text which follows a practical opportunity is offered to all who wish to find out more about the Grail for themselves. In this, as in the section which follows, the printed word takes on a new dimension, and promotes another kind of understanding – that of the interior journey itself.

When a man turns away from God, that is the moment when he starts on the long road towards Him. God surrounds Man, therefore no matter which way he may turn in order to get away from his creative source, inevitably in time, he comes face to face with it. This, then, is the reason for the Grail Quest. It is the Journey of the Racial Hero, the Adventures of the Widow's Son, the Eternal Fairy Tale, the Search for the Golden Fleece. Whatever name the quest goes by, it is nothing more nor less than a return to that source from whence we came,[1] and where we may find renewal. It is an ancient dance in which we must all take part, whether we will or no, though some come to it much later than others.

The Grail Quest is one of many ways that lead to what is

called in the east, spiritual enlightenment. Each tradition has its own path and no one is better than another. For those in the west for whom King Arthur and his knights of the Table Round are racial heroes, the Grail holds a special significance. It is the prime symbol of the English race and of all those who derive from it.

The Quest of the Grail, like all things in this cosmos, has a grand design that must be followed, a pattern, a sequence of steps in the great Dance, steps that are ignored at one's peril. In the Mystery Schools this pattern is followed exactly and the student actually becomes the Hero or the Seeker, and undergoes in his training an interior journey that follows the ancient design. By such means he condenses many lifetimes' experiences into one, and absorbs the understanding that such experiences bring into a shorter span of time. But success depends on his ability to follow the pattern, make the right choice of path when a crossroads is reached, and above all to ask the right questions at the right time.

In this the serious student is helped by a tutor, a kind of personal Merlin, who has already taken this road, and who has returned, and the return is the most important part of the whole Quest. It must be fully understood that the seeker enters upon the Quest not only for himself but for his race, and indeed for all those who cannot go for themselves, those for whom the time is not yet right.

The journey undertaken by the seeker is a paradoxical one; on the one han, it draws the mind inward to the heart's centre, the Hall of the Table Round where sit the many facets of the personalities used by the seeker down the ages. On the other hand, it also projects the mind outward, seeking to bring back to the everyday world an understanding of what has been experienced within. Seeking also to share that experience as far as it is possible with those who stayed behind.

He who seeks, finds, and returns, becomes a Janus-like figure standing at the gateway of many possible worlds. His eyes are unlike those of any other man. They see more deeply, shine with more wisdom, and weep more bitterly. Such a one is forever set apart from those he serves, and it is by his own choice. To serve well one must first learn to stand alone and apart, and to observe quietly.

The Quest has three stages: 1 separation from all that is known and loved. In myth and fairy tale this stage is seen when the young hero/heroine leaves home and family, usually an aged parent who grieves most bitterly. In real life it is the moment when the soul hears the inner call and realizes its need to seek out its source, to renew itself in the Grail of Grails; 2 the journey, the danger, the wonder, the transmutation of the soul through experience. For the student it is a time of training and study during which the student will be severely tested in real life. 3 the all-important return, bearing within the heart's centre, the gift. This gift is a transmuted Table Round, only now it is made concave and fashioned into a personal Grail. It is filled with the essence of Love, Understanding, and Wisdom distilled from the knowledge donated from all those many personality facets, the distillation of myriad lifetimes. Such a Grail is borne with only one purpose, to let all *who can* drink from it. But the bearer of such a Grail can never drink from his own vessel, he must seek another who will give him to drink from their heart's cup.

The wine from such a chalice can be both bitter and sweet, we can never know until the moment of tasting. The true initiate is one who tastes both with equal joy.

The Grail may still be sought and won, each man may be an Arthur, wise, loving, but knowing his own weakness. He may be a Lancelot, brave and strong, but easily led. At the end of the Quest he will be a Galahad combining all the good with less and less of the bad.

Every woman may be a Guenevere, royal but wayward, a Nimue enchanting but heartless, but she too will come to the Chapel Perilous as Elaine the Grail Maiden.

We all go through a form of Quest in our everyday lives, but it is only when we reach a point in those lives when it becomes essential to Seek, to Dare, to Know, and in knowing to keep Silence that we enter consciously upon the inner journey. The Mystery Schools hold the keys to such journeys of the mind and soul. To them in the ancient days were given secrets to hold until man could bear the weight of the knowledge of his own Divinity. Those keys have been held with patience and with courage and against great odds. But in many ways they are no longer needed. In the past hundred years man has grown very quickly, his ability to understand himself on the inner levels has increased a hundredfold. Those still young in soul, and those whose greater experience needs a harder training still need what the Mystery Schools have to offer, but there are others who are capable, with a little help, of finding part of the way for themselves. If this is so, and I believe it is, then we who have held those keys for so long must make them available.

For centuries poets, painters, musicians and dreamers have been in possession of one of those keys. It was an important part of the training of every bard in the Celtic lands. Chaucer and Shakespeare knew it and used it, so did John Donne. It blazes from the works of Coleridge, Wordsworth, Tennyson, and Whitman, it shines from the paintings of Michaelangelo, Da Vinci, Turner, and Constable, and haunts us from the music of that small band of men and women who keep alive the traditional airs and lyrics of our ancient heritage.

Every child who plays with a piece of wood down by a stream, or who sits and gazes out of the window on a wet afternoon holds the very same key that we need to seek out the inner Grail. We call it the 'creative imagination'. Without this one, seemingly simple thing, man has no vision, no dreams, no sense of being more than just a speck of dust. With it he can becomes the ruler of his own inner kingdom, and once established there, that inner sense of achievement and capability will seep through into the everyday world, bringing with it the true magic of self-knowledge. All things have their beginning on the inner levels of existence and work their way outwards. That is why God places Himself both at our centre and at our periphery, so that when, in a mood of spiritual frustration, we feel the need to run from all we imagine He represents, we run in fact straight towards Him. From the inner-most point of the circle of creation, we move outwards in our search. The circle becomes first our own expansion of conscious-ness, then the Table Round where we take our place, and finally, it becomes the Grail and centres itself within us. In the final analysis God is the Grail, containing the Cosmos within what has become an Entity far beyond titles of God or Goddess, or attributes of sex, 'It' is a creative matrix, a life-holder, a Cosmic Grail. Man, life, then becomes the wine that fills this Grail of Grails.

As in all things there is a hierarchy of sacred cups, all valid, all meaningful, and all part of the one Primal Cup.[2] It is the hope of each and every would-be initiate first to seek out and achieve the personal Grail, then the Grail of his race, and through that, the World Grail. Beyond that only those who are called by name dare to go. For those who enter a Mystery School this can mean years of study and discipline, something not always appreciated by those who expect the ancient wisdom to come in a neat package, to which they need only add a few drops of desultory attention.

But there are many who are tied by work, and/or lack of time, teacher, or even a knowledge of their availability. Yet they too have something to offer, and should not be prevented by the pressures of the world from making a start at least on the Quest. For them, there is a key that will open many doors, a form of creative mind work called in occult terminology, pathworking. Although it is used as a training method for high level students, it can also be used by those just starting to discover the world within themselves. It can certainly provide a means whereby any sincere person may achieve his or her own heart's Grail.

It is necessary to explain a little about the techniques of pathworking and their effects, which can be considerable. They have been known to change completely the life patterns of those who attempt them, though so drastic an effect is not usual. But changes they certainly do cause, in ideas, ways of thinking, of living, loving, and not least in understanding. Without change the Grail cannot be achieved, indeed it changes continually itself, from stone, to platter, to spear, to cup and finally to the Divine Child, each change bringing about an equal and opposite effect in the initiate. In achieving the cut and polished stone, he becomes aware of himself as that which needs to be fashioned into the shape best suited to the purpose of those who guide his destiny. When he achieves the platter he learns to carry what must be borne as the platter carries the host. The spear teaches a painful lesson: that which would pierce must first be pierced, must bleed and suffer. But that suffering brings close the achievement of the cup, the giving of self to others, whilst he, the giver, abstains. This accomplished, the last change of the Grail is realized and in the presence of the Sun Child, the seeker becomes the Ruler of his or her own inner Citadel.

Such may be the effects of treading the pathworking of the Grail. To place before untried minds those paths used by students working within a contacted school would be both unwise and cruel. There would always be those who, because of their intellectual abilities could reach further into the underlying truths than others. But sheer mental ability is not what the Quest is about. Such a one would be denied and frustrated when blocks were reached, as there would be in time. Those with less knowledge but more feeling would travel happily at first, but would gradually fail to realize the deeper symbolism and apathy would overtake them. Encompassed by the eggregore of a school and guided by a tutor, such difficulties may be challenged and overcome, but to one with little or no back-up knowledge it would be a daunting task. This being so I have tried to walk a middle way, and give a pathworking that would bring to those using it a sense of wonder and achievement, whilst keeping the deeper effects 'cloud hidden'. Hidden but not totally outside the reach of that one in a thousand to whom the working will act like a clarion call. Repeated workings will gradually uncover an ability to understand on progressively deeper levels, all pathworkings eventually yield their secrets to persistent and observant students.

The actual technique of pathworking is similar to that of a quiet daydream with one important difference; the working is controlled by a disciplined mind with an aim in view. Without some control the whole can become simply wishful thinking on a grand scale. Students in a school train their minds with a series of daily exercises. It would be a good idea to build up to the actual working by doing a week of intensive training first; this would enhance the experience and deepen the effect of the whole thing. Knowing human nature, most will prefer to go straight into the pathworking, but there may be some who would like to try the exercises first, for them I would suggest a simple daily routine for just seven days.

1 Before rising in the morning use just five minutes of your time to build up in the mind's eye as clear a picture of your first schoolroom as you can. Do not rush it, let the mind bring up the details one by one, add a little more each day. It need not be a school room, try your first bedroom, or a room where you stayed when on holiday as a child.

2 Choose a symbol, one with some meaning for you, or a picture so long as it is not over-complicated. For five minutes each afternoon, ten if you can spare it but no longer, just sit and look at the picture, let it imprint itself on your mind for just one minute. Now, close your eyes and allow the image to re-appear on your mental television screen. Once it is there blank it out again, then let it build up again. Keep doing this until you can recall the symbol or picture with absolute clarity and in a fraction of a second.

3 In the evening, or just before you sleep, again using the mind's eye take a walk along a path that you know well. It may be the way you walk to work, or to a friend's house, a favourite country walk, or even one you knew and used as a child. Take it slowly and observe as much detail as you can. Try to remember sound and smell as well as sight, the more real you can get these pictures, the better will be your pathworking when you come to it. Don't worry if you go to sleep halfway through it all, this kind of thing tends to go on working even when you are asleep. In fact this is one of the ways in which an occultist trains himself to dream about a required subject, rather than accepting what the subconscious dishes up.

These three simple steps, if followed for one week, will make the Quest working a vastly improved experience. If you do decide to go straight on with the working, you may like to try the week of exercises later, and then return to the pathworking. You will be quite amazed at the difference.

All pathworkings should be done in a quiet atmosphere away from any possibility of interruptions. A sudden invasion of children or family pets is not conducive to a pleasant experience. It has a similar effect to waking up in the night knowing that someone is in the room. The heart pounds, breathing rate is accelerated, and the ability to orientate is impaired for a few minutes, while your mind tries to sort out where it is, where it was, and where it should be.

Do not use the pathworking more than twice a week. It may seem like an innocuous daydream, but it is not. You will, however, find that with each successive working your ability to understand and cope with the results will deepen. After doing it a few times no doubt it will fade from your mind, to surface only in dreams. But that will not be the end of it. You will find the odd laws of synchronicity coming into play. Books, ideas, pictures, conversation, and people will crop up in your daily life, all of them containing links to your Grail Quest. If you are wise you will keep as detailed a record as possible of the events before, during and after each working.

Finally it will fade from memory, perhaps for years, only to surface when you least expect it, perhaps as the herald of a new change in your life. It is then that you may come to understand the fullest extent of its effect on your life.

Pathworkings are not magical in the Disney sense of the word, they are only magical in the sense that they are signposts towards areas of yourself as yet unexplored. They can also be used as maps for that area. For the unwary they can be traps, for the superficial they can be mirrors, with devastating effects. They are not, and never should be regarded as occult toys.

Time now to approach the Grail working, if you have taken note of the previous pages, you should achieve a reasonable effect on your first try, with each subsequent one becoming clearer. Remember the notes, you are working in an altered state of consciousness, and those notes will help you to evaluate your work. Don't rush it, build all images carefully and as clearly as you can. If you don't do too well at first, keep trying. If certain things are hard to visualize, go and look at them in a museum before you try again, it will get easier.

The journey to the Grail Castle

In order for the experience to be as full as possible, it helps to keep to certain rules. Fairly quiet conditions, no possibility of interruptions and a consistent time factor. All ritual or semi-ritual practices set up a rhythm or wave on the inner sea of consciousness. These waves ebb and flow in a precise pattern, so once a time is selected try hard to keep to it within a few minutes either way. A comfortable chair with a firm back, and subdued lighting are all you need in the way of equipment.

Relaxation is important, the better it is, the easier it will be to alter the state of consciousness. Start with your feet and work your way up to the head, paying particular attention to those areas easily forgotten, like the small muscles behind the ears, and those between the eyebrows.

A series of slightly deeper than normal breaths in a four, two, four, two pattern will help to slow you down to a relaxed, calm state of mind. If you never get further than this, you will have done yourself a great deal of good! Think about the journey you are about to undertake, to the Castle of the Grail, try to recall what you know about the Holy Cup from any preparatory reading you may have done.

Let your mind, now nicely relaxed, ease you into a series of pictures that gradually become clearer and clearer, until they are as real as you can get them. You seem to be standing on the banks of a fast moving river, it looks deep and cold. On the other side you can see a dark forest that seems full of noises and rustling movements. You remember that you have been warned many times against crossing the river, and of going into the forest. Yet you are always drawn towards them, as if some inner voice calls to you to defy the warning.

Somehow you feel that today will be different to any other day. Today that inner voice is stronger than ever before. You feel such a strong compulsion to cross the river and enter the forest, that nothing can stop you. You begin to walk downriver, looking for a shallow place to cross. As you walk you meet other people coming towards you, some are friends, some may even be relatives. When they ask you where you are going, you tell them, 'across the river and into the forest'. A look of horror comes over their faces when you say this, and they plead with you not to go, to stay with them where it is safe. There are strange and terrible things in the forest, monsters that can kill you, or demons that might steal your soul. 'Think of your family', they tell you, 'stay in the village.'

But you turn a deaf ear to all their arguments, and continue to walk steadily downstream. Soon you are alone, and in the silence you begin to wonder if your friends may not be right, perhaps you should go back. But the inner voice starts to whisper of mysteries and honours to be won beyond the dark forest. For a moment you stand and look back towards the village in the far distance. You know deep inside that even if you *do* return, you will never be the same, you will be changed, as one who has broken the boundaries of the known and familiar is changed. You will be an Outsider.

You start walking again. Soon the path is no longer familiar to you, you have gone far beyond the boundaries of the fields and places you have known. You feel happy, lighthearted, as if a weight has been lifted from your shoulders. There is a tingle of excitement down your back, and you unconsciously quicken your steps.

The sun is moving towards noon when you first see the bridge, it gleams like fire and the sunlight dances over it in a rainbow of colours. In shape it looks like any other bridge, but you sense that it crosses more than a river, it crosses a boundary between mankind and . . . something else, something you cannot clearly define as yet.

Now you are nearer and you can see that the bridge is made of glass as clear and transparent as the finest crystal. The sun's rays turn it into a glory of coloured flame. To cross such a thing is frightening, but you know that this is something you *must* do if you are to obey the insistent inner voice that has never ceased to urge you onwards.

As you draw near a figure can be seen standing by the gleaming span of glass. It is cloaked and hooded in black and leans heavily on a staff of applewood, its top cunningly carved into the shape of a hand that grasps a stone of brilliant green.

The figure pushes back its hood revealing a strange and awesome countenance. At first you take it to be just an old woman, but as you look the face changes, now it is the face of your mother, now your sister, now your own face, or that of a loved one left behind in the village. It is young, old, beautiful, and ugly, white as porcelain, now black as jet, golden as a sunripened peach, and the colour of old ivory. The changes

206

follow one upon the other, until you reel back covering your eyes.

When it comes, the voice is stern, but with a quality of love beneath the sternness. You look up and see a woman about the same age as your own mother smiling at you. Gone are the bewildering changes, now she is just like any other woman you know, but with a great dignity of bearing that sets her apart. She asks you why you are so far from your home, and you tell her about the voice that draws you to cross the river and enter the forest.

She asks you what you expect to find on the other side. Think about your answer very carefully. What *do* you expect from this journey? When you have thought answer her, but answer truthfully.

The woman then asks if you will take a gift to her son who lives in a castle a long way away, far beyond the other side of the forest. In return her son will either take you into his service, or allow you to continue your journey and your search.

On your acceptance of her errand, the woman brings from beneath her cloak a leather satchel. She takes the emerald stone from the staff and places it inside the satchel and gives it to you. Then she gives you the staff as well, telling you that it has powers that will help you, if you have done all that you could do, and still need help. Having said this she stands aside and indicates that the way is open to you. You step on to the bridge and walk forward a few paces, then you turn to say goodbye, but the old woman has gone. The river bank has also disappeared and so has the river, now there is only a rolling mist. You know that the step you have made is final, the decision has been made and cannot be undone. There is no way left, you must go forward.

Although made of glass the bridge is firm and safe. Looking down through the transparent floor you can see the sunlight reflected in the mist below. Before you lies the dark, menacing green of the forest, drawing nearer with every step. Already the memory of the life behind you is growing dim, it takes a great effort to remember the village that was once your home, even your own name seems unfamiliar, and by the time you have reached the other side, it has all gone. You have no past, and your future has yet to be fashioned, the present is all that matters.

On the other side of the bridge, the trees open up and close around you leaving only the river, and a simple stone bridge dreaming in the sunlight; you might never have been.

As first the forest seems as black as night, but as your eyes grow used to the dim light you begin to see things more clearly. It is as if you were underwater where everything is tinged with a translucent green. You walk forward looking about you, the trees grow close together like ranks of sturdy soldiers, their branches flashing with sudden bursts of colour as birds move from tree to tree. The undergrowth is very dense and full of the movement of small animals that peer at you from hidden places, their eyes like tiny gleaming jewels.

Gradually you begin to see traces of a pathway through the dense greenery. It is worn and narrow, as if made by single pilgrims over a long period of time. It winds in and out of the trees for many miles and finally you stop to rest a while. Your stomach feels empty, and your throat is very dry. Your need for rest conflicts with your need for food and water.

You sit there almost too tired to move, your staff held loosely in your hand, you wonder if there is any water in the forest, or perhaps some berries to eat. Suddenly the staff moves in your hand, it seems to be pulling at you, trying to make you stand up. You scramble to your feet remembering what the old woman told you about its powers. The tugging gets stronger as if it were getting impatient. Guided by the staff pulling you first one way and then another, you make your way through trees until you arrive in a small clearing, on one side is a stream of clear water, and in the middle is an apple tree full of ripe red apples.

You drink first, the water is very cold, and refreshing, then you reach for an apple. As you do so, the branch moves away, for a moment you stand there foolishly . . . then you reach up again, and again the branch evades your hand, no matter how you try, the tree will not allow you to pick an apple. By now you are very hungry and a little angry. You take the staff to knock down an apple, the wooden hand opens and grasps an apple and pulls it from the branch. Each time you lift it up, it

208

pulls another apple down. You laugh at this, and sit down to eat and enjoy your rest. The staff lies quietly at your side. Obviously this staff has not only powers, but a mind of its own. It feels good, almost as if you have a companion on the long road. You reach out to touch the wooden hand, and it opens and grasps your fingers gently, it feels warm and friendly.

You put some of the apples in the satchel, then, mindful of the help of both staff and tree, you bury the cores a little way from the parent tree, perhaps it will grow and bear fruit for another traveller one day. Already you have changed from the person you once were, you are beginning to realize that you are part of everything around you, and more importantly part of all phases of time, not just the one you happen to be living in. Rested and refreshed you take up the staff and move on into the gathering darkness.

Soon there is no light at all, and no moon either, you stumble and fall many times, but you are determined not to rest. When you fall the next time the staff falls from your hand and you grope around for it in the dark. As you search you feel the wooden hand take yours and guide it to the satchel, then it tugs at the strap. Mindful that it has already helped you once, you open the bag. A brilliant green light streams forth lighting up the trees around you. You reach in and take out the Stone, at once the hand grasps it, as it did when the old woman appeared to you. You stand up and lift the staff, it lights the whole of the path making it easy and safe to walk.

As you move through the forest, despite the light of the Stone, you begin to feel uneasy, there are rustlings and sounds all around you, and the hair rises on your neck. Still, you tell yourself, the staff and the Stone will see you through if you put your faith and trust in them.

As you walk you hear the voice that has haunted you for so long, only now it seems to come from the great Emerald held firmly in the wooden hand of the staff. You forget the strangeness of this and listen intently. It speaks of courage and faith, of determination and understanding. It tells of great deeds and of those who wrought them in the days when the earth was young. Through the forest you move with confidence, the staff warm to your touch, the Stone guiding your feet and your mind.

The dawn comes gently, as the forest thins, although you have not slept, you feel no real tiredness, it is as if the Stone has sustained you through the long night. You stop to drink from a pool and eat an apple, as you bend to the water you see your reflection mirrored there. You hardly recognize yourself, gone is the indecisiveness, the lack of purpose, the face that looks back at you has calm eyes that carry a gleam of emeralds in their depths.

You no longer need the light of the Stone, so you take it from the wooden hand and replace it in the satchel, then, taking the staff you walk out of the forest.

Before you is a high snow-capped mountain, it looks almost unclimbable, but this is just what you must do if you are to carry out your quest. For a moment your heart fails you, you feel lost and frightened, then the staff glows warm in your hand, you look, and one finger of the wooden hand is pointing upwards.

At first the climb is not too difficult, but after some hours of climbing it begins to be agony to cling to tiny crevices, to pull yourself up, inch by tortuous inch. At first you carried the staff strapped across your back, but it would not stay there, so now it helps you to climb, reaching out and up to cling to a handhold too far for you to reach, gripping tightly as you pull yourself a few more precious feet.

Cold is your enemy, and the wind threatens to blow you from the face of the mountain, your fingers are almost too numb to hold on, your limbs no longer have any strength in them. One last effort brings you to a small ledge just below the summit, there you crouch too tired and cold to care any longer about your journey as the cold grips you in a vice.

Suddenly you remember the help of the Stone, perhaps it can help you again, you have done all you could, now you need help. Your frozen fingers work slowly at the strap, but when you reach in there is no Stone, only a plain silver Platter. Now you give way to tears, they slide down your cold face and form slivers of ice. You had hoped for help and now there is none. The sun up here casts a deep orange glow over the snowy peak, but the beauty is lost on you.

The wooden hand of the staff reaches out and grasps the Platter and turns it to catch the suns rays. Thus reflected and doubled in power, they shine on your face bringing warmth and new hope. But more heat is needed if you are to survive. The staff pulls itself into the line of the sun's rays, and before you can act to save it, it bursts into flame. The sudden burst of heat brings back feeling to your hands and feet. But you have lost your friend and companion, the tears of despair are now tears of despair and sorrow almost too deep to be borne. It was as if the staff had been a part of you, now lost forever. The oneness you had come to feel with the wooden staff and the Stone had opened your eyes to the great truth of the oneness of all life, be that life part of a tree, or a crystal from the beating heart of the earth itself.

But the loving sacrifice of the little wooden friend must be made good. You pick up the Platter and put it into the satchel, then you look around you. There is a small cave near the end of the ledge, it proves to be not a cave but a tunnel through to the other side of the mountain. When you emerge, before you is a rough uneven pathway leading down to a barren desert.

You scramble down, missing the feel of the warm wood in your hand, you feel inside that yet again you have changed, you have learned the inner meaning of sorrow and pain and you begin to wonder what still lies ahead. But there is no hesitation when you reach the desert, you walk straight into it, heading by instinct towards a dark smudge on the horizon. As you walk you munch on the last of the forest apples, they provide welcome moisture for a mouth that is soon dry and parched and you think longingly of the snow on the mountain behind you. The heat seems to increase with each step. Then you peer through heat-dimmed eyes at a pile of rocks nearby. There is the wonderful sound of running water, it seems like a miracle. But standing in front of the fountain, now plainly visible, there stands a guardian with a drawn sword.

There is greed and anger in its face, it will not share even with one whose need is so desperate. There seems something strangely familiar in the face of the creature, but your need for water is now so great that you must beg, plead, trick, or fight for it. A fleeting thought goes through your mind about what the son of the old woman will say when the Stone he was expecting turns out to be a silver Platter. Then you remember how it reflected the sun's rays on the mountain, maybe it would work again. You might be able to blind the guardian long enough to get a drink of water and be on your way.

You reach into the satchel for the dish, but there is none, instead you hold in your hand a miniature Spear. For a moment you stand shocked, then the Spear starts to grow in your hand until it is of normal height and weight. With a sinking heart you realize this means you must slay the guardian.

At first you try to beat off the attacks, but soon the lack of water tells and you know the time has come. The thrust is sure and true, but as the point pierces your opponent's body, a terrible pain rips through you also. The fallen body lies still, but the pain and the agony of the wound is yours. There is no blood, no wound, but the pain goes on and one. Some part of you is dying, must die in order to be transformed. You stagger to the pool, the Spear falling from your hand to lie in the sand beside you. The water is sweet and cool and you drink your fill. As you lie there trying to gather your strength again, you think that perhaps the guardian may not yet be dead. Water would be a mercy. You look for something in which to carry it. Where the Spear had lain before, there now lies a silver Cup.

You no longer question the changes, but fill it to the brim and take it to your fallen opponent. Raising the dusty head, you look into your own face, see your own eyes glazing in death, and gently drip water into your own mouth. You wait quietly until the eyes no longer see, then you close them and cover the body with small rocks. This done you pick up the Cup and walk on towards the sheer cliff of granite that now looms quite near.

As you walk you are conscious of a silvery sound, rather like the voice of the Stone. It comes from the cup in your hand, you realize that you have left the satchel behind, but the Cup is clutched tightly in your hand. The voice sings in its silver tones, telling of one who dared a long and lonely journey that out of

the pain and sorrow a new life might emerge. You mourn for
the staff, and you mourn for the self you killed.

As you walk the cup gets heavier and heavier, until it seems
you cannot carry it, but you do, something within you keeps
you going, putting one foot in front of the other. Staggering
now, and exhausted beyond human endurance, you reach the
cliff. The song of the Cup is now a paean of joy, that fills your
being with a sense of belonging to something so vast and so
wonderful that your mind cannot give it shape or words.

From the base of the cliff there winds a steep road, and as
you toil upwards, you feel you may never reach the top. As
you struggle the Cup gives a sweet call of love and greeting, it
is answered by another voice close by you, and walking by your
side is the old woman. She does not seem quite so old now,
nor is she dressed in the same black cloak. Her clothes are of
rich velvet and brocade, and a cloak of blue silk lined with white
falls from her shoulders. She walks beside you encouraging you
to make the last few steps to the top of the path.

The Cup is now so heavy you can hardly bear its weight. But
at the top of the path there waits a litter carried by four strong
men. The woman tells you to place the Cup on the litter, and
this done the procession moves towards a castle set among
gardens and beautiful trees. As you approach the gates swing
open and many people are there to welcome you and those
who come with you.

On into the castle, and into the great Hall. It is six-sided with
windows of crystal in each side. In the centre of the hall just
before the steps that lead to a throne of gold the litter is put
down. The Lady comes forward and waits by the Cup, it glows
and throbs and the light becomes so bright you cannot see.
When it dies down the Cup has gone, and in its place stands
a young boy, His face with all the radiance of the sun itself.

The Lady turns towards you, she has changed again and now
she is young and beautiful. She thanks you for being true to
your promise to bring the gift to Her Son. You ask how this
can be, for what she gave you has changed so many times, and
indeed the last change was the Son Himself. She laughs at this
and the young boy comes to you and takes your hand. He looks
up at you and smiles, 'YOU are the gift my Mother sent me',

he tells you. He walks towards the throne and as He does so He becomes a man, seated on his throne He asks if you will serve Him or go searching again. The answer must be yours.

You ask about the things that have puzzled you, the staff, and the apple tree, the guardian at the well in the desert. The apple tree and the staff, the Lady tells you, are that part of you that lies below your normal knowingness. Like a faithful dog it asks only to serve, and for a little affection and attention to its needs. Sometimes it seems to work against itself, as when you tried to pluck an apple. But with a little thought it can be persuaded to give what is needed. It was also that part of you that belongs to the organic life of the planet, as you grew closer to that part of yourself, it in turn was able to help you. It willingly changed its form to serve you, just as you willingly changed yourself to serve the King.

The Guardian was the Dweller on the Threshold, all that was no longer part of the new you, by 'killing' it, you transformed it, by recognizing and staying with it until it had 'changed' you gave it the power to regenerate in a new form within you. You will be conscious from now on of being many aspects of self within one body. All are under the rule of the Inner King, but you will owe fealty for your kingship to the Divine King who sits before you.

The apple tree whose fruit you took within you is knowledge, the Staff who led you and warmed you is understanding, and the Guardian, transformed wisdom. All these things now have their place within you.

The Lady brings to Her Son the silver cup, the King beckons you to come and kneel at His feet. There He offers to you the Cup of Cups, filled with Himself. It is like drinking pure light, it fills your whole being and knowledge, understanding and wisdom blend into Love within you. The light grows in intensity and when it fades the King and the Lady, the castle and the Cup have all gone. You stand beside a stone bridge spanning a river that runs swift and deep.

Coming towards you are your friends, they have been fishing and are displaying their fine catch. It is as if nothing has happened. They have seen you and call to you to join them. To them you have never left the village, you have just been day-dreaming as usual. But you know inside yourself that you have been farther than the ends of the earth, and you will never be quite the same again.

Some of the memories are fading, but you do not worry, you know they will return when you have need of them. Meanwhile you have something to remind you. You pick up the apple wood staff that lies at your feet, tonight you will carve the top into a hand while you are listening to one of the story-tellers. One day you will be a story-teller, but your stories will hold a wisdom learned from an inner journey taken a long time ago. Maybe one day you will find someone to whom you can tell the real story. Maybe they will take the road that leads across the glass bridge and into the forest. You know also, that when the time is right you will find the bridge again, and this time you will not need to return.

Notes

1 See John Matthews, ch. 4 in this volume, pp. 69ff.
2 See B. Cleeve, Ch. 7 in this volume, pp. 129ff.

:CONCLUSION:

:12:

:GLATISANT AND·GRAIL:

·

PETER·LAMBORN·WILSON

·

Throughout this book we have looked at the power of the Grail imagery and its ability to create changes both inward and outward. It seems fitting, therefore, to end by taking the images a stage further, into the alchemy of a new work created from the old: or rather, as the author prefers, reconstructed from fragments of the old. And here, if we will, we can learn also, keeping vigil with the knights in this story, tracing our quest to its source. What splits the Round Table is the search, in Peter Lamborn Wilson's phrase, for 'higher rites and baser treacheries', dangers that still haunt all seekers after the Grail. Reading between the lines, we learn that as the Grail takes many forms, its essence lies in none of them, or in all of them, and that the seeker must know how to find a path between the mysteries to the common Mystery. In these seeming paradoxes the entire mythos of the Grail is laid bare. For out of all opposites comes harmony, the balancing of all truths within a single Truth – that for which all Grail seekers search. The intention of this book was to give signposts to the goal. Whether it has succeeded is for the reader to discover.

What makes Malory a great poet, and not merely a literary curiosity, is that like Homer and Ovid he stands on the fulcrum between an epic and a literary tradition – he digested the 'matter' of a people, orchestrated a mass of oral and manuscript material in such a way – with such passion, if not precision – that succeeding generations have found him a jewel-mine of archetypes. As for his style, if one reads him in the unmodernized original spelling and punctuation, Malory can be seen to have developed a manner beautifully suited to his matter, a condensed but repetitive cadenced prose or narrative-prose-poem in which nothing is explained but everything is exemplified. Malory's austere musicality forbids any direct intrusion by the author; all his psychological and spiritual insights are embedded in the *story*, in the *surface* of his art, that is, in the style and plot; his imperfections, in this light, seem almost like the imperfections of life itself, in which elements of illogic and unanswered questions always intrude. The *Morte D'Arthur* sprawls, thereby covering a great deal of ground.

The brilliantly drawn and complex character of the Saracen knight Palamydes has always exemplified or at least symbolized for me the *oriental donation* to the Arthurian cycle. Unfortunately the *Palamydes* attributed to Elie de Boron (companion of Robert de Boron, one of the most mystical of the romancers) has never been translated (it was a favourite of Frederick II and of Ariosto); nor have we an English version of the compilation of Rusticano da Pisa, the prison-mate and amanuensis of Marco Polo. (Since I use Ismaili themes in the following text, I find it an intriguing fact that Marco Polo had first-hand experience of the Ismailis or 'Assassins' of Alamut. His fable of the Assassins may not be literally true, but it is symbolically quite sound. It is also interesting to note that the Assassins were known to troubadours and jongleurs, who used them poetically as emblems of the fanatic lover.)

In any case, a scholarly analysis of the Persian and Arabic influences on the romancers must suffer from the total transmogrification of themes and disguising of tropes which the European story-tellers carried out. The West wore blinkers when it accepted anything from the enemy. To disentangle Eastern from Western strands calls for intuition rather than (or at least along with) a textual/historical project. (See Ch. 2.)

For this reason, asked for an essay on the subject, I allowed the request to goad me into carrying out a scheme I'd been contemplating for years, ever since I re-read Malory in Persia while studying Sufism and Ismaili esotericism: to write a sequence of prose-poems or condensed-cadenced linked texts of my own, centred on the figure of the Saracen knight, which would constitute a sort of deliberate fragment (rather like eighteenth century pre-built ruins) of a romance of Palamydes. Tying this theme directly to that of the Grail provided the structure and focus I lacked. I stole some parts direct from Malory, picked up and extended points he only hints at, added elements from other Grail texts such as Von Eschenbach's; the Bedier version of Tristam (a modern masterpiece of romance-compilation); and the *Mabinogion*.

Superimposed over this I laid a grid of Sufi and Ismaili imagery and 'myth', which I pretend is part of Palamydes' Saracen heritage. I use glosses at the foot of some pages to explain historical and doctrinal Eastern elements which the average Western reader might not have come across, and to add information (real and imaginal) which is not contained in the body of the text. A symbol in the margin indicates the portion of text to which a gloss applies.

But I have assumed on the reader's part at least a nodding remembrance of Malory, and have not bothered to develop or identify characters who are basically 'lifted' from the *Morte D'Arthur*. I try to re-tell parts of Malory from the 'Saracen' point of view, and to carry threads of plot dropped by Malory to aesthetically logical conclusions.

Conclusion

I

Sir Perceval, Sir Galahad and Sir Bors, at the lowest ebb of their search for the Grail, stumble upon Sir Palamydes the Saracen, who vanished from Arthur's Court many years since.

For weeks they rode meeting no human, then one midday, blindly following the course of a stream, blundered into a clearing, far from Logres and equally far from Monsalvache, so dazed with the airless heat of the convoluted forest that they failed to notice the glade was already occupied: a knight sat back against moss-cushioned shade-oak, polishing his sword, wearing a rusty black robe of strange design, something like a monk's; black boots held at knees by bands of figured gold; and beside him in the grass a helm and armour of lacquered black and patterned gilt; his skin so dark he could not have been a Briton, his eyes sparkblack, beard curling on his breast in two long swaths like the wings of an angry raven.

The three reined their horses, the knight was on his feet facing them, sword held loosely in one hand; a page all in soft crimson leather leapt up and ran where a great black steed was tethered and shield propped against lightning-blasted stump; the boy began dragging this shield (so heavy he could not lift it) toward his master; the device was a Hand of gold on a field of black.

Perceval at once called out, Sir, we intend you no

The Hand of Fatima, emblem of The Fatimid Dynasty of Cairo (or 'Babylon'), where the father of Sir Palamydes held his demesne. The five fingers represent the Five Pure Ones, the family of the Prophet, and the Hand points down to represent their descendants, the Imams. Black and gold, or black and green-gold, are the colours of the final two circles of Paradise and the last two stages of the alchemical work.

222

injury. I recognize your arms, though I have not seen them since I was a child. If you have not assumed another's colours, you are Sir Palamydes, whom Lancelot called the greatest knight in all Britain and Armorica, save only himself and Sir Tristam.

That is so, Sir, replied the dark warrior; but I fear I cannot return the courtesy of greeting you or your companions by name, for I recognize no one of you, nor do I know the meaning of the device you bear.

When Perceval had introduced himself and his companions, the older knight said, I remember you, Perceval, a child whose excessive foolishness hid an unnatural virtue, not only from others but from your-self – and the three young knights were amazed at these words. I have nothing to offer you but a bit of bread and wine, but please accept them; I've heard nothing of the Court for years, I can see that you are sore with riding and near to suffocation in this heat. Why not refresh yourselves in that stream, then drink while we recount our adventures; and tell me of King Arthur, whose name I shall always serve.

It seemed to them they had been offered no such courtesy for dry seasons, and they wondered secretly at Palamydes – for at Court he would have appeared wild and alien with his darkness, yet here in this trackless wood his words wove a circle of gentle manners. The paradox, it seemed, held something of sorcery – yet they could find no reason to refuse his advice and hospitality. Further, they knew that for them every chance event held significance, each meeting might point the new way of their own adventure, since they had cast themselves like leaves carried on that cool stream, trusting the Grail and its messengers to concoct their fortune.

After they had refreshed themselves and broken bread with Palamydes and his squire, they told him of Logres, of the Queen and Lancelot, of Arthur's

---

Red crosses on a white ground with the Grail in gold at the centre.

sickness and the pall that hung over the fellowship of the Table; and at all this Palamydes wept. Then they spoke of the manifesting of the Grail, and of their quest and failures; at this Palamydes marvelled greatly, and for some time after they had fallen silent he too said nothing, but stroked his beard and stared toward the setting sun (which poured amber in the branches of the trees and burnt acid-blue shadows on the long lawn); birds hunted supper and exulted; the pageboy stole away to gather firewood; and still they waited for Palamydes to speak.

Let us build a fire and keep vigil till morning, said the Saracen at last; for this is Midsummer, a night of power, and we can use these few hours till dawn to trace our adventures to their source, and to recollect our selves. I will not keep company with a sleeping knight.

It has come to me that few of us, perhaps none, will ever see Logres again. The age which Merlin prepared and Arthur ruled is drawing to an end, splitting apart in search of higher rites and baser treacheries. From noon to dusk, you spoke to me of the Grail; and without intending it, guided me on my way. Now from dusk to dawn I shall tell you of my own quest, hoping that you may perhaps learn something useful to your purpose.

And Palamydes struck steel and flint, kindled a small fire, and ordered the boy to pour out wine mixed with cool streamwater; the Saracen keyed his voice to the indigo drone of night insects and nightjars, whippoorwills, nightingales and owls; and began to speak.

II

On certain nights the Caliph of Babylon, the Imam Hakim, secretly left his palace by the Nile and wan-

---

Palamydes foretells the end of the Round Table.

dered disguised and alone, on a black horse and in black robes (such as Palamydes now wore, but of jet silk); under the cleft moon where the palms grew farther and farther apart, past eroded remnants, faceless stone stumps of revenant pharaohs, into the very desert where his gnosis of the stars alone guided him as if at sea, in search of adventure (forest and desert both interlace with the world of the unseen).

* On one such night he happened on the oasis of my father's clan; outside the gate of their keep he found one lone youth, asleep – prodded him with his lance and ordered the gate flung open, that he and his steed might have water. The youth, ashamed of his dereliction, refused; and when Hakim made to ride past, he dealt the Caliph a rough blow with his lance. At once the spear seemed to catch fire in his hands, so that he flung it away in fear; a terrible wind arose, spiralling sand up into maelstroms, and from each of these columns stepped a demon warrior with stag's horns and armour of gleaming fire.

The youth then drew his sword and rushed again upon Hakim, but before the blade even touched the Caliph's shield, the inkblack horse flew up into the air; whereupon both steed and rider seemed suddenly enveloped in flickering green fire. Just then, the djinn seized the youth and disarmed him; the flaming horse descended to earth again, and

---

Concerning the father of Sir Palamydes, a noble of the Fatimid Dynasty. The Fatimid Caliphs were also the Imams of Ismailism, and thus rivals of the Sunni Caliphs in Baghdad as well as the orthodox Shiite Imams. The Fatimids ruled Syria, North Africa, Sicily and even Genoa for a short while, and Egypt for two centuries, until they were overthrown by Saladdin. Tolerant, patrons of the arts, the Fatimids outshone the rest of the Islamic world in splendour. The Nizari Ismailis or 'Assassins' split with the Fatimids over the question of succession, but both branches of Ismailism preached total commitment to esotericism and (at certain periods) abrogation of the Islamic Law.

Hakim said, Tell me your name, guardian of the gate. The youth answered, I am called Esclabor. Because you were bold, said Hakim, against such sorcery, I forgive your dozing, and ask of your courtesy the water which no tribe of the desert must refuse an errant knight.

Though he was held fast by two fanged and spotted-skin monsters the youth said, First you must tell me your name. At this the Caliph laughed, the emerald fire went out, the ghouls stepped into shadows and were gone. If I were a sorcerer I would never tell you, Hakim said, but since I am not, know I am called the Imam Hakim Billah al-Fatimi, seventh Caliph of Babylon.

At this, the youth fell to his face in the dust of the threshold and begged pardon, but the Caliph laughed again, dismounted and raised Esclabor to his feet. For the remainder of the night they sat together before the gate on Hakim's saddlerug, and the Caliph instructed the youth in the secrets of the Five Pure Ones and the Imams. At length he spoke of a certain beast, that appeared in the vast forests of Hyperborea; in shape it had a serpent's head, body like a leopard, buttocks like a lion and footed like a hart; from within its body came a noise like that of thirty hounds (the number of the moon's phases) baying and questing; it was called Glatisant, the Questing Beast.

Then in the hour before dawn, before those of the outer faith are told that prayer is better than sleep, the Caliph knighted Esclabor; he visited the spring, drank deep and watered his horse; resaddled and remounted, rode off silently into the dark desert.

When Hakim later vanished (or was betrayed) Sir Esclabor could abide no longer in Babylon, but took to knight-errantry in the company of several paynim knights. In the course of his wanderings he came to Rome, where he fought for the emperor; then was drawn to Gaul, where the king of that land warred against Uther Pendragon (who was allied with Meliadus of Liones, father of Sir Tristam).

*   While in the service of Pendragon, Sir Esclabor married a Christian girl and had of her three children, of whom Palamydes was the last; in fact, before this youngest son was born, Esclabor was slain in battle; the widow retired to her estate near the marches between Wales and Logres, in the midst of a remote and uninhabited forest, taking her sons with her.

III

Arthur and the Questing Beast.

Once in Caerlion the young King Arthur was visited by the wife of King Lot of Orkney; her real purpose was to spy on him; but Arthur found her beautiful and slept with her. At that time Arthur was still ignorant of his true parentage and thus did not realize he had committed incest with his half-sister, Morgan la Fay. After a month she returned to Orkney, and that night Arthur dreamt a nightmare, a savage metamorphosis of griffins and serpents. In the morning, to dispel the fumes of his terror, he ordered a hunt.

Arthur spied a hart, and spurred his horse in pursuit – but for hours the hart ran just ahead and out of reach, and at length Arthur's horse fell down dead under him and the prey escaped. He wandered till by a spring he found a charcoal burner, and ordered him to fetch back a fresh horse; then, the day being warm, he lay down upon a bank of moss by the bubbling water and fell asleep.

He awoke to the sound of thirty hounds yelping and baying; as if in a vision he saw the strangest beast

---

Segwarides and Saphir were the other two sons of Sir Esclabor le Mescogneu.

in the world crash into the clearing as if pursued –
a beast out of his last night's dream – and realized
the noise of coursing dogs pulsed from within the
belly of the beast. It approached the well and, igno-
ring the king, drank deep – while it gulped, the
baying and barking ceased, but when it had finished,
the chaos broke loose again; the beast ran off and
vanished into the wood.

Despite his terror Arthur half-believed he still slept;
trembling he lay back on the moss again – and soon
was indeed once more asleep.

Some hours passed, and a knight staggered on foot
into the clearing. Seeing Arthur asleep, he prodded
him with the butt of his lance. Have you seen any
sign, he demanded, of a strange beast pass this way?
Astonished, Arthur answered that he had. I killed
my horse chasing it, said the strange knight. Have
you a steed? If so, give it to me at once.

I rode my own to death coursing a hart, said
Arthur. But tell me of this beast – and who are you?

I am called Pellinore, answered the knight, and the
beast is sometimes called Glatisant. It is my quest: I
shall track it or die in the attempt.

Just then the charcoal burner and one of Arthur's
huntsmen returned with a horse. Arthur said, Let
me take on this quest for a year, and if I fail you can
resume it. Then Pellinore fell into a rage and cursed
Arthur for a fool – he seized the horse and mounted
it and rode away after the spoor of the beast, leaving
the young king once more without a mount. Angrily
Arthur sent his servant back yet another time, and
sat down again by the spring to wait.

After a few minutes, a child approached him, a
green-eyed boy of about fourteen dressed in a robe
of midnight blue embroidered with stars and moons.

King Pellinore, *father of Sir Lamorak de Galis, who was later to be
the best-loved friend of Palamydes, and who was slain treacherously
by Mordred. Pellinore also fathered Sir Perceval.*

What did you think of the Questing Beast? asked the boy.

Arthur, who was still too upset to guard his words, answered: I would that quest were mine.

At this the boy laughed and said, The beast Glatisant is not to be attained by you, Arthur, or by any Christian knight. Its mystery belongs to the old pagans like Pellinore or me, or to a Saracen; indeed, it will one day be undertaken by a knight of Babylonian lineage, and achieved by him. For you, there is another fate.

Arthur burst with rage: Who are you, a mere child, to pretend to such knowledge? And how dare you address me by name as if you knew me?

But I do know you, Arthur, said the boy. I know your father was Uther Pendragon and your mother . . .

No one knows that, not even I myself, shouted the king.

. . . your mother was Igraine, who was also the mother of Morgan la Fay, King Lot of Orkney's wife, with whom you slept only two nights since, leaving her with child. Your sister, Arthur.

Arthur drew his sword and would have slain the boy – but he turned and ran into the forest and was lost to sight.

At last the yeoman returned with a horse for the king. Arthur mounted it, and was about to ride back to Caerlion when he heard yet another voice call his name. He turned around and saw, standing in deep shadow near the dark spring, an old man.

Merlin, cried Arthur. Is it you?

Do you know me now? asked Merlin. You were not so keen of sight before. And Arthur noticed the

---

The fruit of this incest will be Mordred, who will eventually wound Arthur and cause him to pass to Avalon, thus bringing about the fall of Britain to the Saxons.

sorcerer was wearing an indigoblack robe strewn with astrological devices. And Merlin, too, vanished.

IV

The youth of Palamydes: he discovers the secret books of his father. His mother, a pious Christian of the Britons, begins to reveal a hidden hatred of her half-black son.

On the verge, the interstice between his mother's lands and the unbounded forest, on the salvage threshold, a liminality, a hedge of mist between worlds, limped the wreck of a tower, once perhaps seven storeys but whittled away now to two – crusted with a living verdigris of ivy – the grey atoms of its stones drifting off into saturated afternoons. To one side were the cellars of a manor that had sunk and vanished, leaving the tower behind like a single owl-infested chimney – these excavations, sunken gardens of weeds, hollyhocks, pharmacopia of astringent herbs, toads in puddles, insect music, lizards, unkempt wild roses, all steamed in breathless sun. On the other side lay a small lake, with antique stone steps disappearing into still algae, reeds and clumped lilies – and beyond this corroded greenglass pool, in a hundred colours language calls green, the hyle, the sylvanian *materia prima* spread itself: the dying and resurrecting forest.

Here Palamydes occulted the books, the manuscripts of black and gold fire-letters his father Sir Esclabor le Mescogneu brought from Babylon. The last of the dead knight's old retainers taught the boy to uncode the script, for this ageing noble made but a pretense of faith, and seduced Palamydes into the path of the mad Caliph Hakim who vanished into

The old retainer is Sir Gyron of Babylon; he alone befriends the boy, teaches him the Saracenic arts of lute and poetry, and the decipherment of Arabic.

the sands beyond Nilus. In the cracked alembic of his tower Palamydes paid out on those texts the fire which another crescenting solitaire of fourteen might have spent in his hand upon the sun-weighted air –

*   or what the pages at Court might have burnt in aping war: he gave, he sacrificed his first eros to that condemned knowledge (heresy even among the Saracens) and in his utter aloofness was converted,

*   as if the books were some hoopoe flown from the orient of half his blood, to hint of undefined paradises, dawn gardens awaiting the shattering of his cage; till one afternoon, standing slowly dazed by the day's adolescence and the transmutations of light, watching dragonflies stitching theorems into the visible breath hung like the smell of sweat sweetly over the austral pond, standing on the stone steps, Palamydes, dressed in velvet, the blackberry tint of his eyes or the bitter anthracite of his Saracenic hair, dreaming dream upon dream till all the crosscurrents cancelled each other out, leaving a still and unnatural geometry of hush in the nexus of the hours, felt rather than heard or witnessed somewhere amid the unspeakable carved jades of oak and elm, fern and tangled bush, a *nothing* like a meridional pandemonium, the non-stamping of goatmen's feet, dog-pitched-whistle and noiseless rattattat of undiluted Panic – so unmixed that in retrospect his fear would seem a sort of ecstasy, a stepping-out and doubling of the self attainable only through sheer non-mindedness; and from across the false perspective of the olivine pool, the unageing dryadic trees bent toward

---

Palamydes is instructed in sword and horse-carried lance by a master-of-arms, but this man hates the boy so much that unwittingly he trains Palamydes into a strong and cunning warrior.

cf. *Sohrawardi the martyr of Aleppo, his* Recital of Oriental Exile; *also* The Hymn of the Pearl.

or did not bend in clockslow terror out and away
from some presence, leaves sucked in or blown out
of a motionless vortex, a Beast barking inside the
skull like pairs of ultrasonic coursing hounds, gaming
for some Anacreonic prey long since (ages since)
vanished into the recesses of the intellect, hiding
behind the black-lacquered armour of successive false
selves, in the very spirals of the blood's memory,
gone to ground in the marrow of thought.

By this Palamydes came to know his wyrd, the
Questing Beast spoken of in Fatimid texts and by
Ostanes the Persian alchemist: a bestial composite
that only an angel can ride. He guessed it had lured
his father from Babylon to this kingdom of Logres,
which seemed an unmappable climactic forest; the
Beast led Esclabor a dark dance in these labyrinths till
he died, and then waited like a buried codicil in his last
will and testament to pass itself on to his inheritor,
the dark boy motionless with fear, in tower-shadow,
glaring as if sightless across the bronze-rot-coloured
pool at the invisible corruscading multiformed zoo-
protean breastfrozen horrorstruck annunciation,
crashing through the underbrush like something dug
up from the gravesites of the sky: crack, thud, and
then silence; the very crows fainted in fear, fell on
their backs, silver eyes turned up in their sockets;
and Palamydes began to tremble with desire.

V

*An incident from the wanderings of Palamydes before he
became one of the Round Table, which he did for the sake
of Sir Tristam of Liones.*

Galahalt, the High Prince of Surluse, once held a
tournament, which Arthur could not attend, but
which was presided over by Lancelot and Guenever.
Arriving in Surluse, Palamydes was offered hospi-

tality by his aunt, a Saracen lady with a beautiful young daughter. This girl begged Palamydes to carry her colours in the jousting, and according to the rule of chivalry he agreed. So exquisite was she that on the first day of the tourney Galahalt himself challenged Palamydes to defend her honour, threatening to ravish her if her champion failed.

This insult Palamydes easily avenged, and that night when his cousin offered him her unripe fruit (like a hard sweet pear) he had no thought to refuse.

Next day the girl approached a Saracen knight of the city named Corsabrin and secretly promised to wed him if he could defeat and slay Palamydes.

When he thrust his pennant, tied to a lance, into the ground before the Queen's pavilion, Palamydes was at once challenged by Sir Corsabrin. They rushed at each other, and each splintered his lance against the other's shield. Before a second pair could be fetched, Corsabrin drew his sword and charged at Palamydes, who raised his shield as he unsheathed his own blade – but Corsabrin slashed at the neck of his rival's eclipse-black horse, cutting through the bone and veins, so that blood exploded over their bright armour, and the steed collapsed. Without giving Palamydes a chance to find another mount, Corsabrin rode his own steel-hung horse straight at the fallen knight, trying to trample him to death.

In a frozen rage, Palamydes leapt up, seized the reins and with one mighty jerk toppled and tripped the living horse in a clanging heap – then waited for Corsabrin to regain his feet, pick up his shield and sword and defend himself. Each time one of them struck the other, a chip of metal would skid through the air like a spark from a smith's forge – within minutes both were bleeding from countless wounds.

Palamydes adopted for his arms at this tourney the emblem of the Questing Beast upon his shield and trappings.

At length Corsabrin waxed stronger and began to beat back his opponent; exulting, he shouted to Palamydes, Your cousin the whore has promised me what she gave you if I kill you. At this Palamydes dashed against him and delivered such a blow to his helm that it raced off, bounced in the dust and rolled toward the feet of the spectators. Yield, commanded Palamydes – but Corsabrin spat in his face and snarled defiance. With one sweep Palamydes cut off his head at the neck; it too bounced and rolled at the crowd, like a living scuttling thing. As the lifeless corpse collapsed to its knees, a charnel stench arose – and as it fell noisily to the earth, its flesh began instantly to decompose as if eaten from within. By the time servants had been ordered to drag it from the tourney ground and dispose of it in unhallowed earth, white worms were beginning to squeeze out from between the joints of its armour.

Lancelot and Guenever were as deeply struck by the prowess of Palamydes as they were horrified by the anti-miracle of Corsabrin's decay; they urged the Saracen noble to be christened at once. For, they said, you see the result of dying outside the church: devils fly to seize the soul and consume the flesh, a foretaste of hell.

Palamydes, who had seen many Saracens and pagans die better deaths than certain Nazarenes, nevertheless pretended to agree, saying that only when he had fought seven true battles would he at last be baptized – for he realized that he remained yet far from his quest; moreover he had betrayed his love of Iseult – and by seven battles he meant the seven stages of the path, which he had not yet begun to travel.

In disgust at what had happened, Palamydes purchased a new horse, and quickly left Surluse, though he was badly wounded. When Sir Mordred noticed this, he gathered six of his close companions to him and suggested that they dispose of the

Saracen just as they had murdered his friend Sir Lamorak – and these conspirators were Sir Dragonet, Brandiles, Uwaine, Ozana, Griflet and Agravaine.

They tracked Palamydes for several days, at last ambushing him – and though they attacked him simultaneously and treacherously, he was able to unhorse four of them and kill two more outright (Ozana and Griflet); Mordred, who had been waiting the chance to thrust at the Saracen from behind (as with Sir Lamorak) gave up and fled.

Palamydes had been wounded even more severely in this battle, and after losing himself in the forest, fell from his horse, unable to keep mounted any longer, and fainted from loss of blood. Thus he was discovered by two peasants, who ran at once to a nearby manor and begged the lady of the house to succor a wounded knight. What arms does he bear? she asked. They described the strange device of a mythic animal on the battered shield. That is Glatisant the Questing Beast, she said, and the knight is my son Palamydes. That he bears this device proves that he still adheres to his unbelief and heresy: a paynim, just as his cursed father before him. I will do nothing to save his life; let him ask elsewhere for hospitality.

But the servants of the house hated this unnatural woman, fearing her sin would destroy them all; so they secretly sent aid, medicines, meat and wine, to their errant lord, and he was soon recovered.

It was then that Palamydes turned his full passion toward Iseult, the wife of King Mark of Cornwall.

VI

Palamydes tells of his unhappy love for Iseult the Queen of Cornwall, and his mingled enmity and friendship with Sir Tristam of Liones.

Why can I not hate Iseult, my opposite the daylight,

235

I that Arthur called a leopard, I that kidnapped her once, I that have killed as paladin too many to remember, unhorsed and unhelmed too many to count, all for the memory of one smile, blood on polished metal?

One cannot serve two beasts, Glatisant and Iseult. I could make an anchorite's boast and emblemize the carnal world as a woman, claim that I cut out the brandmark from my skin, prate that incest and adultery will topple Arthur's arcadia – but no, Tristam and Iseult and I whirled like planets, like angels poisoned with aphrodisiac spinning inside an archangel's brain – the kerubim may go mad, but they do not sin. Those two were each other's quest, they doubled each other. I divided myself.

Tristam and I fought our last duel by Merlin's stony grave, on the very day Galahad appeared to sit in the Siege Perilous, the very day the Grail Quest began; on that day I was purged of envy and resumed the quest of the beast. If I could not hate Iseult, why could I not at least hate Tristam? They were one thing, a hermaphrodite – I loved neither of them so much as I loved their love. When he ran lunatic naked in the forest I searched for him as I wanted her, with the same lust an alchemist knows when Hermes and the Lioness copulate in an athanor.

For all the generosity of your hair, Queen, oil of gold, elixir of bees, you gave me nothing, neither the raging bedlam of utter separation nor the white honey of your saliva; beside some well in the dank woods beautiful as an antiparadise I wept and played
* the lute (which my father in the time of Uther Pendragon first introduced to this land from Babylon) thinking the while: only Tristam and I in all this

---

Arabic: al-'oud, *the lute.*

barbaric country can compose a decently moving lament.

My own eyes were the cause of my sorrow, black as the jewels from a snake's skull – not her eyes, colour of the beast, of the forest – and his were blue, of course, like a child who laughs at a funeral. I let him baptize me that last day, why not? Since my religion permits pious dissimulation, it made an apt symbol to end our story – they were sailing toward their death and I was to vanish into the forest – but they were paynims like me, Dionysus ruled them and only a Saracen paradise of eternal drunken dalliance could ever hold them, if such a thing could exist, all Time in one spasm of released desire.

I looked in the well and saw myself defaded, swore to give up this life for a love I might never get nor recover; I made my last and best poem, almost rejoicing as if music sucked the poison from my wound – but that day Tristam, hunting the hart or hunting me, overheard my work, watched me through the lace of May leaves. Lazy as I am, I would have attained nothing without them to strike against like knife on whetstone. I told him I had as lief die as live – a kind of sanctity. Well uttered, your treason, he said. I answered: Love is free for all men: you and she have the pleasure of your love, but you cannot shut me out from its pain.

All he could offer me then was more jousting, more swordplay – for once he acted the unbalanced envious lover, while I attained something like a vatic elegance. How the three of us danced, witches in a grove, weaving around us an egg of pulsing silk, a spiral pyramid charged with lightning which wakened the night, rays shooting between the branches like swampfire, the prolonged burst of a fallen meteor.

Taqiyya, *which permits Ismailis to pretend to any religion, since all religions are one in any case.*

VII

Palamydes begins his ta'wil, *that is in Arabic, the taking-back-to-the-source of all the adventures recounted during that day and night, his own and those of the Grail knights – the hermeneutic exegesis of the story, the explication of the text their memories have called into being.*

The beast-quester finds the outward form of Glatisant but one of many: each time he comes close, finds the trap sprung, detects traces of its escape or gets a glimpse of it crashing away, then each time the timbre of its bruiting changes, each moment a new station manifests itself, sometimes merely a hollowness in the air, vibrant strumming of voices not yet labelled, tension of light, invisible whirlwind or spout of things about to be born; sometimes a theorem of chaos that suddenly equates, drawing all the trees, moss and lichen into its computations; the light quartered and dented on misshapen rocks and lightning-broke stumps, a spectrum of landscape dropping into focus with sheer ghost-story terror and erotic bliss – click – and the hunter knows that everything he saw till then was but grey and blurred.

When the beast is seen it may also appear in various forms. Palamydes watched it often as a monstrous stag, unkillable; as a Celtic nightmare of a boar; as a raven in a rainstorm. Sometimes it unfolded itself as a sequence of events, a knotted length of time; and sometimes as a vast overflowing, a superabundance, as if just beyond the next ridge the well of images gurgled and spewed up the whole world of palpable things, the patterns of mentation, the angels, the living creatures and elementals.

The very essence of the beast lies in the quality of the hunt – the sportsman is dazzled by the otherness of Glatisant and yet loses the sense of any difference or distance between totem (or prey) and himself: beyond these two clashing rocks he retires and looks on astonished, forgetting his purpose.

Once the beast appeared to him as a herd of deer; as they scattered before his black centaur shape, they transformed themselves into boys and maidens, dressed in white, who turned to laugh at him, like an ironic shower of gold coins, all the dates and inscriptions rubbed and worn beyond decipherment; and once as a child, riding a stag that carried lit opals and garnets strung on gold chains webbed in its antler-tines; and perhaps Iseult was also part of some major apotheosis – if it may be said that such a singularity could be part of any pattern whatsoever: Iseult of the white brow.

Now it is full night, said Palamydes, and we are planets to this little star fire. As he stirred the blaze and added more wood the three knights stretched themselves and swallowed the last dregs of their wine. Iseult is as lost as Eurydice, said the Saracen; her face fades always before my eyes, into an underworld I port with me like luggage, like an organ of the body. The stones and animals sing for me in my quest while I listen, a reader of the Metamorphoses, watching Proteus on the shore of Egypt. Then Palamydes asked his squire for more wine, but the boy was asleep, his head resting on the black-enamelled saddle – and in the firelight the Grail knights remembered the boy's hair was the rarest colour of blackred muskroses, blacklighted scarlet. Palamydes drained the rest of a flask into their cups, last drops luminous in the upblazing.

Pagans such as Merlin speak of a great cauldron that never emptied, but poured out unstinted food and drink – just so does the one become many. At certain powerpoints in forests, deserts or caves such openings suddenly appear or disappear, sluices for the flow of being into our world: Nature naturing

---

The name of the squire was Saphir, like that of the brother of Sir Palamydes.

with a generosity so intense it can drown the unwary
beholder in a surfeit of vision.

* The Persians know of a Cup of Jamshid – he who
possesses it may see reflected in its wine whatever
transpires at that moment anywhere in the world.
Thus the Cup is like a mirror of the Cauldron, which
in turn embodies the always-shapeshifting-moment
of continual creation. The Magians teach that the eye
of the Cup can be turned inward – offering a vision
of the one rather than a spectacle of manyness and
the bending of time. Perhaps if the Cauldron's flow
could be reversed, one might step through it as
through a doorway, or climb down into it like a well,
into the realm of the one.

The Grail you speak of provides food, and is also
a Cup from which the splendour of the one radiates
– a vortex that Janusfaces on two separate lands. I
think the Grail is a Christian's quest, as Merlin
claimed, because its beam shines upward and out of
this world. Yet if you could step through this rent in
the cloth or tear away the veil, what would you find?
Is there more than one real creation?

Glatisant is a paynim's quest, a Saracenic obsession, because it is the quintessence of all nature, the
very palpableness of all that may be touched and
tasted. The beast is the world, but the world as I
have seen it in my errantry, a forest suffused with
the recollection of fauns and satyrs, dryads, water-
nymphs, Priapi and Sileni, amorini riding panthers
* – the world become a *lapis exilit*, a balsam which

The Cup of Jamshid is explained in the Divan *of Hafez of Shiraz,
who is accepted by esoteric Zoroastrians as the expositor* par
excellence *of their doctrines.*

The words lapis exilit *are applied to the Grail by Flegetanis,
Wolfram's Saracenic source for his poem of* Parzival. *They can mean*
stone of exile, *or even* stone that fell to earth, *and by some are
said to refer to the jewel from Lucifer's crown.*

transmutes nothing but the place in which the hunter stands to view the world – and thereby transforms it all beyond recognition. The mercury of Glatisant's mutability must be fixed with the sulphur of an incandescent attentiveness; in the moment the stalker steps forward to achieve this quest, he simultaneously steps back and finds himself again in the forest, perfectly ordinary, still and alone; except that hunter and landscape alike are saturated with presence, like two lovers intertwined in complex embrace, or about to embrace, unknown to those who sleep so heedlessly on nights of power.

At this Palamydes clapped his hands, and the noise reverberated around the crooked columns of the blackswallowed forest in multiple peals of thunder; the three knights started and sat up like gamebirds who hear the hounds; Saphir jerked from sleep and stared about and knuckled his eyes. Palamydes handed the squire his own half-filled cup, and smiled. I will keep company with no sleeping knight, he said.

In the hour before dawn when even the earth yawns and the moon has sunk into a somnolent blur, I drink only certainty, the elixir of wakefulness – and like Merlin, I make prophecy. The quests of Grail and Beast are mirror images of one another. Looking into your glass, I have absorbed a new essence, I have breathed into myself the perfume of your energies. Now look into mine, and you will see the image of a map. The Grail you will attain at Monsalvache is but the prolongation of a more central Grail – and your prophet's blood was not the first to spill in it. * The city of Sarras lies in the farthest East, the Yemen, where once schismatics of my faith hid the stolen

---

The Yemen is identified as the source of the 'oriental knowing' by Mohiyoddin ibn Arabi in his Interpreter of Desires, *and by the author of* The Chymical Marriage of Christian Rosycross. *The Black Stone or meteorite of the Kaaba in Mecca was stolen by the*

Black Stone of Mecca, and where the last of the exiled Fatimid Imams vanished, as Merlin did and as Arthur will, into a cave of silver and crystal.

And I shall move north seeking the beast as the beast seeks me, into Hyperborea, into the land of unending pitch dark – there, at its pole, like a single glowing pearl set in a vast disk of ebony onyx and jet, I shall find the spring or well guarded by angels. There I shall bathe, and put on green robes. And there will begin a new cycle of seven. And there I begin to dance.

Qarmatian heretics and held for some years in the Yemen. The last Fatimid (the twenty-first Imam) Mawla Sabi'l Ashhad al-Tayyib, exiled to the Yemen, vanished in 1132, and like Arthur (or the 'Hidden Imam' of orthodox Shiism) is expected to appear again at the end of this temporal cycle.

RECOMMENDED READING:

·

For those who wish to pursue the Grail through the original texts as well as the interpretations of others, a select list follows. Where possible editions available at time of going to press are included; in all other cases original publication details are given.

Texts

Le Morte D'Arthur: Sir Thomas Malory (edited by Caxton), Harmondsworth, 1969, New York, Penguin, 1970.
Perceval, or Le Conte du Graal by Chrétien de Troyes, trans. N. Bryant, Cambridge, N.J., D. S. Brewer, Rowman & Littlefield, 1982.
Perlesvaus (*The High Book of the Holy Grail*), trans. N. Bryant, Cambridge, N.J., D. S. Brewer/Rowman & Littlefield, 1978.
Peredur (in) *The Mabinogion*, trans. J. Gantz, Harmondsworth and New York, Penguin, 1976.
Parzival by Wolfram von Eschenbach, trans. A. T. Hatto, Harmondsworth and New York, Penguin, 1980.
Queste del Saint Graal (*Quest for the Holy Grail*), trans. P. Matarasso, Harmondsworth and New York, Penguin, 1969.
The Romance of Perceval in Prose, a translation of the E MSS of the Didot Perceval by D. Skeeles, University of Washington Press, 1966.

Interpretations

Ashe, Geoffrey, *Avalonian Quest*, London, Methuen, 1982.
Cavendish, Richard, *King Arthur and The Grail*, London, Weidenfeld & Nicolson, 1978.

Recommended reading

Hall, Manley P., *Orders of the Quest: The Holy Grail*, Los Angeles, Philosophical Research Society, 1976.

Heline, Corinne, *Mysteries of the Holy Grail*, Los Angeles, New Age Press, 1977.

Jung, Emma and von Franz, Marie-Louise, *The Grail Legend*, London, Hodder & Stoughton, 1971; New York, Putnam, 1970.

Knight, Gareth, *Experience of the Inner Worlds*, Cheltenham, Helios Books, 1975.

Knight, Gareth, *Secret Traditions in the Arthurian Legends*, Wellingborough, Aquarian Press, 1983.

Loomis, Roger Sherman, *The Grail: From Celtic Myth to Christian Symbol*, Cardiff, University of Wales Press, New York, Columbia University Press, 1963.

Matthews, John, *The Grail: Quest for Eternal Life*, London, Thames & Hudson, 1981; New York, Crossroads, 1981.

Morduch, Anna, *The Sovereign Adventure*, London and Cambridge, James Clarke, 1970.

Maltwood, K., *The Enchantments of Britain*, London and Cambridge, James Clarke, 1982.

Schmidt, K. O., *The Message of the Grail*, Lakemont, Georgia, C.S.A. Press, 1975.

Weston, J. L., *From Ritual to Romance*, New York, Doubleday/Anchor Books, 1957.

Wyatt, Isobel, *From Round Table to Grail Castle*, Sussex, Lanthorn Press, 1979.

Williams, Charles and Lewis, C. S., *Arthurian Torso*, Oxford University Press, 1948.

Poetry and fiction

Chapman, Vera, *The Three Damosels*, London, Methuen, 1978.

Hunter, Jim, *Perceval and the Presence of God*, London, Faber, 1978.

Jones, David, *The Anathemata*, London, Faber, 1952.

Mitchison, Naomi, *To the Chapel Perilous*, London, Allen & Unwin, 1955.

Monarco, Richard, *Parsifal*, New York, Macmillan, 1977; London, Methuen, 1978.

Monarco, Richard, *The Grail War*, New York, Pocket Books, 1979; London, Sphere Books, 1981.

Monarco, Richard, *The Final Quest*, New York, Pocket Books, 1980; London, Sphere Books, 1982.

Powys, John Cowper, *A Glastonbury Romance*, London, Macdonald, 1955.

Sutcliff, Rosemary, *The Light Beyond the Forest*, London, Bodley Head, 1979.

Recommended reading

Trevor, Meriol, *The Sparrow Child*, Glasgow, Collins, 1958.

Williams, Charles, *Taliessin Through Logres* and *The Region of the Summer Stars*, Cambridge, N.J., D. S. Brewer, 1982.

Williams, Charles, *War in Heaven*, London, Faber, 1930; Oxford, Wm. Eerdmans, 1978.